KT-563-648

■ A F T E R   T H E   L A W

A book series edited by John Brigham and Christine B. Harrington

P R O D U C I N G   L E G A L I T Y

■ *AFTER THE LAW*
A book series edited by John Brigham and Christine B. Harrington

Also published in the series:

Gigs: Jazz and the Cabaret Laws in New York City
By Paul Chevigny

A Theory of Liberty: The Constitution and Minorities
by H. N. Hirsch

Inside the State: The Bracero Program, Immigration, and the I.N.S.
by Kitty Calavita

*Explorations in Law and Society: Toward A Constitutive
Theory of Law*
by Alan Hunt

Virtuous Citizens, Disruptive Subjects
by Barbara Yngvesson

Contested States: Law, Hegemony and Resistance
by Mindie Lazarus-Black and Susan F. Hirsch

PRODUCING LEGALITY

LAW AND SOCIALISM IN CUBA
■ MARJORIE S. ZATZ

■ ROUTLEDGE   NEW YORK   LONDON

Published in 1994 by

Routledge
29 West 35th Street
New York, NY 10001

Published in Great Britain by

Routledge
11 New Fetter Lane
London EC4P 4EE

Printed in the United States of America on acid-free paper

Library of Congress Cataloging-in-Publication Data

Zatz, Marjorie Sue, 1955–
    Producing legality: law and socialism in Cuba / Marjorie S. Zatz.
    p.   cm. — (After the law)
    Includes bibliographical references and index.
    ISBN 0-415-90856-6 (hard : acid-free paper) : — ISBN 0-415-90857-4
(pbk.)
    1. Cuba — Consitutional history. 2. Law and socialism. I. Title. II. Series.
KGN2919.Z38   1994
342.7291'029—dc20
[347.2910229]   94-8847
                                                                    CIP

British Library Cataloguing-in-Publication Data also available

In memory of my sister
Carolyn Zatz
who inspired me in so many ways,

and for Rick, Richie, Patrick and Cameron

CONTENTS

ACKNOWLEDGMENTS

This book could not have been written without the help and encouragement of friends and colleagues in Cuba and in the United States. I owe an inestimable debt to the many Cubans who gave freely of their limited time and scarce resources to make my research possible, and for their hospitality. Special thanks are due Dr. María Luisa Arteaga Abreu, who went far beyond her official capacity as gatekeeper at the Ministry of Justice to encourage others to talk with me, to provide me with documents, and to offer her own thoughts as someone intimately involved for many years in constructing Cuba's new legal order. Dr. Julio Fernández Bulté and Omar Fernández Jiménez, Dean and Vice-Dean respectively, of the University of Havana Law School during the years of data collection, willingly provided me with access, data, and insightful theoretical suggestions. The Law School faculty and staff graciously hosted me as a Visiting Researcher in 1989. I am grateful to them all.

Special recognition is due to my Cuban colleagues who, beyond consenting to multiple, lengthy interviews, also read and commented on drafts of the manuscript: Armando Castanedo, Marcelino Díaz, Milagros Gómez, Lydia Guevara, Miriam Laou, Nancy Pérez, Renén Quirós, and Antonio Rodríguez Gavira. This was a particularly time-consuming task because the manuscript was written in English and our discussions of it took place in Spanish.

James McDonald was the best research assistant imaginable, and I owe him my special thanks. Andy Hall, Heather MacIntyre, and Cheryl Perea spent hundreds of hours compiling the census data for the appendices. Kay Korman gave tirelessly of her time, assisting me with preparation of the manuscript and overseeing the administrative aspects of the grant. Her patience, good humor, and efficiency are without equal. Peg Bortner, Kitty Calavita, Susan Caringella-MacDonald, Drew Humphries, Nancy Jurik, and Michael Musheno offered encouragement and constructive criticisms. John Brigham and Christine Harrington were wonderful series editors. I thank them for their continued interest in the project and their helpful comments on drafts of the manuscript. Cecelia Cancellaro and the staff at Routledge made sure that all of the details of preparing the book for publication went smoothly.

The research was supported by a grant from the Law and Social Sciences Program of the National Science Foundation (#SES 8911816). I thank Felice Levine, Sarah Nerlove, and the panelists of the National Science Foundation for their interest in the project. Travel to Cuba was also funded by a grant from the Arizona State University Women's Studies program. While I thank them all, no U.S. or Cuban agency bears responsibility for any errors or interpretations of the data.

I thank my parents, Ruth and Nathan Zatz, for their support and encouragement over the years. My sister Carolyn was the closest thing I will ever have to a muse. I miss her sorely, and dedicate this book to her memory. I thank my husband, Richard Krecker, for his constant love and support, and for being my intellectual and emotional sounding-board. I also thank Richie and Patrick for their patience when I too often wanted to work "for just a little longer." And finally, my little Cameron, whose impending birth was the impetus to finally finish writing and send the manuscript off.

PREFACE

I was only three years old when Fidel Castro and his *compañeros* marched triumphantly into Havana, but the Cuban revolution has fascinated me for as long as I can remember. In a revolutionary setting, anything seems possible. How, I wondered, does one translate a dream into the reality of a new social order? That was precisely the task confronting Cuba's new leadership.

Over the years my interest narrowed from amorphous questions of how to create a totally new society to more focused inquiries into social and legal change in a revolutionary context. In 1985, I traveled to Cuba at the invitation of the Ministry of Justice as part of a group studying criminal justice and human rights. With the contacts I developed on that and subsequent trips, a study of the Cuban legal order began to appear possible. A grant from the Law and Social Science Program of the National Science Foundation and the interest of the Cuban Ministry of Justice and the University of Havana Law School made it feasible.

This book is my attempt to explain how a new legal order and a new legal consciousness came to be produced in Cuba. It is a story of how law and legality are understood by Cuban legal scholars and policy makers. It provides a window into the official construction of socialist legality in Cuba and how the legal order operates as seen by jurists, judges, and lay people. Throughout the analysis, I examine how contradictory economic, social, cultural, historical, political, and ideological forces originating within and outside Cuba shape and constrain its legal order, and how and why the Cubans have rewritten their laws as domestic and international conditions changed.

I view the production of legality as multifaceted and dynamic. In an attempt to capture, if only momentarily, its multiple aspects for the reader, I play with the word "production." Beyond the obvious modes and means of production, I examine how laws are produced, the training of law students to see how the next generation of jurists is produced, and the ways in which legality is produced and reproduced daily in the courts and the workers' councils. Throughout, I attempt to unearth the underlying ideological bases for laws, as well as how lawmakers, judges, and legal scholars interpret social conditions.

Popular justice is a cornerstone of Cuban legality. The Cubans say, "The closer to the base, the greater the justice." As a sociologist, popular-justice initiatives intrigued me, but everything I read about them sounded hopelessly romantic. Allowing the local community to define and sanction conduct based on the immediate case and local sentiment is not consistent with any internationally recognized rule of law. As I discovered, the Cubans reached this same conclusion, leading them to revamp many of their laws during the 1970s. They wanted to maintain elements of popular participation, both to bring a view of the average person to legal-decisionmaking and to provide a means of educating the populace about socialist legality, while staying within a formalized legal order.

Some legal changes in Cuba reflect and solidify social changes that have already occurred; others are intended to help transform Cuban society in ways that the political leadership views as beneficial. Sometimes social and legal changes keep pace with one another, but the speed with which social conditions shift in revolutionary Cuba means that they are frequently out of sync. As a Cuban colleague exclaimed in one of our many conversations, "One year for us is like 100 years for you!"

Many people in the United States and elsewhere seem surprised at Cuba's steadfast support for some form of socialism, given the demise of socialism in Eastern Europe and the disintegration of the Soviet Union. Economic upheaval generally reaps political discontent, and Cuba is no exception. Many Cubans want to see some changes in their economic and political structures, but they are reluctant to give up the benefits of Cuban-style socialism. Cuba's universal literacy, highly educated citizenry, and free and excellent health care are well known. Another positive outcome of the revolution that is accorded less attention in the scholarly and popular literature is a legal order that is widely respected at home and in international forums.

While the Cubans have made some decisions with which I personally disagree, after seven years of fieldwork in Cuba, I am firmly convinced that policy makers in the legal arena are trying to create a fair, equitable, and just legal order. For this reason, if for no other, I believe that socio-legal scholars would be well served by studying social and legal change in Cuba.

PART ONE

CONTEXT AND THEORETICAL FRAMEWORK

CHAPTER I

THE SOCIAL CONTEXT
DAILY LIFE IN CUBA, 1985–1990

Honest visitors to the island bump into a hallucinating, contradictory and quite earthly reality. The Revolution made of human clay is not the work of infallible gods or evil Satans: it belongs to this world and, being of this world, also belongs to the world to come.

Reality baffles whoever expects to find here a huge concentration camp dotted with palm trees, a punished people doomed to eternal fear. It takes a lot of prejudice not to succumb to the embrace of this loving and grumbling people who complain and laugh out loud and infect whoever approaches them with dignity and freshness.

Anyone who doesn't have spider webs in his eyes can see that the people express themselves openly and that it is impossible to walk one step without bumping into some hospital or school.

But no less baffled are those who honor a date with the purported kingdom of perfect happiness: in Cuba they find empty stores, phones that drive anyone mad, terrible transportation, a press that seems to be from another planet and a bureaucracy that has a problem for every solution.

—Galeano, 1989:3

In every nation law and legality exist as part of daily life. They are not transcendent phenomena, but rather, depend on how they are understood, interpreted, and constituted within a particular social order (Chambliss and Seidman, 1982; Brigham, 1988; Harrington and Merry, 1988; Merry, 1990). This reciprocal, interwoven relationship between law and society is perhaps most visible in a new, revolutionary state. In revolutionary Cuba, law is both a by-product, or mirror, of social change and a catalyst for change. Laws and the legal order solidify past and ongoing social transformations and stamp them with legitimacy. For example, agrarian reform and housing laws were crucial to the construction of Cuban socialism. Law and the legal order also pave the way for social changes, such as gender equality, which the political leadership views as desirable.

This book analyzes Cuban legal policy from the perspective of the policy makers and those implementing the policies. It is not *the* operative reality of Cuban legality, but rather one of several realities. The analysis provides a window into the official construction of socialist legality in Cuba, largely as perceived by those insiders. It draws attention to how policy makers and legal scholars understand the structural, historical, and ideological contradictions and conflicts leading to legal changes, the dilemmas in which they find themselves embroiled, and the strategies chosen by these very human actors as they try to resolve problems within the legal arena.

To understand law and legality in Cuba, we must also understand legal consciousness among Cubans—that is, how law is perceived and used—and how the legal sphere is related to other state institutions and mass organizations. These understandings are culturally and historically specific and only make sense in terms of Cuban culture at a particular moment in time. This book covers the period from 1959, when Fidel Castro and his *compañeros* won their revolutionary war and ousted the dictator Batista, through 1992, when economic exigencies curtailed major advances in juridical institutions. The major emphasis is on events occurring in the period from 1985 to 1990, when the configuration of the world changed dramatically as a consequence of the "velvet" revolutions in Eastern Europe and the disintegration of the Soviet Union.

Although there was a clear socialist bloc until the end of this era, the world economy was defined and controlled by capitalism and capitalist states. In 1961, the most powerful of the capitalist nations, the United States, initiated an economic blockade around Cuba; it remains in place today. During the 1960s and into the 1970s, many of the U.S.'s allies in Latin America participated in the embargo, as did some nations that may not technically have been allies of the United States but were deeply indebted to it and could not risk its wrath. Yet this was also a time of political growth and maturation for the nonaligned movement, and the Cubans provided important leadership for this global organization. Also, Cuba's substantial support to many struggling Latin American and African nations greatly enhanced its prestige internationally. This aid took very visible forms, including teachers, construction workers, and medical assistance.

SOCIALISM AND NATIONALISM, CUBAN STYLE

Unlike the situation in many Eastern European countries where socialism was imposed by the Soviet Union following World War II, the Cuban Revolution was home-grown. By that I mean that Cuba's revolutionary movement, which culminated in the victory over Batista on January 1, 1959 and the declaration of its socialist nature in 1961, resulted from historical events *within Cuba*. The revolution had its antecedents in heroes and martyrs from the turn of the century who fought for independence from Spain and later from U.S. interference in Cuban political and economic life. These historic figures form a major part of Cuban folklore and are continually drawn upon and reinvigorated by the political leadership.

While the Cuban revolution was and remains intensely nationalist, Cuban nationalism does not imply isolationism. At least within the legal sphere, Cuba's leaders have proven themselves to be very much attuned to the international community, and respect in the eyes of that community has consistently been a key consideration in developing domestic policies.

Socialism grew from the tremendous domestic disparities in wealth and opportunity and from Cuba's history of foreign expropriation of much of its human and natural resources. Certainly, there was some pull toward socialism from the Soviet Union and a pushing away by the United States following the revolutionary triumph. My reading of Cuban history and lengthy discussions with Cubans of all walks of life suggest that these were not the defining factors, however. Rather, the move toward socialism was a *Cuban* decision (see also Smith, 1987; Erisman, 1985).

The transition to socialism was endorsed by a huge majority of the Cuban people. As one Havana resident told me, "If we went capitalist we would be like a Peru or Bolivia, not like an Argentina or Venezuela. And you know that many, many people in Peru and Bolivia live in dire poverty." This comment is revealing for two reasons: First, it reflects Cuban perceptions of the effects of socialist versus capitalist political-economic structures on the lives and opportunities of average people. Second, this comment draws attention to another important fact—that Cubans perceive themselves as Latin Americans and use Latin America as their mirror. This is often forgotten by North Americans who assume that Cubans look to the Soviet Union and the United States, perhaps because most North Americans tend to ignore the existence of Latin America. Yet for Cubans, Latin America is their most important referent. In many places throughout this book we will see my Cuban sources repeating over and over again, "We are Latinos."

To understand the role of law and legality in contemporary Cuba, we must have a sense of what life is like in that society. Information on Cuban society is generally unavailable to people in the United States because U.S. government travel restrictions ban tourism and most other travel by U.S. citizens to Cuba; because the U.S. media rarely report on life in Cuba; and because when they do so the reports tend to be highly inflammatory and negative (McCaughan and Platt, 1988; Biancalana and O'Leary, 1988; Prieto González, 1990).[1]

This chapter provides an introduction to daily life in Cuba from 1985 through 1990.[2] I focus primarily upon life in the capital city of Havana, where two million people, one-fifth of the nation's population, live.[3] Where appropriate, the discussion is broadened to include smaller cities and rural areas. Historical factors relating to Cuba's colonial and neocolonial past have led to an uneven development and inequitable distribution of resources between the urban and rural areas. As the census data in the Appendices indicate, since the triumph of the Cuban Revolution in 1959, the new government has sought to reduce this inequality, but differences between urban and rural areas still remain.

The popular U.S. perception of life in Havana, at least as reflected in comments by my students, colleagues, family, and acquaintances, is of a dismal, grim existence where everyone walks around with dour, sullen expressions on their faces, looking fearfully over their shoulders every few moments, dressed in drab clothing. This image does not match the reality of life on the island. Cuba is a Caribbean nation and reflects that culture. Bright colors are visible everywhere, from the rainbow hues worn by the women to the psychedelic T-shirts sported by teenagers to the flowers blooming in yards, gardens, and along the main thoroughfares. Havana is an unusually clean city by Latin American standards. Passing pedestrians and motorists toss cigarette butts and sometimes loose papers into the streets, but little other garbage. The streets, sidewalks, and bus stops are cleaned on a regular basis, adding to the aesthetic appeal of the city. Radios blare contemporary Cuban, Latin American, and North American songs. Afro-Caribbean drum beats and guitar music float from the open windows of Havana's apartments. These sounds compete with the shouts of children playing, neighbors chatting over fences, cars honking their horns at anyone who looks like she or he might dare step onto the street, and the constant noise of cars and buses whizzing by. During the day, the main thoroughfares throng with vehicles; at night lovers stroll arm in arm along the wide sidewalks lining these same streets, stopping to neck under sculpted trees and bushes.

Alongside this imagery of bustle and romance, there is evidence everywhere that Cuba is a Third World country. Most telephones do not work when it rains, and many do not function properly even when it is not raining. Buses use diesel fuel that emits huge clouds of black smoke in their wake. Shortages of basic goods are common, and luxury items (e.g., VCRs, home computers) are scarce and expensive. Water shortages are frequent, largely due to aging pipes, water lines, and pumps. Newspapers, radio, and television carry local, national, and international news, but the favored news source is still gossip, known popularly as *"radio bemba."*[4]

Foods and Consumer Goods

A nutritional diet is commonplace in Cuba. Basic foods and other daily needs (e.g., clothes, soap) are available through the ration system at very low prices, with some as low as the 1959 price. The result is a well-nourished population with a life expectancy at birth of 76 years and infant-mortality rates of 10.7 per 1,000 live births in 1990 and 10.4 in 1992 (Castro Ruz, 1991:4; Lage, 1992:11). This is one of the lowest infant mortality rates in the world—only slightly above the rate of 10 deaths per 1,000 live births in the United States and well below the rate for many states within the U.S.

While the rationed foods (e.g., coffee, beans, rice, flour, meat, chicken, milk)[5] are available at prices which every Cuban can afford, the variety is limited, and residents wait in what are often very long lines. Larger quantities and a more diverse selection of foods, clothing, and consumer goods are available outside the rationing system, but at substantially higher prices. Sometimes key ingredients in the Cuban diet, such as garlic or black beans, are simply not available in the capital city, although they can generally be found in the countryside.

In an effort to aid women in the labor force, families in which the woman works are automatically eligible for what is called *"plan jaba"* if no one in the family unit (e.g., a grandmother) is at home during the day. *"Plan jaba"* is stamped onto the ration booklet, enabling members of eligible families to move through the lines more quickly. The typical method of implementation is through creation of two lines at every store: one for *plan jaba* consumers and one for everyone else, with two people entering from the *plan jaba* line for every person entering from the non-plan line.

Unlike most Latin American countries which have large outdoor markets, in Cuba foods and other goods are sold in stores. In addition to large grocery marts, little corner markets dot the city of Havana. These sell a limited assortment of domestic and imported canned and bottled goods, wine, rum, eggs, fresh fruits and vegetables, rice, flour, cereals, soft drinks, and condensed milk. Specialized stores located in each section of the city sell meat, milk products, and vegetables. Others sell clothing and household goods. Bakeries, which offer a delicious variant of French bread, are widely distributed throughout the city.

In 1984 and 1985, farmers' markets brought fruits and vegetables into the city for sale at prices set by the private farmers themselves. Although this experiment was applauded by most consumers in Havana, it was short lived because some farmers charged exorbitant prices and did not retain enough produce for sale to the state-run markets. These profit-oriented practices threatened the political goal of providing every Cuban with a nutritious diet at low prices. Also, a new class of middle-level entrepreneurs started to emerge. These practices led to Fidel's famous admonition against "garlic millionaires" and to the closing of the markets. The availability of choice food products such as shellfish, shrimp, and some fruits is also constrained by the economic policy of conserving supplies for export, especially those foods which can be sold on the international dollar market.

While the rationing system provides for a relatively even and sufficient distribution of basic necessities, the production and distribution of nonrationed foods and consumer goods is more problematic. Production problems result from natural phenomena such as droughts and hurricane damage, from the need to import petroleum and raw materials and the consequent reliance on shipping schedules that may be delayed, and from shifting consumer demands that long-range planning cannot anticipate. The larger concern for most Cubans, however, is inefficient distribution. As a result, no one knows for sure when a given product is going to reappear. The consequence is a spiraling cycle of hoarding and shortage. It is easy to tell when a particular fruit or vegetable comes into season and is trucked into the capital city. On these days, as soon as you walk onto the street you see people carrying huge bags full of pineapples, grapefruits, eggplants, and so forth. Hoarding arises not only with foods, but with all sorts of products. Stores may run out of shampoo and other nonperishable items because as soon as large shipments are received, consumers tend to purchase the product in bulk to protect against future shortages, which in turn exacerbates the problem.

For example, most Cubans wash clothes at home because the automated laundries, where they exist, are hot, and it is inconvenient to lug baskets of clothes to the laundromat by bus. I was no exception, preferring the relative convenience of washing clothes at home. The house where I lived during much of the data-collection period had only metal buckets, which tend to stain clothes when they rust. After ruining a favorite blouse, I set out in search of a plastic bucket. I checked several stores near my house and near the University of Havana to no avail. Finally, I succumbed to the temptation to buy a bucket at a government run store that caters to diplomats and other foreigners, where all goods must be purchased in dollars. These stores are called "*diplotiendas.*"[6] There I found my plastic bucket. Walking home with it, I was stopped on the street by a police officer at his post. "Where did you find the bucket?" he asked, "Are there any at La Copa?" (La Copa is a nearby group of stores approximately the size of two city blocks). "No," I replied, "I'm sorry, I got it at the diplo." A few days later it became clear that a shipment of plastic buckets had arrived in Old Havana; in the five-minute walk from a meeting in Old Havana to the bus stop, I counted ten people walking by with several buckets swinging from each arm. Clearly, these people did not need all of the buckets they had purchased. But friends, relatives, and neighbors might need them, and one never knew when they would reappear.

Lunches and nutritious snacks such as yogurt are provided free or at very low cost in all work sites and schools. In addition, Cubans often stop into small cafeterias and cafes for lunches, dinners, or snacks. These are conveniently located in every section of the city, but the choices are often limited to grilled sandwiches and eggs. Soft drink stands are set up all over the city, especially around lunch time and during the heat of the afternoon. Pizzerias abound and are a lunchtime favorite since the pizzas tend to be very good, cheap, and the lines move swiftly. Nice restaurants are also frequented. These offer a more interesting and better prepared range of meals than cafeterias. They are more expensive, however, at about ten *pesos* for a meal and a beer, and lines can be long, particularly if the restaurant has beer. Beer is in very high demand and short supply in Cuba. The shortage is apparently due to the limited supply of beer bottles[7] and to a political decision that favors the use of imported grains for direct consumption and feeding of cattle, rather than as a base for alcoholic beverages.

Salaries

The problem for Cuban consumers is a lack of products, not of money. Most Cubans have a high discretionary income and walk around with wads of *pesos* in their pockets. The median monthly salary in 1989 was 188 *pesos*, for an annual salary of 2256 *pesos* (Comité Estatal de Estadísticas, 1990: Table 6.1, page 112; see further

Appendix A). The Cuban *peso* is worth about $1.25 in U.S. dollars at the official exchange rate.

Salary figures are meaningless without a social and economic context. The goal of social justice in Cuba has meant that prices of basic goods are determined by the salaries of the lowest-paid workers, and many social goods are free. Cubans pay no taxes or social security. Where one's home is not owned outright, housing prices are set at a maximum of 20 percent of one's income, and electricity and basic telephone charges are very low. Rationed foods and commodities and bus transportation are also very cheap, with monthly food rations costing around 12 *pesos* a month per person (Benjamin et al., 1985:36) and buses costing 10 *centavos* (roughly equivalent to 12 cents, U.S.) in urban areas and 20 *centavos* for the longer distances in rural areas. Education and health care are free, and old-age pensions reduce the financial strain of retirement. As a consequence, Cubans tend to have a relatively high level of discretionary income. As an example, a dual-worker family of well-educated professionals brings home between 600 and 800 *pesos* per month. They spend 120 to 150 *pesos* monthly for a two bedroom apartment, 15 (without air conditioning) to 40 (with air conditioning) *pesos* for electricity, 6 to 25 *pesos* for telephone, and around 100 to 150 *pesos* for food, including eating in restaurants and food purchases outside the rationing system, for a total monthly expenditure of 250 to 350 *pesos*. This leaves an extra 350 to 450 *pesos* per month. Persons with lower salaries have less discretionary income, but some money remains each month after paying basic household expenses.

The Media

The most commonly read newspaper in Cuba is the official Communist Party paper, *Granma*. The paper takes its name from the yacht in which Fidel Castro and 82 other revolutionaries sailed from Mexico in 1956 to begin the final phase of the Cuban Revolutionary War. The second most widely read newspaper is *Juventud Rebelde*, published by the Young Communists (UJC), followed by the labor-oriented *Trabajadores*. In addition to these national papers, cities in the interior publish newspapers focusing on local or regional events, and the armed forces and other national institutions publish weekly or monthly newspapers or newsletters. Television and radio also provide news several times daily. The quality of radio news reporting is generally perceived to be superior to that of television. Cubans raise the same complaint about TV news that I hear in the United States: an overemphasis on human-interest stories and insufficient in-depth coverage of major national and international news items. In addition to the formal news segment, there are also regularly scheduled news talk shows on Cuban TV, often with panel discussions presenting various perspectives.

Cubans critique their media regularly, complaining in public and private about the poor quality of journalism, and *Granma* serves as the butt of many jokes. A common refrain in Havana is, "Lend me your copy of *Granma*. It'll only take me a moment to read the news." The borrower then quickly scans the first page for headlined national and international stories and the last two pages for international news off the wires, skipping the middle section entirely. What makes Cuban complaints about their written media interesting in comparison to other Latin American countries is that, with rare exceptions, all Cubans are literate. Most Cubans read the newspaper daily, and even in relatively rural areas TV antennae are visible on rooftops. Thus, Cuban complaints about journalism are particularly telling since almost everyone is directly involved in consuming and critiquing the news media.

Transportation

Most Cubans travel by bus. Buses are very cheap, with the price retained at 5 *centavos* per trip from 1959 until 1988, when the fare was raised to 10 *centavos* in the city and 20 *centavos* in rural areas. School children do not pay a fare if they are going to or from school and often do not pay at other times if they are wearing their school uniforms.

Most, although certainly not all, Cubans pay their fares, even if they enter the bus through a middle or rear door where they do not have to confront the bus driver's glare if they try to sneak in without paying. The typical practice if you enter by a middle or rear door is to pass your 10 *centavos* up to the front. This facilitates a favored method for getting small change: as a handful of money is passed to you en route to the front of the bus, you just make change for yourself. Changing a couple of 20 *centavos* coins in this way is easy; with luck and if you are near the front of the bus you can even get change for a *peso*. Since exact fare is required, if you do not have the correct change and are entering from the front of the bus, you simply offer to use a 20 *centavos* coin to pay for another person boarding at the same time and that person gives you his or her 10 *centavos*.

The transportation system is a common topic of conversation among Cubans and the source for many jokes. On every trip to Cuba, within a day or two of my arrival in Havana my friends ask, "Well, what do you think? Are the buses coming more frequently now than the last time you were here?" This is always a difficult question to answer, since it seems that some days they are better, and other days worse.[8] There appears to be an established schedule since bus operators are checked at various points to ascertain that they are on time. However, none of my Cuban friends and acquaintances know what these schedules are. Bus routes, too, are a mystery. Havana residents know a range of buses that will take them to work, to movie theaters, and other places to which they typically travel, but to take a bus outside of one's normal route is always an interesting event. If you ask three people which bus to take to reach a given locale, you are sure to get three different answers. Generally, two of those three routes will take you close to your destination, but there is always some inexplicable mystery route suggested that takes you far off course.

Because buses seem to appear at random, people are often late arriving at their destinations. The usual delays are exacerbated if one bus on a route breaks down. All other buses on that route quickly become overcrowded, and the driver will not stop to admit more passengers. Occasionally, though, you will estimate that you need 50 minutes (30 minutes to wait for the bus and 20 to get wherever you are going); unexpectedly the proper bus will arrive just as you get to the bus stop, passengers will enter and depart quickly at later stops, and you arrive 35 minutes early! As pleasant as the latter experience always is, it is safer to assume that you will have to wait for the bus. Delays are such a regular feature of daily life that the common apology for tardiness is simply to shrug your shoulders and mutter, "*La guagua*" (the Cuban word for bus) in a sufficiently apologetic or frustrated manner. The uncertainty of just when the next bus on your route will appear is a frequent source of spontaneous exercise as people sprint to catch them. Since running in high heels is uncomfortable and can be dangerous, it is fortunate that the women's movement has led many Cuban women to rid themselves of the typical Latin American custom of wearing very high heels. Those women who wear high heels at work often carry them in a bag and wear sandals, sneakers, or flats in the street.

Most buses are huge, red double buses, hinged together in the middle. Counting passengers lucky enough to find a seat and those standing in the aisles, each bus carries a tremendous number of people. The number of passengers is increased further by the boys and young men hanging out the doors—an illegal and dangerous practice which will result in being thrown off the bus if noticed by a police officer, but which is nonetheless a common sight.

Pregnant women have first priority for seats, with the choicest seats near the front entrance reserved for them. In the hundreds of bus rides I have taken in Cuba, I have only seen one occasion in which a pregnant woman did not get a seat. Then, a seemingly drunk man was dozing, and a pregnant woman was standing nearby. Everyone in that section of the bus began pointing and nodding toward him, and urging the passenger standing next to him to get his attention. He looked up, was told that there was a pregnant woman standing, and said, "So? I got this seat and I'm not moving." The other passengers were aghast, mumbling among themselves and yelling to him that he was a *"malcriado"* and *"sinvergüenza"* (i.e., that he was a jerk and had no shame) among other less polite and more colorful names.

Elderly people come next, then mothers or fathers holding young children, followed by any other women. If someone who is not pregnant, traveling with young children, or elderly gets a seat they will brag to friends about their good luck. For a young or middle-aged man to sit down on a bus is jokingly described as cause for celebration.

Cubans are generally quite good natured about delays for buses, using the waiting time to read the newspaper or a book, to gossip or, if waiting at the main downtown bus stop at the corner of 23 and L streets, to savor a coppelia ice cream cone. Delays once en route are not appreciated, but these too are generally met with good humor. For example, I was once on a crowded bus filled with people coming home from work on a very hot day, and the bus stopped for almost ten minutes in front of a little cafe and a blood bank. My fellow passengers were patient for a minute or two, and then everyone started saying, "What is the bus driver doing?" "Is he getting a cup of coffee?" "Has he gone into the blood bank to give a donation?" "Is he going to the bathroom?" Soon annoyance at the delay gave way to laughter, even though three buses covering the same route whizzed past us. When the bus driver finally climbed back into his seat, he was forced to endure a rich mixture of applause and laughing taunts, such as "Were you in the bathroom?" "How was your coffee? Did you bring one for me?"

In mid-1989, another bus system made its appearance on the streets of Havana. These smaller "omnibuses" follow the same routes as regular buses but hold fewer people and ensure each person a seat. Their cost is also greater, at 40 *centavos* a ride. The reaction to them has been mixed. The increased ease of travel is appreciated, but the two-tiered price structure which has resulted is seen as undesirable.

Taxis provide an alternative to the bus system. To everyone's delight, taxi service improved during the last years of the 1980s, and this improvement was very visible by 1989. In the past, catching a taxi was nearly impossible, since regardless of the hour it was always time for the driver to break for lunch or dinner, or else wherever you wanted to go was too far away. These refusals have been substantially reduced, and in 1989 and early 1990 a taxi could be caught within about five minutes on any major street, except at lunch time when they are still impossible to flag down.

Taxis are relatively cheap at a couple of *pesos* for a ride to most locations within the city, though expensive in comparison to bus transportation. The size of the average tip seems to have increased in recent years, perhaps in an effort to reward this "good behavior." The improvement in taxi service is tied to increasingly vocal demands for such service, including an animated film short entitled *"Eh, taxi,"* which pokes fun at taxis which never stop for passengers or, when they do stop, break down.

In addition to this state-run service, there are privately owned and operated taxis. These are easily recognizable because they are old Fords and Chevrolets from the 1950s painted red and white or yellow. They will take you anywhere in the city for one *peso* per passenger, assuming of course that the driver is willing to go to that location, with the decision based on the perceived likelihood of gathering other passengers en route and on the return trip.

A third type of taxi service is reserved for foreigners as part of Cuba's development of tourism. The fares in *turistaxis* must be paid in dollars and cost about triple the fare for regular taxis. These "dollar taxis" are available in front of all hotels and can sometimes be flagged down on streets if your appearance marks you as a foreigner. Their use is generally limited to short-term tourists, since foreigners residing in Cuba for long periods of time tend either to buy cars or to use the buses and regular taxis frequented by Cubans.

Finally, some Cubans are fortunate enough to own cars. These are either old U.S. cars from the 1950s held together by mechanical wizardry or new cars purchased from other socialist countries. New cars are distributed by the workplaces, with the determination of who is to receive a car based on a combination of merit and need. The decision is made by the workplace administration and union, typically upon the recommendation of a committee elected from among the workers. This system results in cars going to the best workers or those who would particularly benefit from them, such as persons with leg or hip problems who have trouble climbing the steep steps on buses. It is, however, apparent that more cars are available to top-level officials, both as a reward or patronage and because top officials are expected to arrive at appointments on time, and having a car is the only way to ensure punctuality.

As late as 1989, Soviet-made Ladas distributed through the workplace cost about 4,000 *pesos*, with long-term payment available at very low interest rates. A Soviet visitor to Cuba lamented that the same car cost twice as much in the Soviet Union. I was frequently told by car owners, "The big problem is not paying for the car, but rather paying for maintenance of it." It is also possible to buy a car from one's savings, but privately purchased cars cost more than those distributed through the workplaces and are beyond the means of the average Cuban. Changing terms of trade with Eastern European countries and the former Soviet Union mean that cars will be in shorter supply and will become more expensive. The desire of Eastern European countries to earn hard currency from their auto exports was evident as early as the fall of 1989, when Poland requested dollars as payment for auto parts.

Cars are not as common in the countryside as in the city, and most cars and trucks in the rural areas tend to be left over from the 1950s. Bicycles, motorcycles, and motor scooters with sidecars for a third person are more common there, and many people travel by horseback. Bus stops can be found throughout the small towns and alongside the highways traversing rural areas.

Interprovincial travel is difficult unless you own a car, and even then gas rationing impedes long-distance travel for pleasure. Buses and trains carry people from one part of the island to another, but access is not easy as advance reservations are needed, and the buses and trains stop only in provincial capitals and other major cities.

Health Care

Health care is one of the most important benefits of the Revolution in the eyes of the Cuban people. Medical care is of very high quality and is available to everyone free of charge. Even surgery (including abortions, which must be performed in hospitals) is free, although the expectation is that someone in the family will donate blood in return. Cuba is a health-care leader within Latin America and the socialist world, and, some would say, in the world in general. The excellent health of the population is due in large part to the nutritious diet available to all Cubans. In marked contrast to my experiences in other Latin American cities, I have never seen anyone in Havana, or elsewhere in the country, who looked malnourished. Nor have I seen anyone under age 40 (i.e., about 10 years old in 1959) with rotting teeth, dental health being indicative of both a nourishing diet and high-quality dental care.

Hospitals and clinics abound. Polyclinics treat minor ailments and give inoculations. Some hospitals specialize in certain types of cases (e.g., oncology, obstetrics, etc.), while others offer general care. The census data presented in Appendix B show that Cuba had a total of

393 medical aid facilities in 1958, only one of which was located in a rural area. By 1985, there were 1,788 medical aid facilities. Of these, 57 hospitals and 281 medical posts serve rural areas. Similarly, the 10 maternity clinics in 1958 grew to 128 maternity hospitals or homes by 1985. Appendix C demonstrates a parallel growth in the number of persons working in medical fields, from 2,404 in 1958 to 125,955 in 1986.

A Cuban woman I met in 1985 told me that she had moved to the United States, but she returned to Cuba because her son had a blood disease and required transfusions on a regular basis. In Texas, it was very difficult to get her son to the hospital as often as was necessary, and the cost of medical care for chronic illness was prohibitive. She returned to Havana because the free health care, large number of polyclinics and hospitals, and willingness of neighbors and family to take her son to the clinic when she was working made it easier to keep her son alive.

Immediately after Castro came to power in 1959, the new government began training large numbers of doctors, in part to replace those who had left the country, and also to provide medical service for the rural population. In 1963, the private practice of medicine was renounced. Upon graduation, medical students worked in the countryside as their *servicio social* (social service)—a means of repayment for the social and economic costs of their training. This practice continues today, although not all new doctors begin work in the rural areas.

Complementing the national network of hospitals and polyclinics, the "family doctor" system was initiated in 1984 on an experimental basis in one Havana municipality. In 1986, it was expanded throughout the country. According to the director of the polyclinic for the Havana municipality "Tenth of October," by May 1989, the ratio of doctors per inhabitants was down to one doctor for every 650 inhabitants (personal interview, May 8, 1989). In March 1990 there were 8,695 family doctors distributed throughout all provinces of the country, a number sufficient to care for 46.9 percent of the population. This figure increased to 10,465 over the next six months, meeting the needs of 60 percent of the population. The ultimate goal is 25,000 family doctors (Rodríguez, 1990:2). The family doctors receive free housing, complete with refrigerator, color television set, and two telephones (one for personal use, the other for consultations), and they have to pay only electric and personal phone bills. This system allows the doctor to get to know the family members in the area and, with this more complete family profile, to better serve the medical needs of the community. In Havana, doctors are located on almost every city block. It is in the countryside, though, where family doctors are most appreciated, since historically medical care in rural areas was lacking. In a farmers' cooperative that I visited in 1990, a family doctor was assigned to three communities totaling about 200 families.

Preventive medicine is very important in Cuba. Regular physical and dental checkups are routine, prenatal care is commonplace, and pregnant women pass immediately to the front of lines so they will not have to stand for lengthy periods of time. Most prescription medicines are free, although there are charges for some scarce imported medicines that must be purchased in dollars. Children receive vaccinations against polio and other diseases that are the scourge of the Third World. Serious efforts have been made to prevent the return of diseases such as cholera and malaria, which no longer exist in Cuba. For example, persons flying to Cuba from Central America, Africa, and other parts of the world where malaria is common are screened for the disease. If they test positive, they cannot board the plane; if they test negative, they must still take a three-day malaria treatment prior to departure in case they have contracted the disease but it has not yet shown up in the blood test.

Cubans are also cognizant of the latest in preventive health care trends. Although cigarette smoking is still common, people talk constantly about the associated health risks, and many people have quit smoking. I was frequently stopped on the streets of Havana by young children who chastised me, warning, "Smoking is bad for you; you should quit." Cubans are also very conscious of the perils of high cholesterol. Cholesterol levels are checked regularly in annual physical exams, and signs on tables in popular restaurants advise consumers to switch to olive oil since it is low in cholesterol. But the most important aspect of preventive health care in Cuba is the availability to the entire population of an adequate diet, drinking water free from contaminants, and a functioning sewage system.

Health care is so good in Cuba that it has developed into a special form of tourism. People from other Latin American and Caribbean countries, particularly, and also from other socialist countries, travel to Cuba for specialized medical care including heart bypasses, eye surgery to correct glaucoma and nearsightedness, and pigmentation disorders. Some of these patients receive free health care while others pay for it, depending upon the patient's financial circumstances and agreements between the countries involved. Several hotels in Havana and in the countryside reserve one or more wings for recuperating international patients and their families.

Leisure Time

Most Cubans work an eight-hour workday Monday through Friday and every other Saturday, for an average work week of 44 hours. After leaving work for the day, many people participate in voluntary construction work or community activities, and considerable time each evening must be spent preparing dinner, washing clothes, cleaning house, and performing other domestic tasks. While Cuban men have responded to the social pressure embodied in the Family Code to share in household and child-care responsibilities, women still do most of this "second-shift" labor. Nevertheless, there is often time for some leisure activity in the evening and on weekends.

Leisure time in the evenings is typically spent visiting with friends and neighbors and watching television. Movies, music videos, and Brazilian and Spanish soap operas appear on TV nightly. Many of the TV movies and videos are made in the United States and captured by satellites. Bus stop conversation suggests that the soap operas are widely watched by both men and women, and they are reviewed weekly in the national newspaper, *Granma.*

Movies are also an important way to spend leisure time, particularly in the summer, since movie theaters are air conditioned. They are easily affordable, at one *peso,* and accessible, with movie theaters located in almost every neighborhood in urban areas. People talk constantly about the films currently showing, and new movies are reviewed in *Granma.* Cuban films are very popular, as are movies from other Latin American countries, Europe, and the United States. The content of Cuban movies is analyzed incessantly. Since the arts, in Cuba as in most of the world, provide a forum for political and social critique, films are a means of expressing new ideas visually. Video theaters are also a popular locale for passing leisure time, although they are not as common as movie theaters. Beyond their entertainment value, videos provide insights into life in other societies and are sometimes watched for professional reasons. For example, on one occasion when I was in Havana, several members of the University of Havana Law Faculty had just seen the video *The Paper Chase,* which is a humorous account of legal education in a prominent U.S. law school.

While movies, videos, and TV are commonly available at relatively cheap prices in the United States as well as Cuba, "high culture," such as ballets, plays, operas, and symphonies, is not generally accessible to the average U.S. citizen. Prior to 1959, such cultural activities were also inaccessible to most Cubans, but a determination was made by the new government to offer cultural events at prices everyone could afford. As a result, seats in the orchestra at the national ballet cost two *pesos,* with the best seats costing three *pesos*. Tickets for other "high-culture" events are similarly priced. Indeed, coming from the U.S. I found it amusing and intriguing the first time I went to a ballet in Cuba and discovered that a glass of wine sold during intermission cost as much as the price of admission. In addition to performances by Cuban artists, there is a constant stream of international artists. Based upon my experiences at these cultural events, attendance is fairly high, ranging from one-third of the seats sold to a full house. As is the case for movies, schedules and reviews of performances are published in the newspaper.

Music is an important feature of Cuban life. Free concerts are held regularly in Havana's huge *Plaza de la Revolución,* the central plaza of the University of Havana, and large plazas in other cities. These are extremely well attended, particularly when the performers include popular *Nueva Canción* artists such as Silvio Rodríguez and Pablo Milanés, or Los Van Van and other Afro-Caribbean musicians. Major performances, particularly those by world-renowned songwriter and singer Silvio Rodríguez, are also televised live for the benefit of those who prefer to watch in the comfort of their living rooms rather than brave the crowds. These performances are open to all, with the exception of some concerts held at the University of Havana for which entry is restricted to students, faculty, and staff. Persons who are not affiliated with the University throng the area, listening from the entrance to the University or streets surrounding it. Occasionally a major artist will stage neighborhood concerts, as occurred for example during the spring of 1989 when Pablito (Pablo Milanés) performed every Sunday in a different neighborhood.

Weekends bring crowds of families to parks, particularly the huge and beautifully landscaped Lenin Park on the outskirts of Havana, with its zoo and botanical garden. Mime acts, puppet shows, and other planned and impromptu shows lend a festive air to Lenin Park every Sunday.

Sports are another common leisure-time activity and are strongly encouraged by the government because of their health benefits. Athletic activities range from the very informal to the highly organized, with open access facilities for both individual (e.g., swimming) and group (e.g., basketball) sports available for all in gigantic arenas. One arena in Havana is so large that it is called "Sports City." In addition to these public arenas, each labor union owns a social center which often includes tennis and basketball courts, beaches, and baseball and track fields, in addition to a social hall for parties.

Basketball courts are in evidence everywhere and are filled with groups of young people playing ball. Jogging has also become a popular means of exercise. In the early mornings and evenings joggers are a regular sight along major and side streets. Baseball, however, is the Cubans' first love. After school and on weekends, a common sight in both cities and the countryside is a group of boys, and sometimes also girls, playing baseball. While adults are not generally seen on the baseball fields in the afternoons, fathers coaching their children are a common sight between dinner time and sunset, and on weekends. As for adult baseball, it is difficult to engage in a conversation about anything else during the national series held each spring! During these games men, particularly, and women stay glued to their television sets, watching the hotly contested series.

Exercise is not limited to the young. In recent years "*círculos de abuelos*" have sprung up. These are aerobics classes geared to the elderly ("*abuelos*" means "grandparents"). *Círculos* of between 20 and 40 elderly women, and some men, are visible throughout Havana's parks about eight o'clock every weekday morning.

But the most common forms of exercise remain dancing and swimming. Rumba, and in 1990 also lambada, dances are held on nonworking Saturdays in Havana, and neighborhood culture houses and night clubs are always filled with young couples dancing. Parties are constant features, with dancing well into the night. Whenever the weather is hot (by Cuban standards this is April through October; visitors from cooler climates would say that it is always hot in Cuba), Cubans vacate the cities for the beaches. A common joke is that if you want to find a Cuban during summer vacation (every worker receives a month of vacation each year) you need to publish a notice in *Granma* asking to which beach they have gone. On Sundays and nonworking Saturdays the beaches fill up by midmorning, and stay packed with roasting bodies until close to dusk.

Going to the beach is so common that Monday morning office conversation consists of "Which beach did you go to yesterday?" rather than "Did you go to the beach yesterday?" I assume there are some, but I have yet to meet a Cuban who does not know how to swim. People travel to beaches by car or bus, often taking along a picnic lunch to avoid the lines at oceanside restaurants. The beaches are fun, as long as you do not mind children racing past, kicking sand onto your towel in their exuberance, ignoring their parents' calls of " *¡oye!*" (listen [to me]) when they know they will be chided to settle down. For Cubans who live relatively far from nice beaches, lakes and lagoons serve as well, with kids swinging into the lagoons from old tires.

Because of the national significance placed on tourism as a means of generating needed dollars, hotels on the prettiest beaches are reserved during the high tourism season for international tourists paying with dollars.[9] The resentment this causes is partially assuaged by the availability of some of these gorgeous beaches to Cuban tourists during the off-season and because all beaches are pretty, with their white sand, coral reefs, and multiple shades of blue and green water.

Finally, the highly literate Cuban population uses spare time for reading. Books, magazines, and newspapers are incredibly cheap and are readily available at bookstores and newspaper stands throughout the city. As Appendix G shows, the number of book titles published in Cuba tripled between 1971 and 1985.

Housing

In 1984, the Cuban government decided to get out of the landlord business. The 1984 housing law (*Ley de Viviendas*) and its 1988 modification made Cubans the owners of their homes. Instead of paying rent, Cubans now pay a mortgage with a maximum duration of 15 years (or 20 for certain types of structures), at which point they own their houses outright. Mortgage payments are limited to a maximum of twenty percent of the family income, an increase from the ten percent maximum under the rental system. Cubans can own vacation homes as well as their primary residences. No Cuban can rent housing to another person, since gaining money without labor and at the expense of another person is contrary to Cuba's version of socialism. Houses can be inherited, and families may trade housing if they wish (Dávalos Fernández, 1990; Article 42 of the 1988 *Ley de Viviendas*).

Nobody is homeless, but shortages are a problem, particularly in Havana. A major platform of the revolutionary forces prior to their triumph was that they would serve the neglected rural areas. They have kept this promise but, some say, to the detriment of the urban areas. In practical terms, this meant that housing construction was emphasized in the rural areas and smaller cities before it was extended to Havana. Appendix D indicates that construction of new housing increased almost ten-fold between 1964 and 1984, from 7,088 to 68,963. Much of the new housing is in cooperatives, generally in rural areas. Between 1981 and 1987, the number of cooperatives increased by a factor of eight, from 610 to 4,802.

In recent years, the government has made a concerted effort to build more new housing in Havana and to repair older homes. Yet as one friend lamented in March of 1989, "The government is working on this problem and many houses have been built in the last two years, but they should have started earlier and it is still a serious problem, especially when a couple has to live with one of their parents."

The recent resurgence of the microbrigades has been a tremendous boon to housing construction. Microbrigades consist of groups of voluntary (or semivoluntary, since it is expected that everyone will do some "voluntary" labor) workers from different state enterprises who build houses, hospitals and clinics, day-care centers, hotels, and schools. They are a response to the shortage of construction workers, which in turn is a consequence of so many youths receiving university educations and gaining employment in intellectual capacities. As I was constantly told, "Everyone wants to be an engineer, not a construction worker." The solution to this dilemma—a problem which developed precisely because the population is so well educated—has been to supplement construction teams with workers from other fields, including engineers!

Depending upon the schedule arranged by the workplace administration and the Ministry of Construction, members of microbrigades engage in construction on nonworking Saturdays, one or two workdays each month, or daily for three- to six-month periods. Some Cubans also do construction work when they leave the office in the evenings if they are not too tired.

Most voluntary workers are quite proud of their efforts, as they see their labor transformed into finished buildings with signs in front of them reading, "This apartment building of 64 residences [or hospital, etc.] is being constructed through the labor of Microbrigade number [whatever] of [name of enterprise]." While some "micros" do better work than others, or are faster than others, particular attention is given to the work of Microbrigade Contingent Blas Roca. The common joke in Havana when construction of a new building begins is, "Who is building this? If it is the Blas Roca Contingent it will be done in two weeks!" While that estimate is rather exaggerated, the Blas Roca Contingent has a reputation for working hard and fast, with members often staying at the work site for 14 or 16 hours. Problems sometimes arise, however, when office workers who know nothing about construction make mistakes which can be time consuming and costly to repair. This reduces the efficiency of the work of the micros.

The housing shortage is particularly acute in Havana. One-fifth of the population lives in the capital city, resulting in a very densely populated area. New housing units are springing up on the edges of the city, but many people who work downtown do not want to live in the suburbs because commuting by bus is so time consuming. The most decrepit parts of Old Havana have been condemned and are being reconstructed, but many residents object to the forced breakup of their communities. The distance not only to work, but also to friends and family, makes relocation unattractive to them.

The housing shortage is so acute in the most desirable areas of Havana that housing has become a major factor contested in divorce settlements (Michalowski, 1989). Sometimes people will wait to get a divorce until additional housing is available, or the divorced couple will simply live in different rooms in the same house. It is difficult to determine whether the frequency of extended families living together in one house is due to the housing shortage, to a cultural emphasis on the family, or both. My sense is that most Cubans would prefer to live close to their parents and extended family but not in the same housing unit, thus affording young couples privacy while maintaining close proximity to other family members. I do know that the mobility pattern among the U.S. middle class, where children often live at opposite ends of the country from their parents, seems bizarre and very undesirable to most Cubans. Indeed, when my friends learn that I live 3,000 miles away from my parents their response is typically a shocked "*¡pobrecita!*" ("Poor little thing!").

Most houses and apartment complexes in the cities are made of concrete. Similar complexes can be found in rural cooperatives, but most houses in the countryside are made of wood, with wood, tile, metal, or thatched roofs. Many houses in the countryside have individual or neighborhood wells, while others have tanks suggesting that water is pumped in from underground water lines or delivered by water trucks.

Almost all houses in Cuba, including those in relatively remote rural areas, now have electricity, running water, and sewage disposal. A few also have hot water. Water shortages are, nevertheless, a serious problem due in part to the insufficient reservoirs of water and in part to pipe corrosion, which reduces water pressure. For example, the University of Havana's faculty guest house, where I lived in 1989, had constant water shortages because of aging pipes leading up to the house from the street. When there is no water, you borrow it from neighbors, filling large buckets and lugging them back to your house for cooking, bathing, and flushing the toilets. The problem was so common in the university guest house that we kept a hose attached to an outdoor faucet in a neighbor's back yard so we would not have to climb the fence or walk around the yard to get water. If the shortage lasts for more than a few hours (because a motor burns out and a replacement part is not available, for example), a water truck can be called to fill the tank set on top of each house. The situation is particularly bad in Old Havana, where it is not uncommon to see water hoisted up to fifth floor apartments.

Many, but not most, houses have telephone lines. If you do not have a telephone, a neighbor often does. This leads to the common practice of giving out your neighbor's phone number so messages can be left for you. When neighbors with phones are not at home and you need to make a call, pay phones are usually available within a five- or ten-minute walk. Some pay phones seem to function on a regular basis; others never seem to work. Because so many people lack phones, and the phones frequently do not work, friends and relatives tend simply to drop by unannounced. This is not generally a problem, unless you have to take a bus or two only to find that the person you wanted to see is not at home.

Education

Education is very good in Cuba. Immediately following the triumph of the Revolution in 1959, the new government initiated a literacy campaign which has garnered international recognition. Teams of young people with some education went into the countryside to teach other youths and adults how to read and write. While the primary purpose of this campaign was to reduce illiteracy, a secondary outcome was an important shift in gender relations. For many girls and young women, it was the first time that they were away from their fathers' control, and this new independence struck a serious blow to the existing patriarchal arrangements.

Education in Cuba is free and compulsory until age 16. There are huge numbers of schools and the student-teacher ratio is quite good, at 12.1 in 1986/87 in the secondary and pre-university schools (see Appendix E) and 11.76 in the technical and professional schools (see Appendix F). School uniforms are purchased through the rationing system at very low prices and are free for students on scholarships. Books are loaned to the students free of charge. The free availability of school books at every educational level is so central to Cuban conceptions of equality and education that when students at the University of Havana sought in 1985 to have their textbooks available for purchase, the constitutionality of that request came into question. Some students wanted to underline passages and write comments in their textbooks, and then keep the books for their own professional libraries rather than return them to the University. Yet selling textbooks was contrary to the constitutional right to a free education. The National Assembly's Commission on Constitutional and Legal Affairs finally determined that textbooks could be sold, so long as a sufficient supply was also available for students to borrow.

The value attached to education is also evidenced by the very low price of books sold in Cuba and their large quantity by Third World standards (see Appendix G). Books are incredibly cheap, ranging from about 10 *centavos* to a maximum of about 15 *pesos* for high-quality art books that would cost well over $100 in the United States. I am constantly amazed when I walk out of a bookstore with two armloads of books, having paid about seven *pesos* ($8.75 U.S.). The popularity of books causes some to be in short demand, however. For example, novels by the Colombian author Gabriel García Márquez sell out in a day or two, and I once watched as a cart of about 200 copies of the autobiography of musician Silvio Rodríguez sold out in three hours.

Cuban education is not only viewed as important, it is quite good by U.S. standards. Children study a wide range of subjects, and when they enter the university, they have a better basic background than is my experience with students in the U.S. Nevertheless, in the early 1980s, the Cuban government and the Communist Party criticized the failure of many professionals to continue their postgraduate studies and urged Cubans to study independently as well as through formal course work. In response, in the mid-1980s the various professional associations began to promote postgraduate work and to offer seminars in their specialty areas at night and on Saturdays.

THE RESEARCH

In discussing "imperialist nostalgia," Renato Rosaldo warns,

> Because researchers are necessarily both somewhat impartial and somewhat partisan, somewhat innocent and somewhat complicit, their readers should be as informed as possible about what the observer was in a position to know and not know (1989:69).

This admonition takes on greater import when readers are poorly informed about the society studied, since with little prior knowledge they must rely almost solely on what the author tells them. The political antagonism between the United States and Cuban governments has meant that the information about Cuba reaching U.S. audiences is very limited and almost completely negative in slant. From the Cuban side, there is a strong distrust of the U.S. government on the part of Cuban officials. As a researcher, I must straddle these two predispositions. Whether or not I have been able to set my "nostalgia" aside is for the reader to determine.

Data collection took place during eight trips to Cuba during the period from 1985 through 1991, including two three-month stays in

1989 when I was a Visiting Researcher at the University of Havana. The other trips were for periods of two or three weeks each. My research was based in the capital city of Havana, but I also traveled into the countryside and interior cities on several occasions.

For the first few trips I stayed in hotels; beginning in 1989 I lived either in the University of Havana's faculty guest house in Miramar, a relatively affluent suburb of Havana proper, or in friends' houses in the city. I lived essentially as the Cubans do—taking buses or walking, waiting in line to enter restaurants and stores, sweating in the heat, trading gossip and jokes with friends. A few times, when I had meetings with high-level officials and wanted to arrive punctually and not drenched in sweat, I broke down and took dollar taxis, but I prided myself on making such instances extremely rare. Thus, to the extent possible for a foreigner, I lived as a Cuban.

The analysis could not have been conducted without immersing myself in the culture. This was necessary to gather the ethnographic data, including understanding the jokes and the gossip, and to make the many contacts necessary to untangle both the theoretic threads of my research and also the Cuban bureaucracies. It was also crucial for gaining the trust of the Cubans. The fact that I was a scholar from the United States never escaped my sources' consciousness, but over the course of many meetings with the same officials and scholars a rapport developed, and with it a level of trust that allowed my sources to become more open with me. It was not until the summer of 1990, during my seventh trip to Cuba, when I finally was assured that I had attained this level of trust. In a meeting with Renén Quirós Pírez (law professor, advisor to two Ministers of Justice, legal scholar, and "father" of all criminal codes from the 1970s to the present) to review draft chapters of this manuscript, we discussed what I thought would be a controversial interpretation of a particularly embarrassing episode in the history of the Ministry of the Interior and its effects on interagency power plays (discussed in Chapter Three). When I asked Dr. Quirós what he thought of my analysis he said, "There are enemies hiding as friends; you are a true friend (*amiga amiga*). You should say what you think, as a sociologist. Your candid interpretations are helpful to us."

The analysis is based on a variety of data sources and types: (1) targeted semistructured interviews with key actors; (2) documentary data and inter and intraoffice memoranda obtained from sources interviewed; (3) census documents; (4) ethnographic data; (5) a comprehensive review of Cuban law journals, newsletters, and books published since 1959; (6) informal interviews and questions asked of a wide scope of people, ranging from high government officials to people crowded next to me on buses; and (7) observation of trials.

Approximately 100 formal interviews of about two hours each were conducted with law and sociology professors; officials and researchers at the Ministry of Justice; officials in the Office of the Attorney General of the Republic, including the Attorney General himself; members of the criminology research team in the Ministry of the Interior; professional and lay judges in municipal and provincial courts and the Supreme Court; members of several commissions in the National Association of Cuban Jurists; criminal defense and civil attorneys working in law collectives; representatives of the Federation of Cuban Women; delegates to the National Assembly, including the chair of the Constitutional and Legal Affairs Commission; members of inter-organizational commissions to study and draft new legislation; and a representative of the State Committee for Economic Collaboration.

These lengthy interviews served as the primary data source for my analyses of lawmaking and legal reform efforts. To better understand the contexts in which particular changes came about, I rely heavily on the retrospective and contemporaneous accounts of those persons responsible for writing the laws and policies. Some of my sources were interviewed only once, others met with me numerous times in differing settings. Some were Communist Party members, others were not. Interviews were conducted in formal meetings and over lunches, dinners, and drinks; in offices, court houses, private homes, and the University guest house.

Most of the formal interviews were taped and then transcribed. When I could not tape them I took careful notes, and following interviews and informal conversations that were not taped, I immediately wrote down my recollections of the discussions. Following every interview, whether taped or not, I noted my general impressions of the source and my perceptions of his or her degree of frankness and openness. All interviews were conducted in Spanish, in which I am fluent. By asking the same or related questions of different sources, I generally was able to obtain data from three independent sources before drawing any conclusions. Where I received contradictory information or interpretations, I have noted the discrepancies in the text.

The law professors at the University of Havana put up with my constant note taking, as offhand comments about meetings they attended inspired what must have seemed to be a never-ending series of questions. Finally, I kept a lengthy journal of my impressions, of events and comments I saw and heard on the streets, in friends' homes, and in offices, of the prices and availability of goods, the latest political jokes, and anything interesting appearing in the media. Where my informal sources could be compromised, I wrote abbreviated reminders to myself and filled in the material upon my return to the U.S.

The analysis was historical and comparative in nature. Content analyses were conducted on the interview and documentary data, along with a more general triangulation of all of the data. Mostly, analysis consisted of a process of sorting through stacks of paper searching for patterns. Data collection and analysis were enhanced by a sharing of observations and data with two other U.S. scholars of the Cuban legal system, Debra Evanson and Raymond Michalowski. The three of us worked on independent but related research projects, and where our sources differed, we were able to confirm information each of us had gathered separately. In 1989 and 1990 I presented preliminary results of my research to Cuban audiences, receiving important feedback from them, and in 1990 and 1991 I reviewed draft chapters with my primary sources to check for accuracy and for alternative interpretations of the data.

The research could not have been conducted without the access provided by the Department of International Relations in the Ministry of Justice and the Law School at the University of Havana. While many interviews and documentary data were obtained through friends or professional contacts made during the course of my research, most of the interviews with high-level officials and access to some documentary data were facilitated by the Ministry of Justice and by the University of Havana Law School. The International Relations Department of the Ministry of Justice and the Law School went far beyond their formal responsibilities for me as a visiting researcher (e.g., approving my visas, arranging interviews), spending countless hours out of their very busy schedules helping me with my work.

As my analysis demonstrates, the upper echelons of Cuban legal bureaucracies are made up of a small and tightly interwoven set of actors, not surprising in a tiny Third World country. What this means is that everyone knows everyone, and has played multiple roles (see Chapter Three, Table 3.2 for a listing). For example, the Director of International Relations at the Ministry of Justice, Dr. María Luisa Arteaga Abreu, previously served as a diplomat, as the first president of the National Organization of Law Collectives (to which all criminal and civil trial lawyers belong), and was one of the law students involved in establishing the popular tribunals in the early 1960s. She also happens to be married to Ramón de la Cruz Ochoa, the Attorney General of the Republic from 1986 to 1993 and former first Vice-Minister of Justice. As a result, Dr. Arteaga was able to go far beyond the protocol of opening doors for me. "La doctora," as she is known within the Ministry, was able, and willing, to offer an insider's view of several key points in Cuban legal history.

Dr. Arteaga's professional biography is not unique. Most high-level legal authorities have a wide range of professional experience and can offer informed opinions about a variety of aspects of Cuban law as it has developed since 1959. Perhaps because of their personal involvement in legal unfoldings over the years, or perhaps because they are so highly situated within the political bureaucracy that they are relatively immune to criticism, I found that these top officials were far more willing to offer candid, and at times critical (and self-critical), assessments of the past, present, and future of juridical life in Cuba than were middle-level bureaucrats.

Why the Cubans permitted and facilitated this research is a question that must be considered. Two reasons suggest themselves. First, several high-level officials and law professors told me that they expected my research to be helpful to them in the course of their own work. Cuban legal scholars clearly enjoyed our sharing of socio-legal theories, and took great interest in my interpretations of their data, including sometimes their own words. In some cases, scholars and officials reviewing tables and figures I had created said, "Oh, you have a complete listing of this! Can I have a copy?" Second, the Cubans are quite proud of the advances that they have made in the legal arena, and they hope that publication of this work in the United States will help fill the information void in the U.S. concerning Cuban law. Certainly, political factors influenced the availability of data, and some elements are undoubtedly missing, yet the diversity of the data sources and the consistent patterns which emerged give me confidence in my results.

I began this work with an overview of contemporary daily life in Cuba, and particularly in Havana, during the period from 1985 to 1990. The Cuban population is well educated, healthy, and generally happy. Challenges to the political-economic system arise from within the citizenry as part of the Cuban people's ongoing efforts to improve their version of socialism. Cuba has not experienced the ossification and overwhelming bureaucratization of the former Soviet Union and some other Eastern European countries, in part because it is still a relatively young Revolution and in part because the population is itself young, vigorous, and energetic.

Nevertheless, serious complaints are raised in private and, increasingly, in public. Probably in large part as a response to drastic changes in Eastern Europe, the Cuban Communist Party leadership in 1990 called for discussions of how to improve political and economic life within the general bounds of a socialist economy and a one-party state. My own sense is that most Cubans would like more consumer goods, a greater variety of food products and restaurants, more taxis, and better service. But, these same people are not willing to give up free and excellent health care and educational systems, nor are they willing to forego the availability of housing and a nutritious diet for all Cubans, or any of the other advances wrought by the Revolution. Cubans of all walks of life are adamant in their refusal to let the exile community in Miami dictate the future of their country.

Part One of the book continues, in Chapter Two, with an introduction to my theoretical model and my stance on some of the relevant debates within the socio-legal community. This provides a framework for understanding the "production" of Cuban socialist legality. I merge a Marxist theory of lawmaking with the literature on the dialectical relationship between formalism and informalism of law. I suggest that changes in both the content of law and the mix of legal formalism and informalism make sense as temporary resolutions to interinstitutional conflicts and dilemmas arising from contradictory structural and historical forces. Ideology is central to my model, since these conflicts cannot be resolved without continual attention to the ideological orientation and immediate as well as long-term goals of the society.

I posit three strategies employed by the Cubans to resolve conflicts and dilemmas. These are the process of law creation, the mix of practical and theoretical legal education, and legal adaptations from abroad. Each of these strategies reflects a means of "producing" socialist legality in Cuba.

The second part of the book elaborates upon these three strategies. Chapter Three applies the broad-based, iterative process of law creation to specific changes in Cuban law. Particular attention is paid to changes in the Law of Criminal Procedure, the Laws of the Organization of the Judicial System and of the Courts, and the Family Code. Each serves as an example of how both the content of law and the mix of legal formalism and informalism are altered through the lawmaking process.

In Chapter Four we move from the production of laws to the production of the next generation of lawyers. Here, the combination of theoretical and practical legal education, designed to prepare future lawyers for the tasks awaiting them, is detailed. The mix of classroom and practical work by Cuban law professors is another aspect of this strategy. Ideologically and practically, it augments their ability to provide students with a blend of theory and practical knowledge, provides an important service to the community, and reduces the risk of an "ivory tower" mentality that could too easily sever the university from the larger society.

Chapter Five focuses upon the strategy of selective legal adaptations. This involves the careful examination of foreign legal models and theories as Cuban lawyers continue to improve both their legal system and their legal theorizing. Interview data are supplemented by analysis of the sources of published influences on Cuban legal thought. In combination with foreign trade data presented in Appendix H, this allows me to determine the extent to which Cuba imports goods and ideas from the same trading partners.

Another way of looking at the "production" and "reproduction" of socialist legality is through the law in action. The third part of this book examines the courts and conflict resolution in the workplace. Chapter Six focuses on the operation of the courts at all levels. Particular attention is placed on the role of lay judges as conveyers of public sentiment into court decisions—and of legal knowledge back to the general public—and on the relationship between lay and professional judges.

Chapter Seven addresses dispute resolution through the labor councils established in each workplace. These councils are the only example of judicial decisionmaking performed solely by lay people, although verdicts can be appealed in court. As I show, one of the most contested features of Cuban labor law is the ability of workers' councils and lower courts to review and overturn disciplinary actions made by administrators. Vacillations in this policy make workers' councils an inconsistent source of power for labor. This discussion sheds light on the structural limits of informalism when the state, be it capitalist or socialist, requires high levels of economic productivity.

Finally, Chapter Eight offers a discussion of the implications of how socialist legality is produced in Cuba—past, present, and future. The importance for the Cubans of respect in the international legal community is highlighted here, as is the relationship between the legal order and other institutional spheres. As in every aspect of Cuban life, economic considerations vie with ideological goals as the leadership attempts to meet the country's multiple and competing needs. The strategies the leadership select are, I suggest, our best indicators of how they translate what are often abstract concerns into visible policies affecting people's everyday lives. Within the legal sphere, these strategies show us how Cuban-style socialist legality is produced.

CHAPTER 2

THE FORM
AND CONTENT
OF LEGALITY
INTEGRATING STRUCTURE
AND IDEOLOGY

One of the first decisions of any newly established government is the content of law. This is determined by the beliefs held by the political leadership and includes those substantive concerns (e.g., agrarian reform, counter-revolutionary activities, gender equality) that they think can be addressed by the legal order. A second and related decision is what form the legal order will take. The essence of this decision is the mix of formalism and informalism that characterizes the judicial arena.

While informalism has become a central concern of legal reformers and scholars (see Abel, 1981:245), empirical research has been hindered by a lack of conceptual clarity. Informalism has been operationalized in various ways, each of which has distinct emphases.[1] Some socio-legal scholars define informalism and formalism of law in terms of ideal-typical poles of a continuum, others see them as homologous, and still others as dialectically interrelated. The most widely studied aspect of informalism is the relationship between local normative orders and the wider social structure, including state agencies, but the multiple nuances of this relationship make any conclusions tentative. Even the criticisms of informalism are inconsistent. Some scholars criticize the informalism movement for expanding the state's social-control apparatus and defusing opposition, others for the risk informalism poses to civil-rights gains that are enforceable only by the state's formal legal order. I suggest that this conceptual vagueness arises from the artificial separation of the form of law from the substantive content of particular laws, and from the failure to locate changes in both the form and content of law within the broader context of structural and historical influences on the society. Furthermore, ideas about legal formalism and informalism developed in the United States and Britain may be biased as a consequence of First World perceptions and experiences (Zatz and Zhu, 1991). These concepts may have little meaning in other parts of the world, regardless of how we operationalize them. These limitations impede research on the nature, sources, and consequences of variation in legal institutions and constrain our understanding of the relationship between legal and social change.

In this chapter I argue that theories of informalism should be integrated with a dialectical theory of lawmaking. This allows us to examine more precisely the relationship between the form and content of law in a particular setting. William Chambliss's structural-contradictions theory provides a useful starting point.[2] He suggests that changes in the content of law, including creation of new laws, are temporary resolutions to conflicts and dilemmas ensuing from contradictory structural forces. Structural contradictions are abstract concepts which cannot themselves be resolved. They are manifested visibly in conflicts between social groups. How best to relieve the tensions they create poses a dilemma for the political leadership.

My integrated theory is consistent with a more general Marxist emphasis on the global political economy in comparative socio-legal research.[3] I see changes in the content of specific laws, the mix of legal formalism and informalism, and the relationship between the form and content of law as reflections of ongoing efforts to resolve conflicts stemming from contradictory structural forces in ways that are ideologically acceptable. I narrow the focus by examining how these multiple factors play out in one particular society—Cuba. The Cuban case sharpens the analysis because it highlights swift changes occurring in a new, revolutionary context.

I begin with the fundamental contradictions within a given society (see Figure 2.1 on the following page). Some contradictions have historical origins within Cuban society; others result from Cuba's place within the larger capitalist world economy. Contradictions create and are manifested in concrete conflicts between social groups and institutions. These contradictions, or at least the determination of which contradictions and conflicts are most central, are dialectically related to the ideological orientation of the political leadership.

The ambiguities, conflicts, and tensions resulting from contradictory demands on the social system are not easily or permanently resolved. Long-term resolution can only occur if and when the fundamental

Figure 2.1 Schematic View of the Theoretical Model

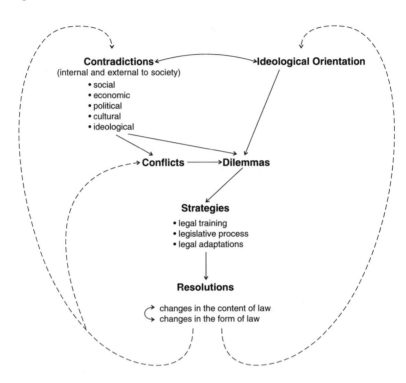

contradictions which spawned the conflicts are eradicated. Even if one set of contradictions (e.g., those caused by a capitalist political economy) is eliminated, a new set is likely to emerge in its place (e.g., those within a socialist political economy), since contradictory forces can be found in all state societies. More typically, conflicts are temporarily contained or smoothed over on a problem-by-problem basis, with new and old conflicts and dilemmas continuing to unfold. Since it is not possible to address all conflicts simultaneously, attention must focus on the most acute conflicts: those causing, or likely soon to cause, major tears in the social fabric.

The leadership thus faces a dilemma: how to resolve these serious conflicts? Multiple avenues exist. For purposes of this analysis, the scope is limited to the legal arena. Resolutions do not arise automatically. Strategies are needed to ascertain which of a set of potential resolutions will work best and to reach those resolutions. Some strategies can be implemented immediately; others require more time. Attention to strategies, including who selects them and why, makes my theoretical model more dynamic and historically grounded.

In the remainder of this chapter, I elaborate on the theoretical concepts and relations that form my model, locating them in the Cuban context. In so doing, I hope to shed additional light on some of the central debates within socio-legal studies.

STRUCTURAL CONTRADICTIONS

I begin with the concept of structural contradictions. Contradictions can be said to exist when a set of social relations serves simultaneously to maintain and to undermine the status quo by producing the very conditions that transform it into something different (Marx, 1971:95; Ollman, 1986). A classic example is the contradiction between the public nature of production and the private ownership of the means of production in capitalist states. Volumes of labor legislation and regulatory law have attempted to resolve, if only temporarily, the class-based conflicts which ensue in an effort to stave off revolts, strikes, and other economic disruptions.

All nation-states, whether capitalist or socialist, are located within and must interact with the global capitalist economy. Accordingly, we must consider those structural and historical forces external to the society that generate conflicts and dilemmas within a nation. For instance, Andre Gunder Frank (1967, 1969) has articulated the relationship between the poverty and uneven development experienced by Third World countries and their peripheral status in the world system as sources of cheap labor and raw materials. Michael Burawoy (1985) has developed a historically contingent model of social transformation that considers how capitalist labor processes vary within capitalist and socialist modes of production. Similarly, Carol Smith (1986) shows how petty commodity producers in Guatemala were historically linked to the capitalist market, with emergence of different forms of commodity production (e.g., artisanal, informal sector) associated with changes in the appropriation of surplus production. These larger forces condition and constrain the potential resolutions available to the political leadership.

Socialist countries are not immune to the many pressures of world capitalist markets. While they historically have traded largely among themselves, they remain tethered to the global economy through a need for hard currency, typically dollars, to purchase capitalist First World exports such as medicines, technologies, and some foods. As a result, changes in the world market can have a tremendous impact on socialist economies (Laclau, 1971; Chase-Dunn, 1982). What hurts the Cubans is not that they have to trade with capitalist nations; it is the *terms* of trade, terms which favor industrialized nations and put agrarian producers of raw materials at a disadvantage. The economic blockade initiated by the United States in 1961 is another burden, both because its geographic proximity would otherwise make the U.S. a desirable trade partner and also because imports from capitalist nations generally require payment in U.S. dollars. Since 1989, we must add the demolition of socialism in Eastern Europe and in the former Soviet Union, which had been Cuba's major trading partners.

Thus, the contradictions and conflicts facing socialist states often differ from those confronting capitalist states. In Cuba, the most notable contradictions are those between the leadership's socialist political and social goals and the economic exigencies posed by the capitalist world economy.

IDEOLOGICAL ORIENTATION

Ideology is critical to both legitimating and challenging conceptions of a just social order and thus is an important force in directing fundamental social change.

While I knew that an understanding of the ideological orientation of the Cuban leadership would be important, my decision to center it in the theoretical model developed in the course of a lengthy discussion with Cuban legal theorist Julio Fernández Bulté, then Dean of the Law School at the University of Havana. Our discussion of ideology, and specifically ideological orientation, began in ethical terms. Dr. Fernández Bulté pointed out that the world's great religions teach their followers codes of morality and ethics. This is perhaps particularly important in the socialization of young people to be good, kind, and considerate of others. "With what," he asked, "do you replace this religious training in a secular society?" Cuba has some Catholics, Protestants, and Jews, and even more adherents to various African, and especially Yoruba, religions, but the majority of the people and almost all of the political leaders are atheist or agnostic. Something besides religion was needed to instill a sense of honor and to teach people what the leadership defined as appropriate behavior—that is, to provide an ideological orientation. For example, when Ernesto

("Che") Guevara called for construction of the "new person," he was offering an ideological orientation for revolutionary Cuban society.

Since that discussion in early 1989, I have thought more about the importance of ideology for an understanding of how legality is produced in Cuba. Antonio Gramsci's (1971) theory of hegemonic ideology, Douglas Kellner's (1978) theory of ideological regions (influenced by Gramsci), and the work within the socio-legal community on legal ideology (Harrington, 1985; Hunt, 1985; the Amherst Seminar, 1988; Harrington and Merry, 1988; Merry, 1990) are particularly helpful in this endeavor.

The dominant, or hegemonic, ideological orientation of a society is generally consistent with the ideology of the political leadership (see Gramsci, 1971).[4] As Kellner's (1978:49–50) discussion of Gramsci's theory illustrates:

> Hegemonic ideology assumes an attempt to legitimate the existing society, its institutions and ways of life. Ideology becomes hegemonic when it is widely accepted as describing "the way things are," inducing people to consent to their society and its way of life as natural, good, and just.

Kellner notes further that hegemonic ideology serves as a means of "indirect rule." It "contains the dominant, most widely shared beliefs and attitudes which are incorporated in social practices and institutions" (1978:50). Gramsci and Kellner suggest that the hegemonic ideology must generally resonate with what people experience in their daily lives if it is to remain credible. It is in this sense that Gramsci (1971:328) referred to ideology as "cement." I would argue that hegemonic ideology does not necessarily mean that the ideology resonates with people's everyday experiences. Indeed, there can be a generalized ambivalence toward it. If that ambivalence becomes transformed into disbelief and hostility, we have the makings of revolutionary resistance (see McDonald, 1993).

Gramsci differed from instrumentalist Marxists who define hegemonic ideology as false consciousness. He argued that a hegemonic ideology could be subverted by an alternative ideology deemed more credible by the people (Gramsci, 1971; Kellner, 1978; Kertzer, 1979; Counihan, 1986). Kellner takes this a step further, positing that in any society several ideologies often coexist. Alternative ideologies may contradict or resist the dominant ideological orientation and may themselves exist in contradiction to one another. Indeed, Kellner (1978) argues that hegemonic ideologies are flexible, adaptive, and often full of contradictions as they make concessions to oppositional groups. Thus, in marked contrast to Poulantzas (1973), especially, and Althusser (1971), Kellner follows Gramsci in seeing hegemonic ideologies as containing "simultaneously cohesive and disintegrating elements . . . as reactive, amorphous, and subject to class struggle [rather than as] an imposed-from-above, monolithic tool of ruling-class domination" (1978:52). Again following Gramsci, Kellner sees contradictions as emerging both within and between the different ideological regions. These contradictions and tensions create an ideological destabilization requiring structural changes and/or a new ideology (Kellner, 1978:57–58).

The importance of ideology is perhaps particularly evident in revolutionary contexts. The revolutionary consciousness does not exist on a one-to-one relationship with specific material conditions. Rather, it exists in a dialectical relationship with them. Based upon her study of the relationship between Indian and non-Indian revolutionaries in Guatemala, Carol Smith (1987:204) concludes, "The revolutionary potential of a class is given by material circumstances, but the potential cannot be assessed by a formula that divorces material circumstances from the subjective interpretation of those circumstances." Explicitly influenced by the work of E. P. Thompson (1978), Smith further argues that the classes that emerge from revolutionary struggles "may or may not hold a single objective interest with respect to their material circumstances, but they will hold a single and opposed interest with respect to those classes that emerge in opposition to them" (1987:204). Smith's argument is particularly helpful in the Cuban case if we substitute for class relations the unifying ideologies of socialism, nationalism, and Latin American regionalism.

The most general and hegemonic ideological orientation in Cuba is that of socialism. Cuba moved very quickly toward becoming a socialist state, declaring itself socialist only two years after the revolutionary triumph of 1959—a very rapid social transformation. Cuban socialism is tightly connected to a second important ideological orientation—nationalism. In expressing its general ideology, the Cuban political leadership draws on heroes of the earlier independence movement (e.g., José Martí, Antonio Maceo) as much as it does on Marx and Lenin. Cuban nationalism is tied to a sense of regionalism. While politically and economically linked to what was until 1989 the socialist bloc, Cuba is also connected politically and economically to Latin America. Also, the Cuban people feel an affinity to Latin America that they do not feel toward Eastern Europe. Cuba's history, culture, language, and geography tie it inextricably to Latin America and the Caribbean.

Legal Ideology

Kellner identifies four major ideological regions, or realms. These are the *economic* (e.g., ideologies of production process, exchange, distribution), the *political* (e.g., ideologies of the state, democracy, civil rights, legal-judicial system, police, and military), the *social* (e.g., ideologies of the private sphere, family, education, social groups, and institutions), and the *cultural* (e.g., ideologies of culture, values, science, technology, philosophy, art, religion, popular culture, and mass media). These regions overlap, interact reciprocally, and are frequently contradictory. Following Kellner's schema, legal ideology would be largely subsumed under the political realm, but it spills over into the social realm, is reinforced by the cultural, and is closely tied to the economic structure and supportive ideologies.

Alan Hunt (1985:13) warns that it is a mistake to use ideology to refer to systematic and total world views. He suggests that when, and if, consistent world views exist, they should be treated as exceptional cases. It is better, he suggests, to situate ideologies historically and culturally. The Amherst Seminar (1988:634) took Hunt's chidings to heart when they concluded:

> Studies of law and ideology direct attention to history, the variability of legality and its conditional nature. Legal ideologies are constituted within particular historical circumstances. Attributions and interpretations are not only a product of particular social interactions, material conditions and institutions, they in turn influence the organization of social interaction in specific contexts. Most importantly, because situations are numerous and variable, there are multiple meanings and multiple ideologies.

Sally Engle Merry suggests that law "exerts both direct coercive power and subtle cultural domination" (1990:10; see also Harrington, 1985; Cohen, 1985; Kairys, 1982; Santos, 1980; Abel, 1981). It is this latter, subtle aspect of law that has led critical legal scholars to argue that law is itself an ideology, or a set of ideologies (e.g., ideologies of formalism, realism, informalism). Law supports a social construction of the world that is acceptable and legitimate because it is legally ordered, even though it privileges some social groups over others. Acquiescence to this world view, and the power differentials that it entails, depends upon compliance and consent to the legal order (Merry, 1990:7).

Nevertheless, there is room for resistance to this hegemonic order. As Kidder (1988:626) stated in his editorial introduction to *Law and Society Review*'s special issue on law and ideology:

Law is ideology, but also an arena where views of society are developed and promoted, so in some sense it seems at times to be a kind of mega-ideology, a taken-for-granted context and language for diverse ideological constructions. Yet it also becomes the object of construction and reconstruction. Ideology in the form of law dominates but is also the medium by which to escape domination.

Ideologies, both hegemonic and alternative, exist in a dialectical relationship with the structural contradictions discussed above. The hegemonic ideology orients and directs the ways in which contradictions are dealt with, such that potential resolutions to the resulting conflicts and dilemmas are met in a manner consistent with the leadership's perceptions of societal goals. Incorporating this element into the theoretical model makes it more dynamic and less reductionist. Visually, the revised model appears as a spiral rather than a closed circle.

CONFLICTS

"Contradictions" and "ideology" might seem to some to be very abstract concepts. They become more concrete when they are played out in conflicts and dilemmas. While much sociological theory over the last two decades has focused almost exclusively on class conflicts within capitalism, conflicts can arise between ethnic groups, genders, and any other social groups whose interests are in direct competition.

Socialist societies are not immune from conflicts. The conflicts which exist between workers and management and between governmental bureaucracies are particularly relevant for this analysis. Although the interinstitutional conflicts in Cuba differ from those identified for the United States, conceptually my criticism is similar to concerns raised by Christine Harrington (1985), Marc Galanter (1979; cited in Harrington, 1985:94), and Kitty Calavita (1992) of potential conflicts between the legal order and other institutional spheres, and between bureaucratic norms and judicial standards.

DILEMMAS

"Dilemmas" refer to the uncertainties faced by various actors, and especially the political leadership, concerning the best way to resolve conflicts. Since no resolution can be perfect given the multiple forces confronting any given society, the dilemma often comes down to choosing the lesser evil and finding a means to reach that tentative resolution. Like conflicts, exactly how dilemmas are constructed, portrayed, and resolved depends in large part on the hegemonic and alternative ideological orientations available and the relative salience of the various contradictions in evidence at that point in time.

STRATEGIES

The dilemmas posed by contradictory demands and conflicts are not just structural. They are also inherently ideological and human. Resolutions to conflicts do not materialize of their own accord. Individuals must decide how best to resolve them, and that decision will be shaped by their beliefs and by the options which they perceive to be available. These options, or mechanisms, are what I call "strategies."

The specific set of strategies selected at a given point in time will depend upon historical conditions, the structural (i.e., economic, political, and social) forces operating within and upon the society, and the ideological orientation of the political leadership. Since many of the contradictions, conflicts, and dilemmas facing capitalist and socialist states will differ, as will the hegemonic (and many alternative) ideologies, we should expect at least some differences in the strategies selected.

Theoretically, this is a crucial stage in the understanding of conflict resolution. Practically, it is an arena for considerable struggle as different organized interest groups or state institutions attempt to influence the process of mediating social conflict, and thus, of shaping governmental policy. Consideration of strategies provides the model with an actor-oriented, dynamic approach to the study of legal transformation. It is here that "human agency" (Giddens, 1982; Henry, 1985) enters most explicitly into the model. Inclusion of strategies into the model recognizes that people make real, often imperfect, decisions.

Within the Cuban legal sphere, three general strategies emerged as I sorted through the data. Each represents a route for resolving conflicts and dilemmas in a manner which is consistent with the ideological orientation of Cuba's political leadership. These are (1) the broad-based, iterative process of law creation; (2) the combination of theory and practice in the training of law students and the work of law professors; and (3) the careful examination of foreign legal models and theories and the selective adaptation of aspects of them. Each of the three general strategies includes what might be called sub-strategies. These emerge as dilemmas unfold in the course of developing and implementing the more encompassing general strategies.

RESOLUTIONS

Changes in the content of Cuban law have been influenced by the political leadership's beliefs about which substantive aspects of life could be changed through law. The most fundamental of these laws have become known as the Moncada Platform (see Chapter Three). These were essentially the promises made to the Cuban people by the revolutionary leaders during the war. Since then, further changes in the content of law have been introduced to induce substantive changes in the material conditions of people's lives.

The structural contradictions theory of lawmaking (Chambliss, 1979) can be extended to include transformations in the form of law and in the relationship between the content and the form of law. Dilemmas surrounding the form of law express a concern with the shape of the legal system and come down to a decision about the mix of formalism and informalism within the legal arena. This includes, but is not limited to, professional and lay participation in judicial decisionmaking.

The Mix of Formalism and Informalism

Alternating trends between formalism and informalism are to be expected, given their dialectical relationship (Abel, 1981, 1982b; Spitzer, 1982). Yet knowing that a relationship is dialectical is not sufficient for assessing when or why one will predominate, nor for understanding the meaning and implications of this relationship. Research on the interconnections between local normative orders and the wider social structures in which they are embedded is one avenue for exploring the linkages between formalism and informalism (Henry, 1985; Cain, 1985; Cohen, 1985; O'Malley, 1987; Merry, 1990). Christine Harrington's (1985) work on delegalization reform movements casts doubt on any total break between formalism and informalism. She argues, "Ostensibly replacing formalism as an ideology, informalism retains a legalistic core that ties it to conventional practice" (1985:2). Similarly, Peter Fitzpatrick (1988, 1992) demonstrates how informal and formal justice can have homologous configurations of power. Discussing the interpenetration of formalism and informalism, Boaventura de Sousa Santos observes, "What appears as *de*-legalization is indeed *re*-legalization" (1980:391, his emphasis).

I use the term "mix" to call attention to the multiple ways in which formalism and informalism are interrelated, and how each requires elements of the other. There may be ideological reasons for naming a system of law formal or informal, but there is little, if any, empirical basis for assuming that either exists in pure form. Depending on one's political-ideological position, formalism can suggest procedural regularities consistent with a "rule of law" in which power imbalances are equalized *or* a mechanism for ensuring that those with power can maintain their privileged position. Similarly, informalism can suggest mob-rule and a legal prop for totalitarian government *or* popular participation in an accessible and affordable legal arena. Both can be seen as expanding *or* contracting the scope of state power over the citizenry and as legitimating *or* delegitimating the legal order.

The term "mix" differentiates my conceptualization of the form of law from that of a continuum. Rather than elaborating a set of characteristics, the presence or absence of which moves a given system closer to the informal or formal poles of an ideal-typical continuum, I see these factors as mingling and interacting in a dynamic, and at times volatile, mixture. It is this complex mix of formal and informal aspects of legal systems that I find theoretically compelling.

Indeed, the Cuban data call into question a polarized view of formalism and informalism. Polarization hinders analysis because it forces the researcher to constantly search for "pure" examples of informalism, perhaps as an outgrowth of anthropological research on informalism in tribal societies (see Danzig, 1982).[5] Given the scale of bureaucracy within modern states, a polarization perspective would suggest that informalism no longer exists. I maintain that this is a premature closure of the analytical field and that it is more likely that some combination of formalism and informalism will coexist and become institutionalized. The Cuban case suggests that it is far more useful to conceptualize formalism and informalism as a dynamic mixture rather than as ideal types. How this mix is constituted can only be understood within a concrete, historically specific context.

It is also only in such specific contexts that we can understand the relationship between the form and content of law. Since political and economic relations differ significantly across socialist and capitalist systems, for example, it is to be expected that not only the form and the content of law (including consideration of which social groupings the legal order favors and other distinctions between socialist and bourgeois law) will vary, but also the relationship between form and content. Aase Gundersen (1992:265) makes a similar point, suggesting, "To assess a system of popular justice it is always necessary to investigate the content of law, and analyze it in terms of how it is created, by whom and for whom."

Critiques of Informalism

Richard Abel (1982a:2) defines legal institutions as informal

> to the extent that they are nonbureaucratic in structure and relatively undifferentiated from the larger society, minimize the use of professionals, and eschew official law in favor of substantive norms that are vague, unwritten, commonsensical, flexible, ad hoc, and particularistic.

In contrast, formal legal structures are bureaucratic, maximize professionalism, rely on rigidly codified law, and are relatively resistant to external pressures or particular substantive considerations (Weber, 1968:654–658; Balbus, 1977:xxi,7–15).

Some theorists locate informal law in a particular context, such as the neighborhood or community. For example, Santos (1977, 1980, 1982b) and Danzig (1982) see informal and community justice as leading to mutually agreed upon outcomes, mediation or conciliation rather than adjudication, deprofessionalized settings which use everyday language, use of nonjurists as arbitrators, and a minimal ability of the legal institution to mobilize coercion in its own name. Merry (1982) and Schonholtz (1985) have portrayed informal justice as, in some contexts, the potential salvation of the community. Others define informal justice largely in terms of lay participation and reliance on informal procedures (Ietswaart, 1982; Isaacman and Isaacman, 1982; Selva and Bohm, 1985; and Hayden, 1986).

The informal justice movement as it is practiced in the United States and other First World capitalist societies has been the subject of extensive criticism. Informalism may defuse and individualize social, fiscal, and legitimacy crises. Its cooptive character enables it to neutralize disputes, disorganize opposition, and undermine collective action before it can effectively organize (Abel, 1981, 1982a, 1982b; Harrington, 1985; Cain, 1985; Henry, 1985).

Informalism also expands the reach of the state's social control apparatus and rhetoric into dispute areas which had previously been outside of state control. In so doing, informalism provides a new basis for legitimating judicial authority and expanding the political and legal domination, including the coercive powers, of the state. Boaventura de Sousa Santos (1980:387) has called this "state-produced non-state power." Yet Santos's critique of informalization in capitalist society concludes on a hopeful note with a nod to its utopian and transcendental potential (1980:393).

Informalism also has come under attack from what has come to be known as "the minority critiques of Critical Legal Studies" (e.g.,

Williams, 1987, 1991; Delgado, 1987; Bracamonte, 1987).[6] Critical Legal Studies (CLS) refers to legal scholarship concerned with issues of inequality, racism, and sexism in U.S. society and its legal order. Politically, CLS scholars tend to be very progressive, seeking to use their professional expertise to advance the causes of those with less power. Yet as a group of mostly white males teaching in elite law schools, they are in privileged positions. The minority critiques center on the argument that CLS scholars do not always know what is best for the disempowered and disenfranchised people for whom they claim to speak. The benefits and drawbacks of informalism are central to the debates between CLS adherents and lawyers of color, many of whom were their students.

From the CLS position, informalism is a means—a strategy in my terminology—for equalizing power. Viewed from below, formalism's emphasis on procedural rights has been a relatively successful tool for gaining civil rights, and informalism represents a dangerous step backwards. Patricia Williams writes, "One's sense of empowerment defines one's relation to the law, in terms of trust/distrust, formality/informality, or rights/no-rights" (1991:148). She continues, "But this failure of rights discourse, much noted in CLS scholarship, does not logically mean that informal systems will lead to better outcomes. Some structures are the products of social forces and people who wanted them that way." Richard Delgado (1987:315) comments further that in the contemporary United States, where these social forces and the power hierarchy (which both sustains them and is sustained by them) are not altered, informalism is

> bad news for minorities. Discretionary judgments colored by racism or other forms of prejudice are made possible by replacing rules, guidelines and rights with fluid, informal decisionmaking. In fact, structureless processes affirmatively increase the likelihood of prejudice.

A "new informalism" is emerging from these multifaceted debates. Sally Engle Merry's (1990) study of how working-class people in the U.S. use and perceive law suggests that the liberal reforms of the twentieth century simultaneously expanded the scope of the state's social control and made law "a source of help rather than . . . an alien institution" for the average person (1990:177). The paradox, as she sees it, of the perception by ordinary people that the law can serve "as the protector of the weak and vulnerable, as a tool for achieving social justice" (1990:178) is that their very use of law increases their dependence on state institutions and this "furthers the subordination of the working class to those who manage and dispense court services" (1990:181).

The "new informalism" exemplified by Merry's work is closely related to my discussion above of alternative ideologies that can grow out of and challenge hegemonic ideologies. In some situations, informalism may be a means of resisting state law, rather than necessarily being coopted by an expanding state social control apparatus and the hegemonic legal ideology. This new informalism leaves far more room for human agency, as individuals accept or challenge the dominant structures and interpretations.

The formalism/informalism debate has proceeded primarily in the United States and Great Britain. Are the arguments and criticisms of each side viable in a totally different context, namely revolutionary Cuba? Simply focusing on the actors and their discourse in what on the surface seem to be informal settings and procedures may lead us to ignore their potential for hidden formalism. If legal norms or procedures are imposed by the state, then the system entails what Lempert (1989) calls a "hidden legalism." What if, however, guidelines or regulations informed by local concerns are imposed by the state? For example, the Cuban popular tribunals discussed in Chapter Three are generally considered to be an example of legal informalism (e.g., van der Plas, 1987; Berman, 1969; Brady, 1981), yet in response to concerns that rose from the bottom up through the legal hierarchy, the Ministry of Justice imposed some regulatory guidelines upon their proceedings. Does this make them legalistic and formal?

It is also not at all clear whether and to what extent the assumptions that (1) informalism increases the strength and scope of the state's social control apparatus, and (2) informalism provides a means of resisting state control, hold true for Cuba. Certainly, informal justice can expand the control of the state, whether that state is structured along capitalist or socialist lines. But, if a new state apparatus truly (and that, perhaps, is the key question) reflects the people as a whole rather than simply the elite, what does expansion of state control really mean, and is it necessarily negative and cooptive? Similarly, we must ask what resistance to the legal order and state power means in such a context. Is it necessarily positive, or can it be the locale for conservative and reactionary counter-revolutionaries? These questions cannot be answered adequately by saying that enhanced state control is cooptive in capitalist states but not in socialist ones, or that resistance is to be applauded in one situation but not in another.

The problem stems from the reality of social and economic differentiation within socialist societies. Although these divisions tend to be far less extensive than in capitalist societies, the quandary remains as to the extent to which all social sectors are represented by the socialist legal order, even with the inclusion of popular participation.[7] In the Cuban case, explicit governmental policies and priorities have greatly reduced social and economic differentiation when compared to the prerevolutionary context and to many other socialist and capitalist nations. The question must, therefore, be reformulated: Does expanded state control resulting from the infusion of aspects of informalism into the legal order create benefits to the majority of the citizens that outweigh the negative and cooptive aspects of this expansion? The question is made more problematic because the forces leading to marginalization, and the categories of people who are marginalized, differ in capitalist and socialist societies.

Even if we decide that informalism has a negative effect because it expands state control, it also has been credited for providing an educational role, especially in socialist societies (Salas, 1979; Selva and Bohm, 1985). This educational role is particularly evident during the initial period following overthrow of regimes whose legal institutions were popularly perceived to be repressive or corrupt.[8]

Additionally, much of the interest in informalism in First World capitalist countries was based on an appreciation for popular participation in socialist legal systems. For example, Brady (1981, 1982), Salas (1979, 1983) and van der Plas (1987) suggest that the most popular and participatory justice systems have arisen in socialist states with ongoing policies of radical social change.

Informalism and Institutionalization

A heavy measure of informalism is common when the legal system is in flux, such as the period immediately after a successful revolution. In these situations the old legal order commands little legitimacy. In addition, the pre-existing legal structure is often highly disrupted when lawyers associated with the old, conservative regime leave the country. In these settings, direct citizen participation typically is combined with mass mobilization through community organizations and structured via informally constituted revolutionary tribunals. The principal activities of these tribunals are organized around immediate social demands (e.g., agrarian and other types of economic reforms, minor crimes, the control of counter-revolutionary activity, and punishment of collaborators with the fallen regime who committed crimes against the people). These conditions in large part explain both the development of popular participation in the Cuban legal system and the relatively lengthy delay (about 25 years) before law reemerged as a prestigious profession.

As new regimes become stable, however, increased legal professionalism and a decline in citizen participation are likely to follow, resulting in increasing formalization of legal processes.[9] This calls into question the relationship between institutionalization of the socialist state and the form of law. Since political and economic relations differ significantly between socialist and capitalist systems, differences should also be expected in the form and content of socialist and bourgeois law (Hipkin, 1985; Hirst, 1985; Spitzer, 1982; Seidman, 1984). Unfortunately, definitions of socialist legality are amorphous. Cantor (1974:12; see also Beirne and Hunt, 1988) sees socialist legality as a transitional set of laws and institutions that protects the interests of workers and peasants, reflects the beliefs and needs of the people, and is flexible to changes in these beliefs and needs over time. Working from somewhat different perspectives, Makhnenko (1976) and Hazard (1969) assert that developed socialist legality is rather formal, with institutionalization of the political and judicial systems representing the apex in the development of the state's legal system.

Blas Roca Calderío, the first President of the National Assembly and head of the Cuban Communist Party's Commission for Legal Studies, was an extremely important force in creating and implementing socialist legality in Cuba *and* in institutionalizing the new state. He argued that "the importance of socialist legality grows with advances in the construction of socialism, with the advance of the institutionalization of revolutionary power, with the perfection of our laws" (in Ordóñez Martínez, 1982:84; my translation). In apparent opposition to Blas Roca's stress on socialist legality's increased importance with stabilization of the new order, Brian Hipkin (1985: 124) argues that socialist legality "can never be in a finished state but rather is a series of changing, shifting demands, struggles and even compromises." This controversy supports my contention that we must carefully consider the relationships between the form and content of law and must tie these to the historical and structural forces operating on a given society at a particular point in time.

CONCLUSIONS

The contradictory structural and historical forces operating within and upon Cuba, in combination with the ideological lens through which they are understood by the political leadership, serve as one way we can interpret the mix of legal formalism and informalism in Cuba, its legal culture, and its laws. While the contradictions may appear abstract, they are manifested in very real conflicts and create dilemmas for those persons charged with resolving them. To be successful, these key actors need viable strategies. I identify three strategies that have emerged in the legal arena. These strategies lead to changes in the substantive content of law, in the mix of legal formalism and informalism, and in the relationship between the content and the form of the legal order over time.

Consideration of the form of the legal order foregrounds debates about formalism and informalism. The benefits and dangers of informalism have been adequately addressed in the literature, yet when applied to Cuba they tend to be overly romantic and not necessarily consistent with how Cuban legal scholars depict their legal order. My approach considers how the *mix* of formalism and informalism has varied historically since 1959, and to what extent elements of each have become institutionalized in Cuba's socialist legality. Like the content of law, the relative mix of formalism and informalism changes as policy makers focus their attention on old and new substantive problems requiring new strategies for their resolution.

PART TWO

STRATEGIES FOR PRODUCING LEGALITY

CHAPTER 3

REACHING
A CONSENSUS
THE PROCESS
OF LAW CREATION

By the way, do you know we broke the law? You didn't know? Who would have known, since we've made so many laws and haven't had enough time to study them?

—Fidel Castro, February 20, 1990[1]

No individual, by him/herself, can successfully conceive a piece of legislation. Collective work is indispensable; especially when you do not have the full sociological background nor modern technological means for forecasting possible future conduct. In these cases, the contribution of everyone is necessary, as is public and honest discussion, as broadbased as possible.

—Gómez Treto[2]

Immediately following the military triumph on the first of January, 1959, the new government quickly enacted a series of legally binding proclamations and decrees designed to solidify the social gains of the revolution. These were, in essence, the promises made by Fidel and his *compañeros* during the revolutionary war. They became known as the "Moncada Platform" because they were announced initially as part of Castro's self-defense when he was tried in 1953 on charges of attacking the Moncada Barracks. The most important of these included the agrarian reforms of May 1959, and October 1963, housing laws, the 1962 educational reform (including the reform of the university discussed in Chapter Four), and the various laws of nationalizations of businesses and banks (Kautzman, May 18, 1989). Together, they radically altered the previously existing social, economic, and political structures.

53

Following this early series of laws there was a marked decrease in legislative activity for about a decade. Some laws were passed, but the creation of legislation was secondary to such revolutionary goals as the literacy campaign, rapid and sweeping advances in health care, construction of housing and schools, and other practical necessities (Martínez, May 17, 1989; Kautzman, May 18, 1989; see also Appendices B and C for growth in the number of medical facilities and personnel, Appendix D for housing data, and Appendix E for increased numbers of schools and teachers).

By the close of the 1960s, the new government was in a position to begin institutionalizing the state. Revolutions themselves cannot be institutionalized, else they cease to be revolutionary. The new state structures and institutions that they bring in their wake can and must be institutionalized, however, if the new order is to be recognized internally and externally as a nation-state. Institutionalization of the new legal order was led by Blas Roca Calderío and the Commission for Legal Studies (*Comisión de Estudios Jurídicos*) of the Central Committee of the Cuban Communist Party, which Blas Roca organized in April of 1968 (Quirós, May 15, 1989; Cuba Fernández, 1974). The commission began its work in 1969, leading most of my sources to cite 1969 as the inception of the period of institutionalization.[3]

The primary task of Blas Roca's commission was to draft a new constitution, but the commission and its subcommittees also developed a series of other substantive and procedural laws.[4] Major laws and policies central to the institutionalization of the Revolution enacted during the 1970s include:

1971 • Creation of the Population Registry and Identity Cards
1972 • Restructuring of the Council of Ministers and creation of its Executive Committee
1973 • Restructuring of the Communist Party apparatus
     • Law of the Organization of the Judicial System
     • Law of Criminal Procedure
     • Private practice of law abolished; creation of National Organization of Law Collectives
     • Experiment with Organs of People's Power in Matanzas Province
1974 • Law of Civil and Administrative Procedure
     • Maternity Law
1975 • Family Code
     • First Party Congress
1976 • Constitution of the Republic of Cuba
     • Law of the Political-Administrative Division of the Republic

- Electoral Law
- Law of the Organization of the Central Administration of the State
- Establishment of fundamental principles of the System of Economic Direction and Planning
- First elections of delegates to Organs of People's Power (municipal through national levels)
- Laws of Migration and Immigration

1977
- New Law of the Organization of the Judicial System
- New Law of Criminal Procedure
- New Law of Civil, Administrative, and Labor Procedure
- Law of the Protection of National Culture

1978
- Child and Youth Code
- Labor activities of sole proprietors legislated

1979
- Criminal Code

The Constitution was overwhelmingly approved in a national referendum in 1976 (see Table 3.1). Blas Roca's commission was dismantled, with its planning and oversight responsibilities passing to the National Assembly's Commission for Constitutional and Legal Affairs (*Comisión de Asuntos Constitucionales y Jurídicos*) and to the Department of State and Legal Agencies (*Departamento de Organos Estatales y Jurídicos*) of the Central Committee of the Party (Quirós, May 15, 1989; Couto, May 11, 1989).

In addition to Blas Roca's leadership role in creating legislation, including his service as the first President of the National Assembly, he was a major force behind the reinvigoration of the legal profession. In his many speeches, Blas Roca repeatedly called for the training of new lawyers and for Cuban scholars to engage in legal scholarship. He also urged creation of self-governing organizations for all jurists (*juristas*) and for trial lawyers (*abogados*).[5] Although Blas Roca was not himself a jurist, his name was consistently mentioned first when I informally polled Cuban legal scholars and practicing attorneys as to the most important influences on Cuban legality.

ORGANIZATION OF THE CUBAN STATE AND LEGAL ARENA

Prior to 1976, the Council of Ministers held legislative authority. The last law passed by the Council of Ministers, the Law of the Organization of the Central Administration of the State (Law No. 1323, November 30, 1976),[6] shifted legislative authority to the National Assembly of People's Power (for *laws*) and to its executive body, the Council of State

Table 3.1.
Modifications and Ratification of the 1976 Constitution.*

Modifications from Popular Meetings*

Total number of participants	6,216,981
Total modifications proposed	12,883
Votes in favor of modifications proposed	685,764
Total additions suggested	2,343
Votes in favor of additions suggested	91,861
Total number of other propositions	1,022
Votes in favor of other propositions	64,020
Total number of clarifications to text requested	84
Votes in favor of clarification requests	1,198

Ratification Votes

Registered voters	Number	% of Registered voters
Voted	5,602,973	98.0
Did not vote	114,293	2.0
Total	5,717,266	100.0%

Votes	Number	% of votes
Yes	5,473,534	97.7
No	54,070	1.0
Blank ballot	44,221	0.8
Annulled ballot	31,148	0.5
Total	5,602,973	100.0%

*   Sources: Garcini Guerra, 1976:103 and *Revista Cubana de Derecho*, 1976:56.
** The following organizations held meetings to discuss the draft Constitution: Association of Cuban Workers (CTC), National Association of Agricultural Producers (ANAP), Committees for the Defense of the Revolution (CDCs), Federation of Cuban Women (FMC), Federation of University Students (FEU), Federation of Middle-School Students (FEEM), Ministry of Justice, Communist Party Nuclei, Communist Party Nuclei outside the country, and the Armed Forces.

(for *decree-laws*), leaving the Council of Ministers with the power only to enact *decrees*.[7] The National Assembly and Municipal and Provincial Assemblies of People's Power began functioning in 1976, immediately following passage of the Constitution and the political-administrative redistribution of the country.

The three central components of the Cuban state are the legislative arena (known as Organs of People's Power, these assemblies run from the national to the municipal level), the ministerial arena (headed by the Council of Ministers), and the Cuban Communist Party (organized hierarchically under the Politburo and its Secretariat). The three branches are structurally autonomous from one another, but in reality they overlap. This overlapping of functions has declined over the years, as has general oversight by the Party, but both are still notable.

As Figure 3.1 diagrams, within the juridical sphere the major agencies are the Ministry of Justice, the Supreme Court, the Ministry of the Interior, and the Office of the Attorney General. Each is organized hierarchically from the national to the municipal levels. The Ministry of Justice has the widest authority, as it is administratively and financially responsible for the courts and the National Organization of Law Collectives, to which all trial attorneys belong. These latter two structures are, however, independent of the Ministry of Justice in terms of their internal organization, staffing, and decision-making authority. Prior to the 1977 Law of the Organization of the Judicial System, the Office of the Attorney General was subsumed under the court structure, but it has been autonomous since that date. The police and prison authorities form part of the Ministry of the Interior.

The Ministers of Justice and the Interior, the President of the Supreme Court, and the Attorney General sit on the Council of Ministers, although only the Ministers of Justice and Interior hold votes. The President of the Supreme Court and the Attorney General are responsible to the National Assembly and must report to it annually.

LEGISLATIVE AUTHORITY

Cuba's legislature is organized hierarchically into three tiers. At the base are the 169 Municipal Assemblies of People's Power, composed of one delegate elected in a secret ballot in each of the 13,860 electoral districts. Electoral districts consist of approximately 1,000 voters. Next come the 14 Provincial Assemblies of People's Power. Prior to 1992, provincial delegates were elected by the Municipal Assemblies, with some but not all delegates elected from within the ranks of the

Municipal Assembly. The highest level of legislative authority is the National Assembly of People's Power.

Until 1992, the Municipal Assemblies elected deputies to the National Assembly, with about 40 percent of the deputies also serving in Municipal or Provincial Assemblies. The selection process changed with passage of a new Electoral Law in October of 1992. Now, candidates for the Provincial Assemblies and the National Assembly are nominated by the Municipal Assemblies but elected by direct secret vote of the citizenry. Delegates at each level are elected from a slate of candidates, must give regularly scheduled accountings to their constituents, and, in theory if not very often in practice, can be recalled. The assemblies meet in regularly scheduled sessions held at staggered intervals twice a year, allowing problems and potential solutions to flow up and down the chain of legislative authority. Special sessions are also called as needed (National Assembly of People's Power, 1981; Martínez, May 17, 1989).

Each assembly secretly elects its Executive Committee and standing committees from within its ranks. Executive Committee members with the most time-consuming responsibilities are paid for their committee work, but most delegates maintain their regular jobs. At the national level, the Executive Committee is the Council of State. It represents the National Assembly between sessions, implements the Assembly's resolutions, and enacts decree-laws. Seventeen permanent standing commissions function as auxiliaries to the National Assembly and the Council of State. The most important commission for purposes of this analysis is the Commission for Constitutional and Legal Affairs (*Comisión de Asuntos Constitucionales y Jurídicos*), noted hereafter as CACJ.

Responsibilities and Composition of the CACJ

The CACJ participates in the entire process of law creation, from planning sessions to analysis of proposed legislation. Whether or not another commission helped formulate and approved a proposed law, *every* proposed law goes to the CACJ for a determination of its constitutionality (Martínez, May 17, 1989). Relating this to the U.S. governmental structure, then, the CACJ is essentially a combined House and Senate Judiciary Committee, with the added responsibility of ascertaining the constitutionality of proposed laws. The CACJ is further charged with translating legal and technical terms into readily understandable lay terminology and circulating this explanation, along with the committee's assessment of the bill, to the rest of the Assembly prior to scheduled debates (Castanedo, May 3, 1989).

Figure 3.1 Organization of the Cuban State and Juridical Sphere

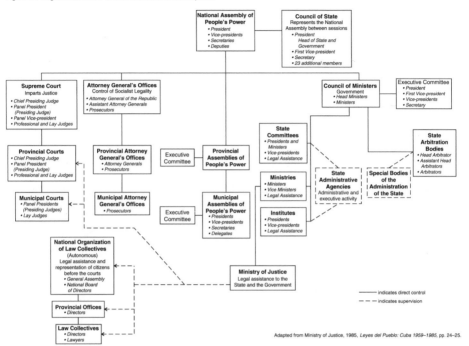

Adapted from Ministry of Justice, 1985, *Leyes del Pueblo: Cuba 1959–1985*, pp. 24–25.

The CACJ has 21 members, geographically distributed to represent the entire country. Its membership in 1989 included physicians, psychologists, psychiatrists, professors, a union leader, and seven jurists, including the vice-president of the Supreme Court. The union leader was also a trained jurist, but did not engage in legal work at his job. The Dean of the Law School at the University of Havana, Julio Fernández Bulté, was a legal adviser to the Commission but was not a voting member.

According to the President of the CACJ, Francisco Martínez, the nonjurists are particularly helpful in writing the Commission's nontechnical interpretations of proposed laws and in providing a non-legalistic perspective on conditions in the country as they affect particular pieces of legislation. For example, when the CACJ analyzed the proposed revisions of the 1984 Housing Law in 1988, its assessment of potential effects on the citizenry was facilitated by the presence of nonjurists. As Martínez told me, the nonlawyers "were able to enrich the legislative process by providing a 'real' perspective on housing conditions and needs" (May 17, 1989).

The CACJ works closely with the Department of State and Legal Agencies of the Central Committee of the Communist Party, the other organization to which planning responsibilities in the legal arena fell when Blas Roca's commission dissolved upon ratification of the Constitution. Since part of the Party Department's role is to help connect the multiple layers of juridical organizations through close contacts with people in the municipalities and provinces, it brings both the party hierarchy's perspective and the views of people throughout the country to bear on proposed legislation.

SCHEMATIC MODEL OF LAW CREATION

The Cuban lawmaking process can be characterized by three contradictory working assumptions: (1) some interorganizational conflicts will arise, even when there is a general agreement that some change is necessary; (2) consensus is desirable and generally achievable; and (3) no law should last forever. Consequently, lawmaking is a slow process of discussing and reconciling differences of opinion and, once passed, the legislation quickly becomes outdated. As I was told,

> You know that elaboration of a law, and especially a law like the Criminal Code, is not an instantaneous act. It's not as though you and I sit here and make a Code and tomorrow it is enacted. For this there is a commission of specialists who write the drafts. They plan the draft bills. Then they are distributed to all the agencies. They are discussed. And this process continues for several years. . . . And that is just the actual work of writing the legislation, not the ideas, which may come years before. Ideas are one thing, and the actual work of writing it is another. (García Alzugaray, April 27, 1989).

As we shall see, the result quite frequently is that work on a new law begins almost as soon as its predecessor is enacted.

Cuban lawmakers perceive law and the lawmaking process as educational, in addition to law's traditional repressive function of telling people what they can and cannot do. Consistent with this ideological goal, the process requires public participation and debate of proposed legislation. As an attorney heavily involved in drafting a new Family Code told me, "When proposed laws are discussed at neighborhood meetings, lawyers living in the neighborhood can talk about what the laws mean and their implications, thus facilitating the educational aspect of law creation" (de la Fuente, December 4, 1989).

Prior to detailing the lawmaking process, three Spanish terms must be clarified. These are *proyecto, anteproyecto,* and *alta asesoría.* From the perspective of U.S. politics, a *proyecto* is comparable to a legislative bill. Draft bills that have not yet reached the National Assembly are known as *anteproyectos. Proyectos* become laws when passed by the National Assembly or decree-laws when passed by the Council of State and ratified by the National Assembly. One agency or organization always takes charge of writing the *anteproyecto* and ultimately presents the *proyecto* on the floor of the National Assembly. This agency or organization is known as the *alta asesoría.*

Anteproyectos are often initiated in annual joint legislative planning sessions of the CACJ, the Ministry of Justice, and other state agencies. They also may be proposed by members or commissions of the National Assembly, by the national offices of the mass and social organizations (e.g., the Federation of Cuban Women [FMC], Cuban Labor Confederation [CTC], Committees for the Defense of the Revolution [CDRs], the National Association of Agricultural Producers [ANAP]), by the Councils of State or Ministers, the Supreme Court, or the Office of the Attorney General, or by a minimum of 10,000 eligible voters. Legislation also may be proposed at the municipal and provincial levels and sent up to the National Assembly.

If the *anteproyecto* is proposed during a joint planning session, a temporary interorganizational work group is then formed, headed by the agency that will be the *alta asesoría.* The Ministry of Justice is typically the *alta asesoría,* but it may be another ministry, national committee, national institute, or commission of the National Assembly.

The *anteproyecto* then goes to the Office of the Secretary of the Council of Ministers (in recent years, Osmani Cienfuegos Gorriaran). The Secretary is known as the *controlador* (controller) and the office as the *Organo Controlador de la Tarea* (Agency Controlling the Task). The *Controlador* circulates the *anteproyecto* to all relevant agencies of the state's central administration (i.e., ministries, national committees and institutes), as well as the Communist Party's Department of State and Legal Agencies and the four law schools.

Proposed laws also go to the mass organizations for public discussion and debate. Technical laws (e.g., laws of criminal procedure) are excused from this wide circulation because it is assumed that most people will not understand them and they will affect only a small proportion of the population. In the interests of speedy passage, however, it is sometimes seen as desirable to bypass popular discussion. The determination of whether a proposed law is technical or nontechnical can be quite contentious. This situation arose in late 1989 with regard to modifications to the Family Code. The Federation of Cuban Women (FMC), *itself a mass organization,* sought to bypass popular discussion in order to pass the modifications as quickly as possible, preferably at the December 1989 legislative session. In contrast, because the Family Code is a law that affects everyone, the Ministry of Justice and the Law School at the University of Havana, along with the CACJ (whose legal advisor it should be recalled was the Dean of the Law School, possibly explaining the similar positions of these two entities), wanted the proposed changes to be publicly discussed in the mass organizations. A situation that several persons referred to as "a war" ensued. The FMC lost, with the revised Code not even being raised as a point of discussion at the December 1989 legislative session.

Next, the relevant state agencies, department of the Communist Party, and law schools write critiques of the *anteproyecto,* known as *dictámenes* or *criterios.* These include the organization's evaluation, concerns, opinions, juridical observations, and relevant practical experiences. A law professor who, as we spoke, had an *anteproyecto* on his desk awaiting his critique, told me,

> This process of writing critiques is very interesting. There are people who think writing a critique is easy. I would say that it is one of the most difficult activities that legal advisors do. I have been writing critiques for the Ministry of Justice for two years. I am of the opinion that it is not possible to write a good critique in an agency office . . . . I can't write a good critique sitting down. I have to go to where the event is occurring, to where the social exigency is . . . . [Referring to a critique he wrote concerning aqueducts and subterranean waters] I sat with the technical advisory council. We debated for eight days . . . [then] I spent a week with the workers [involved in a related construction project]. The experience I had was marvelous. I could never have written a good critique [without it] (Castanedo, May 3, 1989).

The critiques are returned to the office of the Secretary of the Council of Ministers, at which point this office is converted into the *Organo Conciliador de Opiniones* (Agency Conciliating Diverse Opinions). Since differences of opinion are expected and almost always arise, this office arranges meetings for representatives of the agencies with differing viewpoints.

The next version is then written, incorporating critical comments from the *dictámenes* and the outcome of conciliation meetings. If a compromise cannot be reached, the conflicting versions and the criticisms raised are incorporated into the text of the revised *anteproyecto*. It circulates through the same agencies and organizations once again. The conciliation process goes through as many iterations as are necessary.

Once agreement has been reached, or it becomes clear that the parties in conflict will not reach an agreement, the bill goes to the National Assembly as a *proyecto*. It is reviewed by the appropriate legislative commissions[8] and the Council of Ministers for its constitutionality, normative foundations, likely economic effects, correspondence with underlying political, social, and economic motivations, and to ensure that the necessary conditions and mechanisms exist to guarantee its applicability, effectiveness, and compliance.[9] Finally, the commissions recommend passage, rejection, or revision of the *proyecto*. The CACJ's recommendation is the most powerful; if it does not approve the *proyecto,* the process comes to a halt and the bill is sent back for revisions. This is comparable in the U.S. to a bill not coming out of the Judiciary Committee.

Once approved by the relevant commissions, the *proyecto* and the CACJ's critique are distributed to all members of the National Assembly and the date for its floor debate is set. If interorganizational conflicts still persist, the varying perspectives are presented in written form to members of the National Assembly. The *alta asesoría* must also provide an oral accounting of problems with the bill and its rationale for supporting one rather than another version during the scheduled floor debate. When passed by the National Assembly, the *proyecto* becomes law. When *proyectos* are not passed, the National Assembly often suggests that the bill be revised and resubmitted for reconsideration at a later date, usually about three years[10] (Francisco Martínez, May 17, 1989; Armando Castanedo, May 3, 1989; Víctor Kautzman, May 8, 1989; Article 86, *Constitucíon de la República de Cuba; Acuerdo para regular el proceso de elaboración y presentación de proyectos de leyes,* December, 1988).

In reality, floor debate is quite limited. This can be explained by the very short time frame for meetings of the National Assembly, two or three days twice a year, and by the substantial committee activities preceding the bill's arrival at the Assembly. The real debate occurs in these background, interagency meetings, with contentious points already resolved before the *proyecto* ever reaches the legislature as a whole. In the examples that follow, a sense of how conflicting views are hammered out is provided by participants in these interagency workgroups.

EXAMPLES OF LAW CREATION
AND MODIFICATION

Blas Roca Calderío's Commission for Legal Studies was responsible for drafting all major legislation between 1969 and 1976. In essence, the task it set for itself was to create an entirely new, socialist, legal structure. This included the Constitution, substantive and procedural laws found in every country, substantive laws not in place everywhere that attempt to produce profound social changes (e.g., the Family Code), and laws detailing the organization of the judicial system. Although work in all of these areas proceeded simultaneously, as each *anteproyecto* was revised, changes in the other *anteproyectos* became necessary. In some cases these changes were simply stylistic and editorial, but others were more profound. In an effort to achieve consistency, the practice developed in which one law, or set of related laws, would be passed at a time.

I want to turn now to a more detailed analysis of the process of law creation by focusing on three kinds of laws: the criminal code, criminal procedure, and family law. The laws chosen exemplify how the process of law creation is a *strategy* employed by the state for resolving interorganizational conflicts and dilemmas arising from competing demands. They also demonstrate how changes in the substantive content of Cuban law and in the mix of legal formalism and informalism serve as temporary *resolutions* to conflicts and dilemmas. Finally, they show that law is both a byproduct of social change, solidifying past and ongoing social transformations, and a catalyst for social change. As we shall see, changes in criminal law have largely mirrored earlier social transformations, while in family law the legal changes have preceded social change.

The laws I will discuss are: (1) the Criminal Codes of 1979 (Law No. 21, February 15) and 1987 (Law No. 62, December 29); (2) the Laws of the Organization of the Judicial System and of Criminal Procedure of 1973 (Law No. 1250, June 23 and Law No. 1251, June 25), and 1977 (Law No. 4, August 10 and Law No. 5, August 13), the Law of the Courts of 1990 (Law No. 70, July 12) and other proposed reforms in criminal procedure; and (3) the Family Code of 1975 (Law No. 1289, February 14) and its proposed revision. These laws developed as a temporary solution to specific conflicts during the period of institutionalization. By the late 1970s, when the institutionalization process was largely complete, the solutions of the 1960s and 1970s were no longer seen as adequate and the laws were revised. When a new generation raised within the Revolution came of age in the late 1980s, it became necessary once again to revisit these laws.

The laws I have selected offer glimpses into different aspects of the dynamic relationship between social and legal change in revolutionary Cuba. Changes in the Criminal Code reflect where the country has been and where it is going, and analysis of these modifications allows us a profound examination of changes in the operational definition of socialist legality. The Laws of Criminal Procedure and of the Organization of the Courts exemplify how the mix of formalism and informalism was codified and institutionalized in Cuba, particularly, but not exclusively, in the criminal sphere. The Family Code was designed to effect substantive changes in the status of Cuban women— an instance of legal change preceding larger social and cultural changes.

THE CRIMINAL CODES

With independence in 1902, the Republic of Cuba inherited the Spanish Criminal Code. The first Cuban criminal law was the Social Defense Code (*Código de Defensa Social*), enacted in 1936. Following the revolutionary triumph, the Social Defense Code was modified several times to make it more consistent with what was then Cuba's reality. By 1969, it was clear that a new criminal code was needed. As the first "whereas" of the 1979 code stated, its adoption was imperative because the old code, even with post-triumph modifications,

> does not now correspond to the reality of our economic, social, and political development, nor does it have the coherence required of legal bodies of this character. Approval of a new Penal Code is a core part of the basic tasks of the legislative plan for creating the fundamental legal bodies that the new socialist State requires be substituted instead of the old ones. (*Criminal Code*, 1979:1).[11]

The 1979 Criminal Code

The *anteproyecto* for the new criminal code was drafted during the period 1969 through 1973, but it was not enacted until 1979. Ironically, its passage was delayed by the very process of institutionalization that made this new law possible and imperative. The only changes made between 1973 and 1979 were minor alterations to ensure consistency with other laws. Consequently, the ideological principles underlying the 1979 Code were those of the late 1960s and early 1970s. It reflected the social, economic, and political conditions of the country during the 1960s, rather than the late 1970s as its date of enactment might suggest (Quirós, May 15, 1989).

The 1960s were a time of exhilaration and euphoria mixed with extreme hardship for the Cuban people. The era of Batista's tyranny was over, and the Cubans were prepared to pull themselves out of their dependent, neocolonial status. But there was a lot of hard work to be done, and the new state faced many perils. Many Cubans recalled those days to me with variations on, "It was wonderful and it was awful. Everything was so hard but we accomplished so much. No, I never slept much then, but it didn't seem that I needed much sleep. It truly was wonderful. It was an exciting time and I'm proud of what we've done."

Economically, the total blockade against Cuba begun in 1961 by the United States and its allies hurt the country tremendously. Cuba's closest trade partners, the United States and to a lesser extent parts of Latin America, were cut off. This meant that new markets had to be found for Cuban sugar and other export products, and also that new sources for imports had to be located (see Appendix H). While friendlier trade agreements were reached with the Soviet Union and other socialist countries, these countries were poorer than the United States and thus did not have as much to offer, particularly in terms of technological imports. Transportation costs were high, as these new markets were thousands of miles away. In addition to dilemmas of foreign trade, the Cuban economy was seriously harmed by sabotage and other economic crimes committed by U.S.-sponsored Cuban exiles. Military incursions by these exiles and the very realistic fear of an invasion meant that funds which could otherwise be spent on economic development had to be rerouted for defense purposes.

Beginning with the triumph and escalating further following nationalizations of foreign enterprises in the early 1960s, U.S. businesses began pulling out of Cuba. They took not only their businesses, but also U.S. *and Cuban* engineers, technicians, and other skilled workers. In addition, many doctors, lawyers, and other professionals ran for the United States and other countries where they could maintain their comfortable lifestyles with greater ease. This left Cuba with deficiencies in both economic and human resources.

The most immediate ideological goals and social priorities of the revolution were to make every Cuban literate and healthy. The literacy campaign, while a tremendous feat, was relatively easy compared with meeting the health care needs of the population. Every educated Cuban could teach others how to read and write, and they did so quickly and effectively, making the Cuban literacy campaign of 1961 an international standard for Third World countries. Some health care needs could be met by unskilled labor (e.g., clearing swamps where disease-carrying mosquitoes bred, disposing of sewage, constructing adequate housing), but other aspects of health care required professionals. Accordingly, training of doctors, nurses, and medical technicians was a high priority for the new state (see Appendix C for growth in the numbers of health-care professionals). Engineers, technicians, and teachers were also desperately needed to take over and modernize businesses, infrastructure, and agriculture, and to train the next generation of professionals (see Appendix F).

Politically, the new Cuban state was exploring who it was and what it wanted to be. Fidel Castro and his *compañeros* had developed a revolutionary platform during their years of fighting, and the socialist nature of the revolution was publicly proclaimed by Fidel in 1961 just prior to the successful rebuffing of the Bay of Pigs invasion. But political transformations require far more than public statements and platforms. The transition from dependent capitalism to socialism necessitated changes in the social and economic realms along with a new institutional structure. In other words, the basic ideological principles of the Revolution had to be operationalized. Much of this operationalization occurred during the 1960s, with its sweeping social and economic advances. Institutionalizing these social policies in the form of more durable laws, however, had to wait until the 1970s.

The social and economic progress made by the Cuban people during the 1960s was remarkable. That it occurred at a time when every other aspect of life had to be secondary to national defense makes this progress even more amazing. It meant, however, that when institutionalization began in the late 1960s, the mindset of the people was still that of "living in a permanent situation of war" (Quirós, May 15, 1989). It was not only money and human resources that were devoted to the physical defense of the revolution; everything, including criminal law, had to be a weapon for defense. That is precisely what the 1979 Code was, and that is also why it was already outdated by the time it was enacted into law.

Professor Renén Quirós Pírez, generally considered to be the "father" of the 1979 Criminal Code and subsequent modifications of it through the 1987 Code, explained it in this way:

> The 1979 Code still reflected the situation of war and fighting. In those times we had to use all of the weapons that we could to resist [spies and saboteurs]. And one of those weapons, logically, was the sanction of criminal law. Our military resources were not what they are today and therefore we had to use all of the weapons, and one of these was criminal law, the criminal sanction.

Reminding me that the Code was really written in the early 1970s he continued,

> Perhaps there was some failure of foresight. We didn't take into account the changes that had been produced in economic conditions that made it less necessary to resort to criminal sanctions . . . . Almost immediately after passing the Code in 1979, we began to understand that we had arrived at a criminal code with very severe sanctions, without the necessity of very severe sanctions, that we had widened the scope of "crime" beyond the limits of what really constituted crime. We began to understand that other means, social influence, could assist us. This did not occur in the year 1979, but we began to see it early in the decade of the 1980s. By 1983, the ideas were clear as to where we should go (May 15, 1989).

Similarly, former Minister of Justice Juan Escalona Reguera has acknowledged that by 1983,

> we intuited that the criminal policy we had been applying in the country did not fit the social, political and economic conditions we had attained . . . and that the response we had given to this problem [of crime in Cuba], based solely on repression, would not permit us to overcome [it] (Escalona, 1988:30,32).[12]

Modifications of the 1979 Code: The 1987 Code

The 1979 Code embodied the view that lengthy incarceration should be the primary mechanism for crime control. Further, it defined a very wide range of unacceptable behaviors as criminal. For example, under the 1979 Code "robbery of socialist property" was a different crime from "robbery" and carried a harsher sanction than did robbery. With passage of the 1987 Code, "robbery of socialist property" no longer exists as a separate crime category.

The ideas formulated by 1983 reserved use of the criminal sanction as a last resort, and within that, incarceration as *the* last resort, to be used only when alternative sanctions would not be adequate or appropriate. The new code mandating these major changes was not enacted until late 1987 and did not go into effect until April 30, 1989. To some extent, delays in its passage can be attributed to Cuba's commitment to housing and jobs for all of its people, translating concretely into the need to locate jobs and housing for all persons who would be released from prison earlier than had been anticipated.

However, some steps were taken in advance of the law's passage. In 1985 the Council of State approved a process for judicial review of previous sentences with the explicit aim of diminishing many of them (Decree-law No. 87, July 22). Cuban law allows for a sentencing range for each offense. The 1985 decree-law granted judges the discretion to reduce average or maximum sentences to minimum sentences under the 1979 law, or under even earlier law if the 1979 minimums seemed excessive. More than 35,000 cases were reviewed by the courts in 1985 and 1986, resulting in conditional release of 15,000 prisoners and full release of others (Quirós, May 15, 1989; see also Evanson, 1994). Also, in 1986 the Council of State passed an accord which restricted the use of pretrial detention to the most serious cases (e.g., murder, rape, drug offenses).

Although many Cubans are skeptical of these changes, arguing "once a thief, always a thief," by 1989 only 10 percent of the prisoners released early had recidivated, none of the defendants released pending trial were arrested for new crimes, and only 5.4 percent of those awaiting trial returned to jail for violating the conditions of their release (Escalona, 1988; Quirós, May 15, 1989; Amaro Salup, 1989). Thus, the more lenient standards put into place in the late 1980s appear both warranted and successful.

The legal changes incorporated in the 1987 Code reflected contemporary social conditions in which the family, neighborhood, and workplace were seen as more conducive to the prevention of crime and resocialization of criminals than incarceration. According to Renén Quirós Pírez, the new law had three immediate consequences: (1) reducing the number of acts that had been defined as criminal under the old code by about 29 percent; (2) reducing sentence lengths, often by a large proportion; and (3) offering alternatives to incarceration (e.g., probation with varying degrees of scrutiny and suspended sentences) for offenses that carried short periods of incarceration, with "short" defined in 1989 to mean a three-year maximum. By Quirós's personal calculations, incorporation of these measures into the new law has meant that judges can now apply alternatives to incarceration in 85 percent of the cases that come before them (Quirós, May 15, 1989).

What accounts for these radical transformations in the perception and use of criminal sanctions? Cuban legal scholars and policy makers argue that the objective reality and the subjective interpretation of both the crime problem and of the appropriateness of repressive criminal sanctions changed as a response to changing social, political, and economic conditions (Quirós, May 15, 1989; Kautzman, May 12, 1989; Kautzman, May 15, 1989). [13]

Social conditions within Cuba changed substantially during the 1970s and 1980s, even though the external conditions (e.g., threat from the United States, problems resulting from Cuba's largely agrarian economy, necessary imports that could only be purchased with foreign currency) were not altered significantly. The revolutionary achievements of the 1960s (e.g., guaranteed food, clothing, education, housing, health care, and employment) were consolidated and institutionalized in the 1970s through the Constitution and other laws that better organized the state's activities. These gains were augmented during the 1980s, leading to an improved living standard for all Cubans. Additional advances could be seen in the sociocultural realm, with attempts to eradicate discrimination based on sex and race manifested concretely in greater educational and occupational opportunities for all. This meant significant increases in the number of day-care centers (see Appendix I) and admission of women into the more prestigious and higher-paying professions (see Appendix J).

Politically, the revolutionary leadership had matured greatly. As Quirós explained,

> The situation that existed in the first years after the triumph, especially the mobilization of everyone for war, did not permit us to dedicate ourselves to perfecting the state apparatus. But, also, I don't think we had very clear ideas of what, for example, criminal law should be. At the end of the 1960s we began the process of institutionalization—in 1969 to be precise. At that point the direction of the country had matured to the point that a new epoch could begin. This was when lawyers began to play their roles as lawyers with greater intensity. Until that moment jurists played the same role as the rest of the people—as people constructing a society (May 15, 1989).

Alongside these political and social transformations came increased efforts to fortify the economy. During the 1960s the military threat, combined with the blockade and the "brain drain" of professionals, meant that economic and human resources had to be dedicated to defense. In this situation of very real scarcity, the Cubans trained new doctors, teachers, and technicians for the paralyzed industries (see Appendix F). Women's liberation represented both an ideological shift and an economic strategy, since the labor-force participation of women was crucial to reinvigorating the economy. By the end of the 1960s, the situation had stabilized sufficiently to allow for reorganization of the state apparatus and reprioritization of goals and necessities. With these internal transformations,

> we could dedicate to the defense what had to go to defense, and designate to the economy what had to go to the economy. That is, we could now designate people, resources, et cetera, for economic fortification of the country. For this reason there was a change in our economic conditions in the decade of the 70s (Quirós, May 15, 1989; also Kautzman, May 12, 1989).

These changes were further strengthened during the 1980s through the Cuban process of "rectification" (*rectificación de errores y tendencias negativas*). "Rectification" sounds more negative in English than in Spanish, but even in Spanish it indicates that serious errors were made that must be redressed, that the Revolution was becoming sidetracked. Serious problems certainly arose in the economic realm and in many administrative sectors. Whether the legal arena faced such extreme inadequacies and tensions is debatable, leading one prominent Cuban legal scholar to say that he is "allergic" to the term "rectification." My own assessment and that of many Cuban legal scholars is that "improvement" better describes the kinds of changes that occurred in the legal sphere during the 1980s.

Rectification as a formal state policy was publicly announced at the Party Congress in 1986, but substantial improvements in the juridical arena began earlier, with most sources suggesting 1983 as the point of departure (Quirós, May 15, 1989; Kautzman, May 18, 1989). 1983 was an important date in Cuban legal history. It was in this year that the basic principles of the new Criminal Code were established. Juan Escalona Reguera became Minister of Justice in 1983, a post which he retained until February 1990, when he resigned to become President of the National Assembly. Escalona Reguera, who is a member of the Party's Central Committee, is a very forceful administrator and policy maker. Very much influenced by international events and adept at using international forums to further programmatic changes he envisions, Escalona and his colleagues (particularly Professor Renén Quirós Pírez and former First Vice-Minister of Justice, and later Attorney General, Ramón de la Cruz Ochoa) brought very positive international recognition to Cuba's legal system due to its liberal policies (e.g., decriminalization, depenalization, reductions in pretrial detention) that are in line with United Nations recommendations.

For all of these reasons, criminal sanctions were still seen as a weapon for defense in the late 1980s, but only in the sense that a few activities (e.g., spying, sabotage, assassinations, treason) represent "enemy" actions that must be dealt with through a repressive criminal justice system. By 1987, when the new criminal code was passed into law, the most common crimes were petty theft, minor assaults, and traffic violations. Using internal data from the Office of the Attorney General of the Republic of Cuba, Michalowski (1992) demonstrates that in 1987 robbery occurred at the rate of 13 per 100,000 inhabitants, burglary and theft each at rates of 101 per 100,000, and all personal crimes combined at a rate of 190 per 100,000. To put this in perspective, he presents comparable rates for the U.S. in 1986: 225 robberies per 100,000 inhabitants, 1,345 burglaries per 100,000 inhabitants, and 3,010 per 100,000 for theft. As another indicator of the changing nature of crime in Cuba, the state security section of the provincial court for the city of Havana was turned into a traffic court. Renén Quirós Pírez maintains, "We have to ask ourselves, then, do we need to use weapons so strong, so powerful, against these types of delinquencies?" (May 15, 1989).

The interpretation of criminal justice as a weapon for defense of the state changed in the early 1980s. With that change in legal consciousness, a repressive criminal justice system was transformed into a system that relies more heavily on education and resocialization than on incarceration.

LAWS OF THE ORGANIZATION OF THE JUDICIAL SYSTEM AND OF CRIMINAL PROCEDURE

Immediate Post-Triumph Court Structures

The Revolutionary government inherited two court structures. One of these, the Urgency Tribunals (*tribunales de urgencia*) used by Batista against the revolutionary forces, was dismantled on January 5, 1959. The old Spanish system of audiences (*audiencias*) and correctional judges (*juzgados correccionales*), organized hierarchically under the Supreme Court, was maintained until December, 1973. The seven audiences (one in each province and a seventh in the city of Holguín) tried cases with potential penalties of six or more months of incarceration, and correctional judges heard less serious cases (Kautzman, 1988, May 18, 1989; van der Plas, 1987; Fernández Guerra, December 1, 1989).

Two additional court structures quickly emerged. The first was the system of revolutionary tribunals (*tribunales revolucionarios*). Castro's forces had established these in the Sierra Maestra Mountains during the war, and in January 1959, they were extended to all of the provinces. Between January and July of 1959, they adjudicated accusations of torture and other crimes against the Cuban people committed by Batista's police, soldiers, and officials. By the summer of 1959, most of these cases had been processed and all criminal cases went to the regular system of *audiencias* and *juzgados*. Very quickly thereafter, upon passage of the first set of revolutionary laws (e.g., urban and agrarian reforms and nationalizations), crimes of aggression and sabotage by the U.S. and discontented Cubans began to appear. The revolutionary tribunals were reconstituted in November of 1959 to deal with such crimes. They remained in effect until December 1973, when the first Law of the Organization of the Judicial System was enacted (García Alzugaray, May 23, 1991).

The revolutionary tribunals were the only courts with authority to sentence a person to death. They were staffed by a mixed bench of professional and lay judges. The lay judges were soldiers, members of the Ministry of the Interior, and civilian members of the militia. A prosecutor made the accusations and an attorney defended the interests and due process guarantees of the accused (Kautzman, May 18, 1989).

The second new court structure was created *de facto* in October 1962, when Fidel Castro suggested to the University of Havana law faculty and students that they organize popular tribunals (*tribunales populares*; also known as *tribunales de base*). These courts began to function in 1963, first in the Sierra Maestra, then in the Escambray region, and finally spreading to the city of Havana and the rest of the country. Soon there were "hundreds and hundreds" of popular tribunals (Kautzman, May 18, 1989).

The popular tribunals were characterized by a high degree of informality. They were staffed by a panel of three regular citizens elected from the local communities to serve as judges. No special dress was required, and trials were open forums held at night. The decision to hold trials at night was based on two concerns. First, the judges worked at other jobs during the day so as not to further disrupt the already devastated economy, and they tried cases on a voluntary basis after completion of their work day. Second, the educational role of the popular tribunals was enhanced by holding trials at night when all interested members of the community could attend them, thereby seeing how socialist legality actually worked. Given the corrupt reputation of Batista's judges, it was important for the people to witness for themselves how revolutionary justice differed from the prerevolutionary form of legality.

Suspects could choose to be defended by lay persons or attorneys. The mass organizations, particularly the neighborhood-level Committees for the Defense of the Revolution (CDRs), were involved in all phases of the trial, from initial accusations through sanctioning and re-education. The popular tribunals had jurisdiction over minor civil and criminal cases with a maximum potential penalty of six months of incarceration. The judges, none of whom had formal legal training, took a short course of legal study prior to assuming office and were assisted on an "as needed" basis by legal advisors from the Ministry of Justice and the law schools. These judges were far more creative than the correctional judges, using sanctions such as compulsory schooling and other means of community-based rehabilitation and resocialization whenever possible (Kautzman, 1988, May 18, 1989; Marimón Roca, 1981; van der Plas, 1987; Berman, 1969). As I will discuss more fully later in this chapter, it was this innovativeness in sanctioning rather than the judges' lack of formal training in law that made the popular tribunals informal in the eyes of Cuban legal scholars (Díaz, June 28, 1990). The inconsistencies between the laws and these innovative sanctions meant that the flexibility of the popular tribunals had to be curtailed if an internationally recognized state of law was to exist (Fernández Guerra, December 1, 1989).

While the popular tribunals became a viable *institution* during the 1960s, they were never *institutionalized* in the form of a law, decree-law, or decree. Rather, "they were created 'de facto' as a revolutionary method of resolving a problem that could not await much time and so it was decided to use this experimental mode . . . . It was an experiment that became institutionalized" (Kautzman, May 18, 1989; also Arteaga, April 19, 1989). Basic procedural norms for their operation were laid out, however, in the form of *Manuals for Popular Tribunals* written by the Ministry of Justice in 1966 and 1968.

Two aspects of this experiment were later institutionalized: popular participation in judicial decisionmaking and the multiperson judicial panel. The experimental use of lay judges grew out of ideological goals and economic exigencies. Ideologically, popular involvement was perceived as educational and as a means of enhancing justice. Economically, it was a response to the serious shortage of trained lawyers. Many lawyers had left the country, others assumed nonjudicial tasks seen as more immediately necessary, and only a very small number of students were trained as lawyers during the 1960s (see Chapter Four). The experiment was generally viewed as successful, and many principles underlying the functioning of the popular tribunals were incorporated into the new court structure created in 1973 (Kautzman, May 18, 1989).

1973 LOSJ and LPP

In 1973, the Law of the Organization of the Judicial System (*Ley de la Organización del Sistema Judicial*, Law No. 1250; hereafter LOSJ) collapsed the three autonomous jurisdictions (the traditional audiences and correctional judges, revolutionary tribunals, popular tribunals) into one judicial structure with four layers: supreme/national, regional, provincial, and community/base. The principal reason for this revision was organizational coherency, with economic considerations also contributing to the decision. Once the new political organization of the country became institutionalized, integration of the three jurisdictional structures came to be seen as both desirable and possible. Organizationally and economically, it made no sense to have three court structures, complete with three sets of personnel and buildings, duplicating one another's functions. In addition, the traditional system and the revolutionary tribunals were no longer necessary, since police tended to bring minor cases directly to the popular tribunals rather than to the correctional judges, and because of the marked decrease of invasive military activities by the CIA and Miami-based exiles (Kautzman, May 18, 1989; Quirós, May 15, 1989).

Another objective of the new judicial structure was to expand and institutionalize the popular participation and multijudge structure that had been so successful in the popular tribunals. The correctional judges had operated as one-judge benches and the *audiencias* were composed of three-judge panels in which each judge was a professionally trained lawyer (Díaz, June 28, 1990). Thus, the combination of lay participation and collective panels was new to Cuba. Popularly elected multiperson benches were thought to democratize the administration of justice and to provide greater guarantees of reaching proper judgments (Merino, 1972; Dórticos, 1973).

Two days after passage of the LOSJ, a new Law of Criminal Procedure (*Ley del Procedimiento Penal*, Law No. 1251; hereafter LPP) was enacted. These two laws are tightly interwoven, since the LPP regulates how cases are to be handled by the courts, and the LOSJ defines the jurisdiction of the court layers. Thus, fundamental changes in one law require corresponding changes in the other. For this reason, the two laws are treated here as one set of laws.[14]

Under the 1973 laws, the community level courts, by that time commonly referred to as *tribunales de base,* retained total jurisdiction over minor civil and criminal cases. "Minor" was operationally defined as carrying a maximum penalty of six months incarceration or a fine of 100 *cuotas.* Each *cuota* can range from fifty *centavos* to 20 *pesos,* although one *peso* (roughly 75 cents U.S.D.) is the most common (Díaz, November 17, 1989). The *tribunales de base* were staffed by three lay judges. The regional and provincial courts and the Supreme Court handled increasingly more serious civil and criminal cases as well as labor and state security cases, and the Supreme Court also heard military cases. Each heard appeals from the court immediately below it in the judicial hierarchy. These higher courts had mixed bars composed of lay and professional judges, with a professionally trained lawyer acting as president of each judicial panel.

When the *tribunales de base* were transformed from an experiment to a judicial institution with the 1973 laws, trial times moved from evenings to days. This change was in large part reflective of the professionalization of the courts with the greater availability of trained jurists. The sense was that courts, like all other offices, should operate during the daytime. It was also a response to the very real exhaustion the Cuban people felt when they left work at the end of the day, only to go back to work in the evening as judges in addition to their other voluntary labor. The educational role of the courts suffered since fewer people could attend trials, but something had to be done to relieve the exhaustion of people who had been working day and night for 14 years. In addition, the authority of popular tribunals to engage in innovative sanctioning was restricted, and the prosecutor was allowed to intervene in serious cases (Prieto Morales, 1985; van der Plas, 1987; Kautzman, 1988).

This latter change resulted from the restructuring of the court system in 1973, in which the Office of the Attorney General gained administrative independence from the Supreme Court (Garcia, April 27, 1989). The new Office of the Attorney General was charged with control of legality, prevention of crime, prosecution of enemies of the State, assisting and advising the police during the preparatory phase of criminal processing, and oversight of criminal sanctions (Cuba Fernández, 1973). At the same time, the private practice of law was eliminated. All trial lawyers were integrated into law collectives (*bufetes colectivos*). The National Organization of Law Collectives is an autonomous national organization; neither it nor the individual attorney is subordinate to any other state agency or authority (Roca Calderío, 1974).

1977 LOSJ and LPP

The 1976 political-administrative reorganization of the country eliminated regions and created 14 provinces and 169 municipalities. The LOSJ and LPP were revamped to be consistent with this new organization (Laws No. 4 and 5, respectively).

While organizational coherence was the major rationale for the new laws, the 1977 laws also altered the administration of justice in two important ways. First, they modified the composition of the bench and the responsibilities of judges. Judges were elected by the new municipal, provincial, and national (for the Supreme Court) legislatures. The mixed bench of professional and lay judges was formalized into three-judge panels in municipal courts (two lay judges and one professional judge who serves as president of the panel) and five-judge panels in provincial courts and the Supreme Court (two lay judges and three professionally trained judges, one of whom is president). Each court has its own sphere of original jurisdiction and appellate review of lower court decisions. Municipal courts were empowered to adjudicate minor civil cases and criminal cases with a maximum penalty of nine months, an increase over their prior six-month maximum, and fines up to 270 *cuotas* rather than the prior 100 *cuotas* limit.[15] The provincial courts and Supreme Court retained jurisdiction over more serious civil and criminal cases as well as administrative, labor, and state security cases. The incorporation of labor disputes into the court system was new with the 1977 law (see Chapter Seven). As was established in 1973, the Supreme Court is also the highest appellate level for military cases and hears all cases involving the death penalty.

Second, consistent with the 1976 Constitution, the courts and the Office of the Attorney General gained further autonomy from other state agencies and institutions (Ordóñez Martínez, 1982; Escasena, 1984; Prieto Morales, 1985). Each of these changes had important theoretical and practical effects.

The Mix of Formalism and Informalism of Law

I proposed in Chapter Two that it is theoretically most fruitful to conceive of historical and contextual mixes of legal formalism and informalism, rather than classifying them dichotomously or as poles of a continuum. Adele van der Plas (1987) appears to take the latter perspective, lamenting the loss of informalism when professional judges work alongside lay judges at each court level. She sees this as the end of the era of informal, popular justice in Cuba. In contrast, I suggest that the mix of formalism and informalism was altered with the 1973 and 1977 laws, but not in any simple way that allows us to say that before or after passage of these laws the system was closer to one or the other end of a formalism-informalism continuum.

Prior to 1973, minor cases tended to go to the popular tribunals rather than to the correctional judges, but serious cases during that era went to the traditional audiences presided over *solely by professional* judges. From 1973 through 1976, all judges in the *tribunales de base* were lay judges, and lay judges joined the judicial panels of higher courts. In 1977, a professional judge was added to the judicial panel at the local level, but the jurisdiction of the local court, *where lay judges form a majority,* was increased. Thus, even with the increased number of trained lawyers, making it possible for lay judges to be eliminated from the system, the Cubans made the decision to retain popular participation in judicial decisionmaking. They see such participation as crucially important for the very reasons that many theorists and community activists elsewhere favor informal justice—because of its pedagogical potential and the human perspective of ordinary people that it brings to judicial decisionmaking. Christine Harrington (1985:2) has suggested the theoretical possibility of institutionalizing informalism. Similarly, I suggest that the laws of the 1970s institutionalized a key characteristic of informalism, use of lay judges, throughout the judicial structure.

Beyond the purported loss of informalism when professionally trained lawyers are merged with lay judges (based on the questionable assumption that the presence of professionals limits the decision-making autonomy of lay judges and constricts popular participation), informalism can be seen as disappearing when it is codified. The experiment in popular tribunals began in a *de facto* manner at Fidel Castro's suggestion and was never incorporated into any formal body of law. Nevertheless, case processing was made more systematic by the *Manuals for Popular Tribunals,* published by a state agency, the Ministry of Justice. Thus, even before passage of the LOSJ and the LPP, there had been some state involvement in and codification of the popular tribunals.

Some Cuban legal scholars see the closing of the popular tribunals as reducing or eliminating informalism. Their definition of informalism has nothing to do with lay involvement or lack of institutional oversight, however, because they do not equate informalism with popular participation. They see informalism as the ability to impose sanctions outside the bounds of the criminal code. It does not matter whether the sanctions are viewed positively (e.g., mandatory schooling) or negatively (e.g., public self-criticism); the key factor is whether they fall inside or outside the sanctioning range mandated in the criminal law (Díaz Pinillo, June 28, 1990). The laws of the 1970s substantially reduced this flexibility, although discretion in sentencing has not followed a clear temporal chronology. The judges in popular tribunals certainly had considerable discretion in sanctioning, but within the constraints of the cases they handled: minor cases, equivalent to misdemeanors in the U.S. system. Also, the Ministry of Justice exercised some oversight functions. To enhance equality in sanctioning, this innovativeness was reduced in the 1970s. Yet the 1985, 1986, and 1989 modifications in criminal law discussed above expanded judges' flexibility by allowing them to use probation and suspended sentences instead of prison terms. For these reasons I suggest that these laws did not eliminate informalism, but rather, *institutionalized* a new mix of informalism and formalism.

A polarized view of informalism and formalism can easily lead to an overly romantic notion that is inconsistent with reality. It also leads us into a theoretical straitjacket. With stabilization of any new regime, increased legal professionalism and a decline in citizen participation are likely to follow, resulting in greater formalization of legal processes.[16] If the legal structure of a nation is not institutionalized in a codified, bureaucratic manner, its enemies can accuse it internationally of not being a "state of law" and allowing for mob rule. Yet when a stable new regime formalizes rules into codified law and employs legal professionals, it can be charged with giving in to the wishes of the professionals, with professionals forming an elite stratum in most societies.

Inquisitorial versus Adversarial Nature of Criminal Law

The second significant outcome of the 1973 and 1977 LOSJ and LPP was the increased autonomy and responsibilities of the Office of the Attorney General (Pérez Sarmiento, 1989). This has important theoretical and practical implications because it reflects a break from the old Spanish inquisitorial-accusatorial system toward a more adversarial system.

The inquisitorial system had its roots in the Spanish tribunals of the *Santa Inquisición,* dating from 1198, which were used to prosecute, judge, and sanction heretics accused of crimes against the Christian faith. Preventive detention was commonplace. Detention facilitated torture, which was generally the basis for confessions. This system reached its apex in the late 1600s in France. In its purest form, the inquisitorial system collapsed with the triumph of the French Revolution in 1789, the Napoleonic Code of Criminal Instruction of 1808, and the Declaration of the Rights of Men and Citizens. French law during the Napoleonic era reestablished the principle of judicial debate between parties (based on the earlier Roman and Greek accusatorial system) and created a role for defense attorneys. When the Spanish incorporated these modifications from French law into their inquisitorial procedures, the emergent judicial system became known as "mixed," or "formal accusatory."

The mixed system was imported to Latin America with colonization and formed the basis for criminal procedural law throughout most of contemporary Latin America, including Cuba (Arranz, November 9, 1989; Bodes Torres, 1988:9–30; Prieto Morales, 1982:15–33). The most inhumane, obsolete, and unjust aspects of the inquisitorial and ancient accusatorial systems were rejected. The mixed system allowed for private (through complaints) or state initiation of the criminal process, oral and written presentation of evidence at trial, lay and professional participation in the criminal process, and either pretrial detention or liberty (depending upon the particular case).

The Cubans altered a key aspect of this system during the 1970s. The old Spanish system had a *juez instructor* (instructor judge) who conducted the accusation, and gathered and analyzed evidence. The Cubans discarded this judicial position in the 1970s, replacing it with a high-ranking police officer, the *instructor policial.* The work of the police instructor is overseen by the prosecutor's office, which is responsible for ensuring that the police do not violate due process guarantees and individual rights. The mixed system divides criminal procedure into two major parts: the preparatory phase and the oral trial. The preparatory phase is dominated by the inquisitorial system and the trial phase by the accusatorial system. The break between the two systems occurs in the intermediate stage, still formally within the preparatory phase, when the police instructor turns the case over to the prosecutor (Pérez Sarmiento, 1989; Prieto Morales, 1982; Arranz, 1989).

While the arresting party, prosecutor, and judge are no longer rolled into one official in contemporary Latin America, or Cuba specifically, the preparatory phase affords the police tremendous discretionary powers and relatively few guarantees to the accused. The police have 24 hours following arrest to decide if they want to charge the person. Then, the police instructor has three days to investigate the case and gather evidence before determining whether or not there is sufficient evidence to warrant passing the case on to the prosecutor. The prosecutor has another three days to dismiss or formally charge the person. Once the prosecutor files charges, the court has another three days to decide whether to try the case or dismiss it. Only then is there formally a "case."

Thus, as many as ten days may pass following arrest before a formal case is established. During this period the suspect is not formally accused. The result of this inquisitorially based definition of when a case becomes a "case" is that the suspect sits in jail awaiting the decisions of the police instructor and prosecutor; the suspect is not officially entitled to legal counsel since s/he has not formally been accused of a crime; the state, but not the defense, can collect any available evidence; and many due-process guarantees do not officially come into effect, although in practice most do, especially in recent years (Arranz, 1989).

While the Cuban police still exercise tremendous discretionary powers, the 1973 laws, the 1976 Constitution, and especially the 1977 laws empower the Attorney General's Office (the *Fiscalía*) to oversee the activities of the police instructor to ensure that investigations are conducted legally and properly (i.e., without abuse of police powers and in accordance with due-process guarantees). As a result, the power wielded by the police instructor is largely determined by the discretion of the supervising prosecutor. In particularly sensitive or important cases, the *Fiscalía* may take complete charge of the investigation. Thus, some of the discretionary power of the police, who in most societies are the legal actors most apt to abuse their authority, has been removed, with that discretion moving to the prosecutor's office and the courts.

The increased power and responsibilities granted the *Fiscalía* in the 1970s were not immediately visible. They increased gradually until 1986, when the relatively young and dynamic former First Vice-Minister of Justice, Ramón de la Cruz Ochoa, was appointed Attorney General (see Table 3.2). Under de la Cruz, this office made fuller use of its mandated powers (Díaz Pinillo, November 17, 1989). Asked why his office has increased its scope of responsibilities in recent years, de la Cruz Ochoa conceded that in the first 20 or 25 years of the Revolution, the *Fiscalía* did not break away sufficiently from the court structure, where it had been located under the old Spanish system. Under his leadership the *Fiscalía* has begun using more of the powers granted it by law, particularly as these concern control over the police. De la Cruz Ochoa hopes to further modernize the concept of the Cuban prosecutor and to grant both prosecutors and defense attorneys greater responsibilities at the municipal level where their presence at trial is not now required (de la Cruz Ochoa, December 5, 1989).

1990 Law of the Courts and Proposed Changes in Criminal Procedure

Following passage of the 1987 Criminal Code, new laws of criminal procedure and of the functioning of judicial agencies were needed for internal consistency (Rodríguez Gavira, 1988, December 4, 1989; Díaz, May 9, 1989, November 17, 1989). It was decided in the late 1980s to separate the juridical institutions, regulating each under a separate statute. This was facilitated by 1984 legislation (Decree-law No. 81) detailing the self-governance of the law collectives (*bufetes colectivos*). In July 1990, the Law of the Courts (*Ley de los Tribunales,* Law No. 70) was passed. The 1977 LOSJ then became officially defunct, although the Office of the Attorney General is to be governed by the old LOSJ until a new Law of the *Fiscalía* is enacted. As of the summer of 1991, the *bufetes colectivos* and the *Fiscalía* were drafting their new laws, but neither can proceed very far in this process until the new LPP is finalized, since proposed modifications in the LPP have major implications for both institutions.[17]

Speaking of the need for a new Law of Criminal Procedure, one lawyer said that the most recent criminal code gives Cuba "criminal concepts that are among the most advanced in the entire world. Now we need to change criminal procedure to keep up with them" (de la Fuente, December 4, 1989). Similarly, the "father" of the criminal code told me:

> We have to have a criminal procedure for this time. The new laws of procedure must be adjusted to current condi-tions . . . . I don't think the Law of Criminal Procedure can be a simple modification. It has to be a global revision, to adjust it to these current conditions (Quirós, May 15, 1989).

When asked why such radical policy shifts appear to occur so quickly in Cuba, yet another legal scholar (also a judge and member of the commission to write the new LPP) replied, "Ten years is a lot when you are in the middle of major transformations—it is like 100 years for other countries" (Díaz Pinillo, May 9, 1989). As will be elaborated below, there are also organizational, economic, and ideological bases for these innovations.

Plans for reform of the judicial system and criminal procedure began around 1985. The interorganizational commission to write the new LPP is headed by the Office of the Attorney General. In addition to a representative of this office, the commission includes a representative of the Ministry of Justice, two University of Havana law professors, a representative of the Supreme Court, and two representatives from the National Organization of Law Collectives.[18] Initially a representative from the Ministry of the Interior (which includes the police) was invited to attend relevant meetings. Police representation was formalized when the point at which the defense attorney would enter the case became a major concern of the commission (Rodríguez Gavira, December 4, 1989; Díaz Pinillo, June 28, 1990). During the spring and fall of 1989 I interviewed most members of this commission, meeting with some members again in 1990 and 1991.

A major alteration expected in the new LPP is the earlier involvement of defense attorneys in case processing. This was initiated by the National Organization of Law Collectives (to which all defense attorneys belong) in their *anteproyecto*. While their *anteproyecto* will not be the final document, and indeed the commission moved a step back from this *anteproyecto* to spend several years elaborating the basic principles of the new law, it was a successful strategic move by the law collectives since many of their points have been incorporated into the basic principles underlying the new legislation and are expected to remain in the final version of the law (Ceballos, November 22, 1989).

Exactly *when* defense attorneys will enter the process is the crux of the interorganizational conflict. The defense attorneys want to begin their formal participation on day one, when the police first begin their investigation. As a prominent defense attorney who serves on the commission to rewrite the LPP told me, "We want to enter in the first hour of the first day" (Ceballos, November 22, 1989; also de la Fuente, December 4, 1989). The Ministry of Justice and Office of the Attorney General are also committed to seeing defense attorneys enter at "the earliest possible moment." The police would prefer that the defense enters at day seven, when the case goes to the court for determination of whether to try the case or dismiss it. At a minimum, the police want to preserve their four days (24 hours for detention and 72 hours for the police instructor's investigation), the clear implication being that they fear the activities of defense attorneys will make collection of evidence more difficult.

Commission members uniformly stressed the collegial nature of their work and the norm of proceeding whenever possible on the basis of consensus. Yet, in the words of the Attorney General of the Republic, "at the policy level there is consensus, not conflict, [but] in day-to-day, concrete cases of course there is some conflict" (de la Cruz, December 5, 1989). Similarly, in discussing proposed changes in criminal procedure the vice-president of the National Union of Cuban Jurists told me "there are always contradictions, but not antagonisms" (Martín, April 18, 1989). In practical terms as it affects this piece of legislation, this means that every agency, including the police, agrees that defense attorneys must enter the process earlier than they do. Or, as I was told by the Attorney General of the Republic, the police have been "persuaded, convinced" that a change must occur, something that would have been "more difficult four years ago" (de la Cruz, May 9, 1989).

In December 1989, expectations of the compromise position differed, with two members of the commission estimating the compromise point as following day four (when the case moves from the police instructor to the prosecutor), another as somewhere between day one and day four, and another after day one or day two. By May 1991, discussion had centered around the first two days; either day one, immediately following arrest, or day two, when the police turn the case over to the police instructor. A representative of the Attorney General's office (the *Fiscalía*) told me that a consensus had essentially formed that the defense attorney should enter on day one, although the police still do not like this idea (García Alzugaray, May 23, 1991). The *Fiscalía's* support for this change is extremely important for three reasons: it oversees the work of the police instructor; the court rarely dismisses a case that the *Fiscalía* has brought; and the *Fiscalía* ensures the legality of state action, not the court.

In April 1992 the Society of Penal Sciences held a meeting to discuss the *anteproyecto,* and it was submitted to the Council of State in the fall of 1992. This version states that the accused person formally becomes a part of the process, and thus, the defense would enter, at the moment the defendant is instructed of the charges (i.e., by day two).[19] At that point the defense attorney could begin an independent, parallel investigation of the case, rather than leaving initial collection of the evidence in the hands of the police instructor and prosecutor.

While this modification in the law is crucially important to defendants and defense attorneys (and that is why the *Fiscalía,* the Ministry of Justice, the law schools, and the National Organization of Law Collectives are actively seeking a redefinition in law) the *reality* is that defense attorneys frequently begin their work immediately after the accused is arrested, when a member of the family of the accused contacts the law collective.

The change also has profound implications in terms of the philosophical bases underlying court processing. What the defense attorneys, the Office of the Attorney General, the law schools, and the Ministry of Justice are calling for is nothing less radical than the elimination of both the inquisitorial and mixed systems in favor of a more fully adversarial system. A key question underlying debate over a new LPP is precisely *who* will direct the investigation of the case. In some societies (both socialist and capitalist) it is the police, in others the prosecutor's office, and in others the judiciary. In the United States, for example, it is the judiciary, since judges must approve search warrants and other aspects of the police investigation. Removing this power from the police, including the police instructor, is critical for movement toward a more adversarial system and away from an inquisitorial system (Arranz, May 2, 1989).

An organizational analysis offers another possible explanation (see Table 3.2 for a listing of heads of major juridical agencies). There has clearly been some jockeying for power among the various criminal justice agencies. The picture that emerges is one in which the police are losing power and the Ministry of Justice and the Office of the Attorney General are gaining power. The police are structurally subsumed under the Ministry of the Interior. Traditionally, this has been a very powerful Ministry. It still is, but its respect has waned somewhat in recent years due to internal scandals and abuses of power that led to the replacement and criminal sanctioning of the Minister of the Interior (José Abrantes Fernández) in the summer of 1989. The related "Ochoa trial" of 14 members of the Armed Forces and the Ministry of the Interior convicted of drug smuggling, abuses of authority, and treasonous activities resulted in death penalties for four persons, including two high-ranking officers in the Ministry of the Interior. Although members of the police were not implicated in these crimes and scandals, the Ministry as a whole, and especially its top leadership, lost prestige. The respect accorded the average police officer was not reduced markedly by the scandal, but the Cuban people did not previously hold the police in very high esteem. The police in Cuba are not feared any more than they are in the United States; they just are not taken very seriously.

In contrast, since the mid-1980s the Ministry of Justice and the Office of the Attorney General have experienced tremendous gains in authority, prestige, and respect, and this is evidenced in both international and domestic relations. The judiciary, under the leadership of the Supreme Court and its President, Raúl Amaro Salup, was and remains an influential institution. Juan Escalona Reguera, Minister of Justice from 1983 to 1990, sits on the Central Committee of the Party (as does the new Minister of the Interior). When Escalona Reguera left his post as Minister, it was to become President of the National Assembly. This position is very influential, particularly at that time since heady discussions were underway concerning an increase in the professionalization and authority of the National Assembly. Also, the number of lawyers in the country doubled during the mid-1980s, adding significantly to the number and relative clout of defense attorneys and prosecutors. For these reasons, I predict that the new LPP will markedly increase the power of all other judicial actors *except* the police, whose relative power will decrease.[20]

Table 3.2:
Heads of Major Juridical Agencies (1959-1991)

Agency Heads	Dates	Key Former Position
Ministers of Justice		
Ángel Fernández Rodríguez	Jan 1959–Feb 1959	
Alfredo Yabúr Maluf (a)	Feb 1959–1973	
Armando Torres Santrayll	1973–Jan 1980	
Osvaldo Dórticos Torrado (a)	Jan 1980–Jun 1983	President of Cuba
Hector Garcín y Guerra (b)		
Ramón de la Cruz Ochoa (b)		
Mercedes Castro (b)	Jul 1983–Sep 1983	
Juan Escalona Reguera	Oct 1983–Feb 1990	
Carlos Amat Forés	Feb 1990–	First Vice-Minister of Justice
Ministers of the Interior (c)		
Ramiro Valdés Menéndez	Jun 1960–1973	
Sergio del Valle Jiménez (d)	1973–Dec 1979	
Ramiro Valdés Menéndez	Dec 1979–1985	
José Abrantes Fernández (e)	1985–Oct 1989	
Abelardo Colomé Ibarra	Oct 1989–	Army General
Presidents of the Supreme Court		
Emilio Menéndez y Menéndez (f)	1959–Nov 1960	
Enrique Hart y Ramírez (a)	Nov 1960–Jul 1980	
Raúl Amaro Salup	Jul 1980–	
Attorneys General of the Republic		
Mario Fernández	Jan 1959–Jul 1959	
José Santiago Cuba Fernández	Jul 1959–Jan 1980	
Idalberto Ladrón de Guevara (g)	Jan 1980–Apr 1984	
René Burguet Flóres (h)	May 1984–Dec 1985	
Ramón de la Cruz Ochoa	Jan 1986–	First Vice-Minister of Justice
Presidents of the National Assembly (i)		
Blas Roca Calderío	Dec 1976–Jan 1980	
Raúl Roa García	Jan 1980–Dec 1981	Vice-President of National Assembly
Flavio Bravo Pardo (a)	Dec 1981–Feb 1988	
Severo Aguirre del Cristo (j)	Feb 1988–Feb 1990	
Juan Escalona Reguera	Feb 1990–	Minister of Justice

(a) died in office
(b) upon the suicide of Dórticos, these three Vice-Ministers collectively headed the Ministry until appointment of Escalona
(c) the Ministry of the Interior was created in June 1960
(d) resigned to become Minister of Public Health
(e) left office in disgrace, convicted of abuse of power in the aftermath of the Ochoa affair
(f) resigned, sought asylum in a foreign embassy and left Cuba
(g) removed from office following a tragedy in which a boy died
(h) Acting Attorney General following removal of Ladrón de Guevera from office; served provisionally until appointment of de la Cruz Ochoa
(i) the National Assembly was created in 1976
(j) Vice-President of the National Assembly since July 1985; assumed the responsibilities of the President from the death of Bravo in 1988 until election of Escalona

Another major innovation expected with the new LPP is greater guarantees for victims and a formal role for them in court processing and sanctioning. The commission as a whole agreed that this change would be positive, since, as several members commented, "they are victimized by the crime and by the law" (Rodríguez Gavira, December 4, 1989; Ceballos, November 22, 1989; Díaz Pinillo, May 9, 1989, November 17, 1989). Surprisingly, since militaries are usually rather regressive, the Military Law of Criminal Procedure affords victims greater rights than does the civilian law. A basic operating principle accepted by the commission is that victims should have a formal part in criminal procedure. Concretely, this means expanding their representation from the prosecutor (who, as in the United States, represents society as a whole rather than a specific aggrieved party) to independent counsel if they so desire.

When asked if greater rights for victims will reduce defendants' rights, Mario Ceballos, one of Cuba's most respected defense attorneys and a member of the commission, replied, "The victim is a citizen too, and deserves the same rights as the defendant" (Ceballos, November 22, 1989). Another commission member said, "The accused person has a great many rights and guarantees; the victim has practically none" (Díaz Pinillo, November 17, 1989). The Attorney General added that increased guarantees for victims would allow for greater democratization of criminal procedure (de la Cruz, December 5, 1989). The opposing position holds that victims make the initial accusation and are defended by the police, the prosecutor, and the courts. "What more," some ask, "do the victims need?" If victims are to be represented by attorneys, the regulations governing law collectives will need to be modified to include consistent prices for victims, as is done for defendants. That, however, is seen as a minor and easy revision.

Another possible change with the new laws is increased jurisdiction for municipal courts to adjudicate cases carrying penalties of up to three years' incarceration. If the competency of municipal courts is altered, it will have interesting implications for the mix of formalism and informalism. In keeping with my argument above that lay judges remain a cornerstone of Cuban judicial decisionmaking, it means that cases decided by lay judges, or in which lay judges predominate, will increase in number and importance. Until 1977 lay judges only handled criminal cases with a six-month maximum. In 1977 the municipal panels gained jurisdiction over all cases with nine-month maximums, and in 1987 over cases with one-year maximums, comparable to misdemeanors in the United States. With this change, panels in which lay people predominate would decide what are essentially minor felonies.

The primary reason for considering this is organizational efficiency. It would reduce the caseloads of the provincial courts and the number of appeals to the Supreme Court. Currently 15 to 20 percent of all cases adjudicated in provincial court go to the Supreme Court on appeal (Ceballos, November 22, 1989). Many of these are relatively minor cases. As one scholar told me, "It is absurd for the Supreme Court to be hearing petty theft or minor assault cases; that should not be the function of a *modern* Supreme Court" (Díaz Pinillo, November 17, 1989, his emphasis). If more cases are decided at the municipal level, appeals would go first to the provincial courts, relieving the extreme congestion in the Supreme Court. Provincial courts could focus their attention on complex cases that often require lengthy trials and longer deliberations. Simpler cases would be handled at the municipal level, which is less bureaucratized and much faster (Díaz Pinillo, November 17, 1989; de la Cruz, December 5, 1989).

A contrasting position holds that because judges in municipal courts have very limited experience, they should not have decision-making power over cases that may result in substantial prison terms. Surprisingly, municipal court lay judges espouse this position. I had expected them to welcome additional authority, but in interviews they consistently raised concerns about their abilities to adjudicate serious cases.

By the summer of 1991, economics had become a crucial concern in policy creation. If the municipal courts assume the burden for more cases, they will need more judges, secretaries, security staff, and space. As a result, a change in the competency of municipal courts is unlikely at this time (García Alzugaray, May 23, 1991).

The new Law of the Courts (*Ley de los Tribunales*, Law No. 70), which was enacted July 12, 1990, and went into effect January 1, 1991, enhanced organizational efficiency in a different but equally startling way: by shifting the balance of lay and professional judges in provincial courts. Under this new law, most provincial court panels are composed of two lay and one professional judge, instead of two lay and three professional judges. Consequently, the mix of lay and professional judges in provincial courts is now the same as in the lower, municipal courts where lay judges have traditionally formed a majority. The professional judge retains a major role as president of the panel and by deciding technical points of law, so as to avoid arbitrary decisions, with the lay judges offering their opinions and their votes (Rodríguez Gavira, May 22, 1991). In cases where the maximum sanction is imprisonment for more than eight years, or death, or where the President of the Court (equivalent to the Chief Presiding Judge in U.S. courts) determines that the case is especially important or complex, the previous composition of two lay and three professional judges remains in effect.

The point at which five-judge panels would be reinvoked was a source of considerable discussion, with some commission members suggesting cases with maximum sentences of six years, and others eight years. The final decision was based on a quantitative analysis of the number of cases that would be affected by the change. The vast majority of criminal cases handled in provincial courts in the late 1980s, about 80 to 90 percent, carried sanctions of eight years or less. (The percentage of serious crime increased in the early 1990s in response to the very difficult economic situation.) A contentious decision was whether to split the provincial courts into two sections, one for less serious and the second for more serious cases. Proponents said that if the courts were formally divided, appeals from the less serious section could go to the other section, further reducing appeals to the Supreme Court. Attorney General Ramón de la Cruz Ochoa adamantly opposed this position. He felt strongly that all appeals from provincial courts should be heard by the Supreme Court (de la Cruz, December 5, 1989). Consistent with his view, the new law stops short of dividing the provincial courts into sections, thus ensuring that all appeals go to the Supreme Court.

In practical terms, this new composition means that the same number of judges can handle more cases (e.g., fifteen judges can hear five cases concurrently rather than three). This makes case processing faster and more efficient at the provincial level, and allows more time to be spent on complex cases (Díaz Pinillo, May 9, 1989; de la Cruz, December 5, 1989). Another basis for this change is the success of the municipal model. Since panels with one professional and two lay judges worked so well there, it was decided to expand that structure to the provincial level. Consistent with the Cuban leadership's ideological orientation, it was thought that panels dominated by lay judges would make more just decisions (Rodríguez Gavira, May 22, 1991).

Lay judges are not the *only* indicator of informal justice, nor is involvement of lay people in judicial decisionmaking equivalent to informalism. But, it is probably a necessary condition for informalism, and is an important factor in assessing the relative mix of formalism and informalism in any given legal system.[21] The role of lay judges is an integral part of my argument that we are seeing a new mix of legal formalism and informalism in Cuba, rather than a decrease in informalism as van der Plas (1987) suggests.

The new Law of the Courts also formally modifies the term of office for lay judges from two months per year to one month. This had already been established by judicial norm, and was simply formalized under the new law. The primary reason for this change was economic, since it disturbed production when workers served as judges for two non-consecutive months, in addition to their one-month vacation each year. A secondary rationale was ideological in nature. By doubling the number of lay judges, the number of people who learn about socialist legality in action and who can use that knowledge to help resolve disputes in the neighborhoods and workplaces is considerably augmented (Rodríguez Gavira, December 4, 1989; Fernández, December 1, 1989).

At the same time that the 1990 law reduced the number of months served by lay judges, it increased their term of office from two-and-one-half to five years, equal to professional judges. While these stipulations may at first appear contradictory, they ensure that even if the same person is repeatedly re-elected, she or he only works as a judge for one month each year. Thus, the possibilities for doubling the number of people acquiring experience as lay judges remain.

Law was also made more consistent with organizational reality when the 1990 Law of the Courts formalized the practice of using substitute professional judges. Substitutes are needed when, for example, a judge becomes pregnant and temporarily leaves the bench, or when a person serves part time as judge and part time in another capacity (e.g., law professor or official in the Ministry of Justice) (Rodríguez Gavira, May 22, 1991). The new law also specifies more precisely the structural relationship between the Ministry of Justice and the courts. The relationship itself was not altered by the law; rather, the new law formalized the existing relationship in which the Ministry of Justice handles organizational and financial matters affecting the courts. The idea is that "courts should be concerned with imparting justice, not with fixing a leaky roof" (Rodríguez Gavira, May 22, 1991; Arteaga Abreu, July 5, 1990).

The short-term effect of this new law, as of May, 1991, has been to make case processing more flexible, to reduce the backlog of pending court cases, and to increase the speed of case processing. These effects are all attributable to the reduced number of judges on panels, from five to three. This allows the same number of judges to hear a larger number of cases and establishes a new majority of lay judges on each panel.

THE FAMILY CODES

The Family Code of 1975 (*Código de Familia,* Law No. 1289) and its proposed revisions exemplify legislation intended to substantially alter culturally prescribed gender relations.[22] In the eyes of Cuban legal scholars and policy makers, the Family Code is a conscious political tool for modifying, transforming, and developing the society, and for creating a new social awareness of the family as a viable institution (Gómez Treto, 1988). Except in those few instances where another civil or criminal law also applies (e.g., divorce, rape), the Family Code is not enforceable through legal means. In this sense it is a symbolic law, in which the credence and legitimacy of the state are lent to a policy position—here, gender equality—but no formal penalties are invoked if it is violated (Edelman, 1964; Schneider and Ingram, 1990). Nonetheless, over time the Family Code has become a very influential statute, with its provisions having been cited as the bases for Supreme Court decisions (de la Fuente, 1989:87–88, 99–101).

The Family Code developed in response to the contradiction between the Latin American cultural norm, placing responsibility for the home and children solely on the shoulders of women, and the economic necessity for women to enter the paid labor force, if desired economic and social progress was to occur, particularly in the wake of a brain drain in the early 1960s. Most women in this Third World country did not have access to such consumer commodities as washing machines and disposable diapers, making labor in the home even more arduous and time consuming. The political leadership thus faced a dilemma: something had to be done to relieve women's burdens. The Family Code was their answer.

The Family Code of 1975

Margaret Randall, who has written extensively about women and revolution, was living in Havana in 1975. She wrote of the mood just prior to passage of the Family Code:

> This general feeling among working women, and the population in general, that old ideas about women's roles simply have no place in the new society, had reached an unofficial peak when the draft of the new Family Code was first discussed in the newspaper and became subject matter for interminable street-level discussions. I say street level as opposed to the official discussions of each new law which take place in workplaces, military units, mass organizations, and schools. A lot of unofficial discussion goes on first—in grocery stores, on buses, in waiting rooms . . . . The street-level discussions of this new code have been lively. Cuban women and men, always outspoken and opinionated, go at it anywhere and all the time. Often men try to put forth "historical" or "biological" reasons for

objecting . . . . In markets and on buses there are always plenty of women on hand, with well-founded arguments borne out by their own experience to defend their imminent legal gains (1979:296–297).

The Family Code was passed by the Council of Ministers in 1975. The *anteproyecto* was written by the Commission for Legal Studies, led by Blas Roca Calderío, and was carefully examined by all of the ministries and other central state agencies. The final draft was publicly discussed and critiqued by more than five million people in neighborhood and workplace meetings organized by the Committees for the Defense of the Revolution (CDRs), the Cuban Labor Confederation (CTC), the Federation of Cuban Women (FMC), the National Association of Small Agricultural Producers (ANAP), the Federation of University Students (FEU), the Federation of Middle-School Students (FEEM), and other mass and social organizations (Ribas, May 10, 1989; González, May 10, 1989). It was approved by 98 percent of the participants in these meetings and assemblies. Even with this general approval, the Commission for Legal Studies examined each of more than 4,000 comments raised concerning 121 of the Code's 166 articles, incorporating some suggested revisions into the final *proyecto*.

The Family Code is considered to be Cuba's first truly "socialist code," lending it additional political legitimacy (Ribas, May 10, 1989; González, May 10, 1989; Roca Calderío, 1975). The date when it went into effect, March 8, 1975, was chosen purposefully. 1975 was the International Year of Women, and March 8 is celebrated worldwide as International Women's Day. Thus, Cuba's first socialist code passed into law on International Women's Day during the International Year of Women. Equally important symbolically to the Cubans, the Family Code passed into law during the year of the First Communist Party Congress.

The Family Code emphasizes the family unit and what is best for children, treating all children equally whether or not the parents were married when the child was born. It speaks specifically to equality between women and men, and to the need for both to share in household chores and in the raising of children. It does not, however, go so far as to mandate that they must share *equally* in these tasks (Ribas, May 10, 1989; González, May 10, 1989). As a legal scholar specializing in civil and family law told me,

It is complex. We are Latin women. The Family Code has moral authority and it has helped change consciousness, but the first thing we need to do is to educate women, as mothers. They need to learn that they should teach boys to do household chores, not allow the boys to go out and play baseball while the girls are doing all the chores. The boys can go to the store to buy milk as well as the girls can (Pérez Sixto, June 21, 1990).

The legal equality between men and women has been reinforced in concrete terms by structural changes in Cuba since the Revolution (Gómez Treto, 1988; Valdés, 1985; Hart Dávalos, 1985). For example, many Cuban women have told me that the economic security that has resulted from vastly increased educational and occupational opportunities for women (see Appendix J), in combination with cultural changes in the perceived societal roles for women, has meant that they can and do leave men who are physically or psychologically abusive.

The very real changes in men's and women's consciousness as a result of the Family Code and the educational efforts surrounding it are evidenced in a series of jokes. These have attained a level of folklore, with numerous Cubans telling essentially the same story:

At first after the law was passed I didn't want to do any household work. What would my friends and neighbors think! I would shut the front door so none of the neighbors would see me vacuuming. But pretty soon everyone's door was shut, because the men were all vacuuming! So then I purposefully kept the door open, letting everyone see that I was vacuuming. Now I am so accustomed to doing some of the work that I don't notice whether the door is open or shut!

Another piece of folklore tells of Raúl Castro (Minister of the Armed Forces, brother of Fidel and, at the time, husband of FMC President Vilma Espín) hanging up laundry to dry, thus publicly setting the example that housework was a "manly" thing to do.

Real changes have indeed occurred, with men now doing some household labor. Nevertheless, from the perspective of most Cuban women, the stories that men tell are somewhat exaggerated. According to my Cuban friends, both male and female, the men see themselves as "helping" their wives, rather than viewing work in the home as their responsibility. Young men are more willing to shoulder household duties than older men, but the reality is that Cuban women are still responsible for most of the household labor and child care, in addition to their paid labor or studies. This perception was reinforced by a study conducted by the Cuban Academy of Science in 1989. It surveyed 1,123 couples who married after 1975 and who had children between the ages of 12 and 19. These couples had vowed in their wedding ceremonies to comply with the Family Code, yet the Academy of Science found that less than five percent of the men shared *equally* in household duties (Rodríguez Calderón, 1990:13).

A New Family Code for the 1990s

As representatives of the Federation of Cuban Women told me, the Family Code was very advanced for its time, but not for today. From the contemporary vantage point, the 1975 Code has discriminatory elements that must be corrected (Ribas, May 10, 1989; González, May 10, 1989). Further, many Cuban adults were children or adolescents when the *anteproyecto* for the first code was discussed, and there is a general sentiment that it is time for that generation "to have its say" (de la Fuente, December 4, 1989). Finally, with changes since 1975 in related laws (e.g., the Law of Social Security, the Civil Code, the Housing Laws, and the Registry of Civil Status Law), parts of the Family Code have become outmoded and must be adapted to new social conditions. Interestingly, a minority view espoused by some legal scholars suggests that these revisions, and particularly the Registry of Civil Status Law, make a new Family Code unnecessary. This side lost out to the majority position that a new law is needed.

A new Family Code was proposed by the FMC (an organization of 3,200,000 women) under the personal sponsorship of Vilma Espín (President of the FMC and member of the Politburo and the Council of State), with support from the University of Havana Law School and the Ministry of Justice. Representatives of the Federation told me that the FMC leadership decided not to write the *anteproyecto* themselves; instead, they raised their concerns and suggestions to the Ministry of Justice, which typically takes the lead as *alta asesoría* in writing *anteproyectos*. The Ministry of Justice then conducted a study of the problems faced by women and drafted the legislation (Ribas, May 10, 1989; González, May 10, 1989). In addition to the Federation of Cuban Women and the Ministry of Justice, the interorganizational commission formed to write the new code includes representatives of the Office of the Attorney General, the Supreme Court, the University of Havana Law School, the National Direction of Notaries, the National Assembly's CACJ, and the Communist Party's Committee on the Status of Women (Pérez Sixto, November 9, 1989; de la Fuente, December 4, 1989).

The changes expected with the new Family Code do not alter its scope or legal status, and primarily affect marriage and divorce. The ideological principle of "whatever is best for the child" has been invoked by all sides to the debate. Divorce proceedings will probably be simplified when the parties are in agreement and there are no children. They may be streamlined if there are minor children when the parents are in agreement, although such cases might still have to go to the courts for resolution. Child custody, child support, and visitation rights are also being discussed, but the strong cultural norm that mothers retain custody of their children is not likely to be altered. The minimum age for marriage is expected to increase in an effort to reduce the number of adolescent women bearing children, and thus leaving school and reducing their training and employment capabilities (with social as well as individual costs), as well as to reduce the high rate of divorce among young people. Finally, possibilities for adoption, which is very unusual in Cuba, are likely to be enhanced under the new code (Gómez Treto, 1988; de la Fuente, 1989; de la Fuente, December 4, 1989; Pérez Sixto, November 9, 1989).

The *anteproyecto* for this new law will be discussed in a series of neighborhood and workplace meetings prior to being finalized. This step was contested by the Federation of Cuban Women because it will delay approval of the new code. Ironically, it was a mass organization (the FMC) that sought to avoid the popular discussion stage built into the Cuban lawmaking process, and it was the governmental bureaucracy (the CACJ and Ministry of Justice) and the law schools that argued for it. The decision to submit the *anteproyecto* to popular discussion was based on the two-fold rationale that popular discussion would both enrich the law and provide a means of educating people about it. Since the intellectuals serving on the commission have a different lifestyle from the average citizen, it is assumed that people with diverse experiences and points of view will raise concerns that commission members would not have contemplated. Widespread discussion and debate at the neighborhood level also facilitates the educational function of the code. This is especially important since the primary value of the Family Code lies in its potential to create social and cultural changes. Finally, as mentioned above, adolescents and young adults did not have the opportunity to participate in development of the 1975 code and should have a say in legislation of such magnitude.

For these reasons, the FMC's attempt to thwart popular discussion of the new code appears on the surface to make little sense. One explanation for the Federation's actions rests with its President's status as a political insider. Vilma Espín was at that time a full member of the Party's Politburo, member of the Council of State, and sister-in-law of Fidel Castro. Accordingly, she would have been privy to sensitive information concerning political upheaval in the Soviet Union and Eastern Europe and to Fidel's thoughts about how these tumultuous changes would affect Cuba. It is reasonable to speculate that Vilma Espín surmised that if the Code did not go forward immediately, it would become bogged down by more critical political and economic issues—as it did. Thus, the controversy surrounding efforts to bypass popular discussion of the new Family Code provides yet another example of political and ideological contradictions and the conflicts they create.

In the fall of 1989, the FMC hoped that the new Family Code would go to the National Assembly in July 1990. The CACJ, the Ministry of Justice, and the law schools expected that it would go forward in December 1990. By the summer of 1990, however, it was clear that the draft probably would not reach the National Assembly in the near future. As was the case with the Law of Criminal Procedure discussed above, the new Family Code was put on hold until more serious economic and political concerns, including a national food plan, have been resolved.

CONCLUSIONS

Cuban policy makers see law as simultaneously reflecting existing social, economic, and political conditions and as a means of altering these conditions in a manner that is consistent with the ideological goals of the political leadership. In introducing the Cuban law-creation process, I proposed that it is characterized by three contradictory assumptions: some interorganizational conflicts will arise, consensus is desirable and generally achievable, and no law should last forever. The consequence, as the examples presented in this chapter demonstrate, is a policy of widespread discussion and reconciliation of differences of opinion. This is achieved through multiagency working commissions, followed by popular discussion in neighborhoods and workplaces. This practice facilitates consideration of a range of perspectives and serves an educational function, but it also makes the process rather slow.

In revolutionary Cuba, reappraisal and modification of laws begin almost immediately after they are enacted. As the criminal codes demonstrate, some laws are outdated as soon as they are passed. Legal scholar Renén Quirós Pírez (1988:5) has argued that the creation of juridical norms "demands the objective interpretation of the level of social conditions reached at a specific historical moment," and if a law is to have positive effects it "must be elaborated and re-elaborated with a historical sense and subordinate to the fluid course of events, without aims or purposes of long-term durability."[23] Similarly, then First Vice-President of the Ministry of Justice Ramón de la Cruz Ochoa (1985:50) has stated, "We must rid ourselves of the idea that laws last forever, or for a very long period of time. This is impossible in the current stage of constructing a new society."[24]

It is precisely because the Cuban lawmaking process incorporates these principles that I suggest it is a *strategy* for temporarily resolving interorganizational conflicts and dilemmas arising from competing demands on the state. It is through examination of strategies that the actions of real people, i.e., human agency, enter into what might otherwise be an overly mechanistic theoretical model.

The creation of legislation is but one method of producing socialist legality in Cuba. The eminent legal theorist Julio Fernández Bulté defines socialist legality as a method of state direction of the society inspired and oriented by the Communist Party. It is characterized by regulation of social conduct through juridical norms corresponding to the interests of the working class and its allies (e.g., the peasantry). In this way, Fernández Bulté conceptually separates legality from legislation, with socialist legality representing a form of social life belonging to socialism and legislation being the expression of those principles in a form that is binding on all (1985:41–42).

The laws discussed in this chapter show explicitly how changes in the substantive content of law and in the mix of formalism and informalism are responses to specific social, economic, political, and ideological forces and goals. This multifaceted context sometimes seems to require incompatible solutions, while at other times the same policy change will ameliorate problems in several spheres. This is clearest in Renén Quirós's reflections on the history of criminal law in revolutionary Cuba.

The decision to make law creation a broad-based process is itself ideological. Changes in the mix of lay and professional judges over time, and changes in family law that facilitate larger numbers of women entering the paid work force, exemplify how economic and ideological considerations converge.

In each example discussed in this chapter, we see the importance of history and culture. Cuba inherited its legal form from Spain, but it has been moving away from the old Spanish system in recent years. Socialist legality in Cuba reflects the tension between the culture and history it shares with the rest of Latin America and its ideological ties to the socialist world.

CHAPTER 4

PRODUCING JURISTS
LEGAL EDUCATION
IN CUBA

You can change the laws, but if you do not impart these
new ideas, the ideas that serve as the basis for changes in
law, to students, to those persons who will fill the positions
in the legal sphere, then what good are the changes?

—Omar Fernández Jiménez, April 13, 1989.

A legal system can only be as good as its jurists. If the legal order is to
be transformed, the training of future legal professionals must be
changed as well. In other words, "producing" the next generation of
jurists is critical to the production of socialist legality. It is in this
context that legal education becomes a *strategy* for altering the content
of socialist law. Since the relationship between legal professionals and
nonprofessionals is a key aspect of the mix of formalism and informalism, changes in legal education also affect this mix.

The Cubans employed multiple substrategies to rebuild legal
education along socialist lines. The substrategies I will discuss in this
chapter include sending law students into the countryside to create
popular tribunals; holding night-school classes for bureaucrats, police,
and others peripherally involved in the legal sphere; later eliminating
night school in favor of an enhanced day-school curriculum, when the
requirements of a sophisticated legal system made night school look
like a one-room school house; improving curricula and postgraduate
educational forums; and better integrating theoretical and practical
work for both law students and law faculty. Each of these substrategies was a response to new and previously existing conflicts
resulting from structural, historical, and ideological contradictions.
They posed dilemmas for the political leadership, and increasingly, for
those entrusted with running the legal sphere.

In calling for comparative analyses of legal training and socialization, Lawrence Friedman (1989) observed that the role and relevance of lawyers varies cross-culturally, depending on the unique experience and history of each country and its legal profession. We must examine the direct impact of lawyers' work on the society and the role of lawyers as bearers of ideology, including the social meaning assigned to their work, their symbolic behavior, value systems, and positioning in the society's ideological structure (Friedman, 1989:10).

These concerns are closely intertwined in revolutionary Cuba. Law and legal education are not portrayed as value-neutral. Law is defined as serving the interests of the working class, and most Cuban lawyers self-define their roles in these terms. This is in marked contrast to prerevolutionary, bourgeois law which supported the interests of capital and of the political and economic elites. The ideal of serving the interests of the working class becomes complicated, however, when most people coming into direct contact with the legal system are members of this class, and the government is constitutionally empowered to act on behalf of the working class. Cuban jurists, and particularly criminal defense lawyers, resolve this ideological conflict by seeing themselves as responsible primarily to their clients (Michalowski, 1989). Serving their clients well furthers respect for the legal order, thereby also enhancing the legitimacy of the state.

Increasingly, legal education encourages future jurists to think critically—not to accept law as immutable, but rather as something that should change as the society matures. This effort to instill critical thinking in young lawyers is a central tenet in the new plan of the universities, Plan C, discussed later in this chapter. First, however, we must consider how and why the shortage of lawyers and the call for improvements in legal education came about.

THE POST-TRIUMPH ERA: "LAWYERS FOR WHAT?"

With the triumph of the revolutionary forces on January 1, 1959, the legal profession lost its traditional prominence in Cuban academic and political life. Lawyers did not fully regain their prestige until the late 1970s and early 1980s (Kautzman Torres, May 18, 1989). Explanatory factors range from the idealistic to the practical.

First, by 1961 the new Cuban government had publicly declared the socialist nature of the revolution. The leadership rather idealistically assumed that radical social transformations (e.g., adequate food, clothing, housing, full employment, free and accessible health care and education) would rid the society of crime and other social harms. Nonjuridical means, it was initially thought, would be sufficient for maintaining contractual agreements and resolving disputes (Escalona, 1985).

The highly esteemed Cuban jurist Francisco Varona y Duque de Estrada argued that law would disappear in communist society, but also that this prediction must be understood in dialectical terms and from a historical perspective (1972:85). Law, he theorized, would vanish with the disappearance of the state, but this would require a relatively lengthy transformation of the material base of the society and of social consciousness, i.e., creation of the truly new person. Moreover, the disappearance of law would not leave a normative vacuum or a situation of anomie. In its wake, a new system of cultural norms would develop and become internalized into the revolutionary consciousness as a natural outgrowth of the end of exploitative social relations. This ideological construction creates an interesting contradiction: the revolutionary development of law would contribute to producing a normative level that would supersede it. During this transitional period, laws would facilitate the technical and cultural development that would make them obsolete. By the early 1970s, the Cuban leadership recognized that such transformations would not be complete in the foreseeable future and set about institutionalizing the state apparatus and the place of law in Cuban society.

Second, with very few exceptions, prerevolutionary jurists were seen as corrupt men who maintained Batista's hold on power. More damning, many of them were in complicity with the atrocities committed by the Batista regime. In revolutionary Cuba lawyers, and even the practice of law, were viewed as remnants of the bourgeois life which was eschewed by the revolution.[1] It was in this context that Fidel Castro, himself a trained lawyer, proclaimed soon after the triumph, "Lawyers for what?"

In prerevolutionary Cuba, as in the rest of Latin America, jurists traditionally have been culled from the social, political, and economic elite. One ramification of the law-state-capital nexus typical of capitalist societies has been to make law one of the most politically conservative and traditional professions (Lorey, 1988; Lynch, 1981). As a result, with few exceptions, lawyers were not trusted by the revolutionary leaders, especially, or by the people (Kautzman, May 18, 1989). Also, the practice of law was far removed from the life of the average person. As was the case elsewhere in Latin America, Cuban lawyers worked for the wealthy and the urban population, not *campesinos* in the countryside (Lorey, 1988; Kautzman, May 1989).

Given the revolutionary government's plans to concentrate on the concerns of the average citizen, and particularly those in rural areas, producing more lawyers was not a priority.

Third, it was far more prestigious and showed much more *conciencia* (political and social conscience) for a student to enter practical professions rather than the esoteric field of law. The health care and educational goals set by the revolutionary leadership generated a tremendous and immediate need for doctors and teachers. There was also a severe shortage of technicians to run the newly nationalized infrastructure (electricity, telephone system, roads, etc.), banks, and major industries, including sugar refineries (see Appendix F). The "brain drain" of professionals and technicians also left a critical shortage of chemical, industrial, geological, electrical, and telecommunications engineers, veterinarians, physicists, biologists, mathematicians, and economists (Rodríguez, 1987a:499,502,504; Kautzman, May 18, 1989).

Consequently, there were too few lawyers and law students to handle the citizenry's legal concerns, particularly outside of major urban centers. As the National Union of Cuban Jurists (*Unión Nacional de Juristas Cubanos;* hereafter, UNJC) summarized the situation at that time:

> The underestimation and certain abandon (of the role of jurists) also resulted over several years in a reduction in the number of students graduating from the Universities, including some years in which no jurists graduated. Only the night-school courses for workers, whose graduates did not generally study with the idea of practicing the profession, functioned (UNJC, 1987:9).

Fourth, many law professors left the country or were expelled in the years immediately surrounding the triumph. The University of Havana Law School had closed on December 2, 1956, when Fidel Castro and his *compañeros* landed in the Granma (Carreras y Cuevas, July 5, 1990). It reopened in early 1959, but soon after, in July 1960, the law professors remaining in the country were faced with a demand by the counter-revolutionary bar association (*el Colegio de Abogados*) that they stop teaching classes. Violation of this order, they were told, would result in permanent expulsion from the bar and their right to practice law.

Four jurists who had fought against Batista and opposed the *Colegio's* decision came to the law school and taught classes. Because of their courageous physical presence, the University of Havana's Law School could not be closed. They convinced other revolutionary jurists to join with them, thereby reestablishing classes. The new faculty was staffed by lawyers who had graduated before the triumph, identified totally with the Revolution, and who, for the most part, had participated in the insurrection. The 100 or so students and handful of professors at the nation's second law school, the University of Oriente in Santiago, moved to the University of Havana (UNJC, 1987:19; Castanedo Abay, July 4, 1990).

Consistent with the Law of the Reform of the University of Havana (Law No. 859) of 1960, the University was reorganized in 1962 under the three-person rectorship of Armando Hart (later Minister of Culture), Carlos Rafael Rodríguez (later a vice-president of the country and probably the most highly esteemed intellectual in the government), and Regino Boti. The new university structure consisted of departments housed within schools, which in turn were subsumed within faculties. Law became a school within the Faculty of Philosophy (Rodríguez, 1987a:509). With later changes in the University's organization, it has since become its own faculty with departments but no schools.

In articulating his conceptualization of a reformed university, Carlos Rafael Rodríguez argued that instead of the traditional elitist lawyer, the country needed to train jurists to serve the nation, the people, and the revolutionary government. These legal "technicians," as he called them, should have solid legal training as well as very clear political orientations (Rodríguez, 1987a:506). Accordingly, courses in dialectical materialism, history, and political economy were added to the curriculum of all university programs in 1962 (Rodríguez, 1987a:506-507). In an initial effort to merge theory and praxis, a new pedagogy that combined lectures with seminars, debates, and practical experience was also central to the university reform.

The newly reopened University of Havana Law Department assumed additional responsibilities in October, 1962. During a now famous meeting with students and faculty, Fidel Castro suggested that the law students organize local level courts throughout the country, beginning in the interior. These courts would be staffed solely by lay judges. In 1963, the students set out to organize these courts, known as *tribunales populares,* and Cuba's system of popular justice officially began.

THE 1970S: THE NIGHT-SCHOOL ERA

Throughout the 1960s and 1970s, Cuba's political leadership did not perceive a pressing need for traditionally trained jurists. Only a handful of students graduated in law during these years. In the late

1960s night classes, known as *cursos para trabajadores* (courses for workers), provided basic legal education for persons whose jobs required some knowledge of the law.

Technically, two types of *cursos para trabajadores* led to law degrees. These were *cursos por encuentro* (courses with meetings) and *cursos libres* (correspondence courses). When Cubans speak of *cursos para trabajadores,* however, they are almost invariably referring to the former. These classes met two nights each week and on weekends. Their sole purpose was to eliminate logistical and technical limitations among persons working in areas related to law. Students included police officers and others in the Ministry of the Interior, military personnel assigned juridical work, managers of state businesses, and bureaucrats in the various agencies involved in the administration of justice (Varona y Duque de Estrada, 1972:84).[2]

Night-school courses began in 1969, the same year that Blas Roca's Calderíos's Commission for Legal Studies began writing the laws that institutionalized the new state order, and were expanded in the 1970s. Regular day classes were reduced simultaneously, to the point where in the 1977–78 and 1978–79 academic years not a single day student matriculated in the country's law schools, while 409 law students matriculated in night school (Fernández, April 13, 1989). Night-school courses were offered in all four law schools (Havana, Santiago, Santa Clara, and Camagüey), and also for a five-year period during the 1970s in Pinar del Río.

Reflecting on the night school courses and the reasons for ending them, a University of Havana law professor told me:

> The *cursos para trabajadores* existed in their historical moment . . . They provided people working in the judicial sphere, especially in the Ministry of the Interior, with juridical information. *This was a way to resolve some immediate problems. In their historical moment these courses were a positive response, a correct response; now they would not be* (my emphasis).

This negative evaluation largely reflects the deficient training that night-school students received. Students reviewed summaries of course materials with the only apparent goal being to pass the courses rather than to learn as much as possible and obtain a solid grounding in legal culture (Machado Ventura, 1984:210).

The decision to eliminate this program, rather than simply to improve the curriculum, is intriguing. During the era of institutional-ization, night school became a temporarily viable resolution to the problem of an insufficient number of people trained in law. In the next phase in Cuba's development, greater numbers of lawyers were not sufficient; they also had to be better trained. By the end of the 1970s, the night schools had closed, the prestige of the profession was rekindled, and the number of day students began climbing steeply (Kautzman, May 18, 1989). A contradiction thus becomes apparent: institutionalization required both the creation and the cessation of night-school classes. That is, the night-school program was an outgrowth of the institutionalization process which made more lawyers necessary. The result of this process, however, has been greater professionalization and elitism of law, and with it a desire on the part of the legal community for regularized day classes geared toward training specialists in law, rather than providing a service for police and others in law-related fields.

THE 1980S: A RENEWED NEED FOR WELL-TRAINED JURISTS

In the process of writing the laws of the 1970s, jurists essentially wrote a role for themselves in Cuban society. The restructuring of the courts necessitated more lawyers, as did creation of the System of Economic Direction and Planning (*Sistema de dirección y planificación de la economía*) (Machado, 1984:210; Arteaga Abreu, April 19, 1989). Economic development and trade diversification brought an impressive growth in the number of state-owned factories and other economic enterprises. Lawyers were needed to write contracts between Cuban enterprises, and between Cuban enterprises and the foreign businesses and governments with which they collaborated. This required expertise in contract law and in international public and private law. Also, as Cuba sought to become a leader of the Third World and the nonaligned movement, jurists trained in international law were needed to analyze international accords and agreements.

However, two factors continued to undermine the relevance of law in the construction of Cuban socialism: (1) the inadequate training of jurists; and (2) the lack of a general culture of respect for law, due largely to the perception that bourgeois law defended the privileged interests of exploiters rather than workers (UNJC, 1987:6; Rodríguez, 1987b:572).

Speaking of the paucity of adequately trained jurists, Politburo member José Ramón Machado Ventura noted in 1984:

> It is known that for many years the teaching of Law did not receive the best attention, the immediate consequence of

which was seen principally in the weakening of the teaching in the Law Schools, in the absence of texts, materials, [and] adequate programs of study; the results of which were reflected clearly in the deficient preparation of those who graduated in this specialty from the halls of the University (1984:210).[3]

As early as the First Party Congress in 1975, it was recognized that a legality appropriate for revolutionary Cuba was needed to replace the old legality of the exploiters. This meant substituting socialist juridical norms for some old laws (UNJC, 1987:4–5). The lack of a culture of respect for law was sufficiently grave to warrant discussion by Fidel Castro in the July 1984 legislative session (UNJC, 1987:5). The importance of law and the role of lawyers in fortifying socialist legality and guaranteeing strict compliance with it continued to be a political and strategic theme, with a new emphasis on the role of lawyers visible in the Third Party Congress, held in February 1986 (UNJC, 1987:5).

It was at this time that "rectification" became a particularly serious concern of the political leadership. A little over a year after the Third Party Congress, then-Minister of Justice Juan Escalona Reguera referred to pedagogical deficiencies that contributed to a general lack of respect for law. In his speech at the closing of the National Union of Cuban Jurists' Congress in June, 1987 he acknowledged:

> the perceptible absence of courses in our plans of study for the middle-school level and including in the university, in which some aspects of law and the state are explained, and as a result we frequently encounter in our university graduates and technicians a great juridical ignorance, which also affects a certain number of state managers who are not capable of distinguishing between a law, a decree-law and a decree, nor are sufficiently knowledgeable about the labor legislation that they are obliged to apply or demand be applied (Escalona, 1987:187–188; see also UNJC, 1987:6–7).[4]

Through the mid-1980s, legal training lacked a coherent structure that could incorporate legal research, studies for advanced candidacy, and university coursework and theses. This was not solely the fault of the law schools and the juridical agencies. It also was conditioned by the absence of a national strategy for overall development of scientific work in law, the very gradual establishment of socialist legislation, failure of the citizenry to adequately understand legislation, problems with the nation's juridical organization, scientific isolation vis-à-vis juridical work in other socialist countries, and a scarcity of legal research, whether conducted and published in Cuba or elsewhere (Fernández Bulté, 1989:1–2). This situation led the Politburo to write a set of important accords in 1982 and later to assess how well these recommendations had been implemented.

Communist Party Recommendations
Concerning Legal Education

Since 1982, the Cuban Communist Party has conducted annual analyses of all spheres of Cuban life, including the legal realm. These reports, known as *"acuerdos"* (accords, or agreements) when they come from the Politburo and *"resoluciones"* (resolutions) when they come from the Central Committee, contain evaluations of state and government agencies and suggestions for alleviating problems noted. The reports have become shorter each year, as more and more of the remedies are in place. Víctor Kautzman Torres, who is the Assistant Director of Legal Affairs for the Foreign Ministry, legal advisor for the Ministry of Justice, member of the Juridical Affairs and Foreign Relations Committees of the UNJC, and professor of Constitutional Law at the University of Havana, described the process for me:

> One year the accords might say that there is a shortage of legal texts, and in the next year books should be published on criminal law, civil law, and some other branch of law. The next year the Politburo would review what was done and say, "OK, books have been published on criminal law and some other branch of law, and these are the titles, but we still need a book on civil law and that should be published this year." Then the next year it will check to see if that was done or not. Basically what the Politburo does is to suggest remedies and examine which of these have been followed thus far. This is why the report has become shorter and shorter each year, as more and more of these measures have been met and no longer have to be discussed. The Politburo gives a chronology for when to finish which things (Kautzman Torres, May 8, 1989).

Within the legal sphere, the Politburo in October of 1982 suggested the following measures:
1. create legislation;
2. modernize legislation;
3. support the study of law by revising curricula, establishing

short- and long-term programs of retraining, and providing practical experience for advanced law students;

4. incorporate Adjunct Professors into the law faculties;
5. evaluate and increase publications in law, especially for student use;
6. increase the professional-scientific capabilities of judges and others involved in juridical work through retraining; and
7. determine the projected demand for jurists through 1985 and, consistent with this demand, the number of students who should be studying law and increase the number of scholarships and lecture halls accordingly (Kautzman Torres, May 8, 1989; Machado Ventura, 1984:218; UNJC, 1987:11–12).

To meet these demands, the Politburo asked the Ministry of Higher Education to create the necessary conditions for improving the quality of teaching, programs of study, and texts, and to provide additional scholarships. It also called for evaluation of university professors to determine who should continue teaching and who should not, the immediate pedagogical needs of the faculties, which practicing jurists should become Adjunct Professors, and how adjuncts should be remunerated for their additional responsibilities (Machado Ventura, 1984:211–212).

Within the next year some changes were made, leading the Central Committee to state as point 25 in its Resolutions of the Sixth Plenary:

> Continue to fortify socialist legality and the fight against crime. To elevate the quality of judicial work, emphasizing the tasks related to the preparation and formation of juridical corps and demanding fulfillment of the work norms of judges, prosecutors, police investigators, and lawyers (Central Committee of the Communist Party of Cuba, 1983:10).[5]

In its Eighth Plenary, held on December 19, 1983, the Central Committee resolved that there was still a need:

> To increase the efforts under way to fortify socialist legality. To improve work in the areas of legal education and the publication of laws and other juridical norms among the masses. To execute and adequately control the program of political-ideological training of jurists. To work on the elaboration of new laws in accordance with the character and objectives of our society . . . elevating the efficiency and quality of the activities of corresponding agencies and

institutions (Central Committee of the Communist Party of Cuba, 1984:18).[6]

In 1984, the Politburo analyzed compliance with its 1982 accord and reprioritized its concerns based upon the extent to which stated goals had been met. The greatest advances were in areas that did not require outlays of scarce resources (e.g., paper). For instance, the University of Havana Law School evaluated all Assistant and Associate Professors. The Department of Law at the University of Las Villas was granted further resources and autonomy by becoming a College of Law in its own right in 1984, rather than a department housed administratively within the College of Economics. By that time, growth in the number of day students was apparent, as was a gradual increase in professional retooling by jurists (Machado Ventura, 1984:216, 217; UNJC, 1987:12). Also in 1984, the Politburo expanded its earlier request for an estimate of the demand for jurists to encompass the country's projected needs through 1995 (UNJC, 1987:12).

Progress in planning for and obtaining course texts and other bibliographic materials and in other law-related publications was particularly evident, with increased publications by both Cuban and foreign scholars (see further Chapter Five and Appendix G for law-related publications). By 1984 an editorial plan was in place for selecting foreign books for publication in Cuba, as well as books by Cuban authors. The plan included receipt of 45 texts and complementary teaching materials for publication, reprinting of others, and contracts for another 42 books, all intended for student use. Publication of additional books was defined as an immediate and crucial need because there were still some university courses that did not have basic texts. Students in those courses were forced to rely solely on lectures and class notes (Machado Ventura, 1984:217; Kautzman Torres, May 8, 1989).

The issues raised in the 1982 and subsequent accords retained their importance in later years. In his closing to the Third Congress of the National Union of Cuban Jurists in 1987, then-Minister of Justice and Central Committee member Juan Escalona Reguera tied these accords to development of a new Professional Plan of Study (Plan C) for the law schools. Minister Escalona Reguera stressed the importance of complying with the party accords concerning the teaching of law if Cuba's plans in the legislative realm and the ongoing process of rectification were to succeed. He continued:

> No one doubts that in these moments positive advances can be seen in this direction, but we are all also conscious that

we still have a long way to go. With this pledge to work toward elaborating a new plan of studies for the Faculties [of Law], which must guide us toward a more integral [legal] preparation which abandons rote memorization and the normativist teaching of laws and that reaches, fortunately, to the knowledge of the socialist juridical institutions and succeeds in giving to our students an understanding of the philosophical and political bases that explain the necessity for their existence . . . . (Escalona, 1987:191).[7]

Escalona Reguera also spoke of the need for legal education to attain the level of other sciences, and for the country's jurists to become convinced of the importance of continuing to advance their knowledge of law by consulting scientific texts in law, philosophy, economics, and politics. "Only in this way," he concluded, "will it be possible to reach the cultural and technical development indispensable for answering the demands that the Direction of the Party formulated for us in 1982" (1987:192).[8]

THE 1990S: A PEDAGOGY FOR THE FUTURE

By the mid-1980s, rectification was well underway in the legal sphere. The Communist Party recommendations supported a greater professionalization of law and legal education, including increased attention to legal theorizing and research. With more students and better-trained faculty, the law schools set out to create an innovative pedagogy for the 1990s.

I will elaborate on the specifics of this pedagogy as they were laid out in Plan C of the Plans for Professional Study later in this chapter. Briefly, they entail a more coherent mix of theoretical and practical work designed to prepare students to be critical consumers and analysts of law. Legal education would emphasize the philosophical principles and the political, economic, social, and historical bases for laws, rather than forcing students to memorize statutes. This solid grounding in legal theory, it was hoped, would instill a spirit of creativity in future jurists, enabling them to better interpret and refine legislation to meet the country's juridical needs as it moved toward the twenty-first century.

To set the stage for this larger analysis of legal pedagogy, I first want to discuss the composition of the student body and the administrative and political organization of the law schools.

LAW STUDENTS: WHO ARE THE FUTURE JURISTS?

Most students entering Cuba's universities today are about 17 years old. Those students who served in the military are a little older, about 21, when they begin their university studies.[9]

Admissions decisions generally follow the European model, in which the students' high-school records and entrance exams weigh heavily. Applicants' career preferences are matched against the enrollment plans of the different faculties. The most desirable disciplines, including law in recent years, tend to have their pick of the best students. In addition to academic record, law-school admissions are based on results of an interview with a panel of law professors, law students, and members of the National Union of Cuban Jurists.[10]

Variation in the Number of Students

As of May 1989 there were slightly over 8,000 jurists in Cuba, including those with night-school degrees. Most are young lawyers who graduated from law school during the 1980s. This was a rapid climb from the 3,000 jurists in Cuba in 1977, and even the 5,624 jurists in 1982. In a country of 10 million, it represents one lawyer for every 1,250 citizens.

The size of entering cohorts fluctuated until the Politburo's call in 1982 for a systematic analysis of the number of future jurists needed. For example, there were only slightly over 600 students enrolled in the University of Havana when it reopened in 1959, and very few of these were law students (Carreras y Cuevas, July 5, 1990). By 1984, at least 2,290 students had enrolled in the country's regular (day) law school classes since the revolutionary triumph (Machado Ventura, 1984:218). In 1985 this figure had risen to 3,000, almost double that of 1982 (Escalona, 1987:192; UNJC, 1987:13). Following the plans developed in 1982 and 1983, the number of students enrolled in the law schools remained high through the 1990–91 academic year, with the greatest number of students enrolled in that year, including 200 first-year students. Admissions began to taper off in 1991–92, with a cap of 100 first-year students (Fernández Bulté, May 22, 1989, May 15, 1991; Fernández Jiménez, April 13, 1989). Table 4.1 presents the number of students graduating each year.[11]

These data are informative for several reasons. The 1960–61 graduating class was the first after the triumph, and students graduating in this year were those whose studies had been interrupted by the closing of the University of Havana's Law School in 1956. The 1963 graduating class is more than double the size of the 1962

Table 4.1.
Cuban Law School Graduates, by Year and Type of Program*

Academic Year	Day School	Night School (Courses for Workers)
1960–1961	252	0
1961–1962	63	0
1962–1963	133	0
1963–1964	336	0
1964–1965	0	0
1965–1966	43	0
1966–1967	31	0
1967–1968	56	0
1968–1969	37	0
1969–1970	74	0
1970–1971	22	0
1971–1972	17	0
1972–1973	6	112
1973–1974	44	87
1974–1975	50	292
1975–1976	47	55
1976–1977	58	496
1977–1978	0	124
1978–1979	0	285
1979–1980	62	0
1980–1981	172	0
1981–1982	**	0
1982–1983	366	0
1983–1984	396	0
1984–1985	332	0
1985–1986	347	0

* Source: UNJC, *Tésis sobre la vida jurídica del país,*
1987:19–21. Figures include graduates from the Law Schools
or Departments at the Universities of Havana, Camagüey, Las
Villas, Oriente, and for five years during the 1970s, night-
school students in Pinar del Río.

** not available

graduating class, and the 1964 class more than doubles the 1963 class once again, but then it drops to zero in 1965. The low number of day-school graduates in 1965–70 is indicative of the general lack of interest in the study of law and the societal need for professionals in other career tracks (see Appendix F). These numbers dropped even further in 1971–73 when it was thought that night-school classes could resolve the problem of too few lawyers. Contrast the 112 night students graduating in 1973 with the six day students graduating that year. These night students were the largest group of students graduating since 1964.

Easy entrance exams facilitated the admission of inadequately prepared students. At the same time, some of the most qualified professors left the university to perform other revolutionary tasks. They were replaced by new professors, most of whom did not have much professional experience. In combination with reduced programs of study and elimination of basic courses needed to properly prepare lawyers, use of student teaching assistants as teachers, poor quality texts and other teaching materials, and easy exams, this situation further impoverished legal education in Cuba during the 1960s and 1970s (UNJC, 1987:20–21).

Most of the country's law students, whether day students or night students in the *cursos para trabajadores,* attended the University of Havana. While historical data on student enrollments are not generally available, Politburo member José Ramón Machado Ventura offers some figures for the law department at the University of Las Villas. He reports that between 1977 and 1981, 97 jurists graduated from night school at Las Villas, and, in 1980 and 1981, 129 students enrolled in day courses and 130 in night courses. The first 46 day students graduated in 1983. By 1984, the total number of day students at Las Villas was 470 (Machado Ventura, 1984:213). This figure was expected to increase further over the next few years, with plans for 140 or 150 students to enter the law school at Las Villas in 1985 and an average of 90 students entering each year between 1986 and 1990 (Machado Ventura, 1984:214). The actual growth was a little slower, with 510 law students enrolled at Las Villas in 1988–89 and a jump the next year to 700 (see Table 4.2).

The 1982 and 1984 assessments of the future need for jurists concluded that 5,500 more jurists would be needed by 1995, almost doubling the 5,624 lawyers in the country in 1982. This necessitated entering classes of at least 600 students per year for the period 1984–1990, distributed across the country's law schools according to geographic needs (Machado Ventura, 1984:211). The scarcity of jurists was found to be particularly acute in the provinces of Sancti Spíritus, Cienfüegos, and Villa Clara (where the University of Las Villas is located), each of which, according to Politburo member José Ramón Machado Ventura (1984:213), needs more than 900 additional jurists by 1995. The disproportionate geographic dispersion is evident in 1982 figures showing that 2,464 jurists, or 43.81% of the nation's lawyers, were in the city of Havana. In contrast, 76 jurists (1.35% of the nation's total) practiced in Sancti Spíritus, 83 in Cienfüegos (1.48%), 110 in Ciego de Avila (1.96%), 149 in Granma (2.65%), and 154 in Las Tunas (2.74%). Consequently, the proportion of jurists to the population was as low as 1 per 5,000 in some provinces (UNJC, 1987:9). This is consistent with Lorey's (1988: 905–908) findings of an unequal geographic distribution of professionals throughout Latin America and the United States.

Table 4.2 presents the distribution of students in the nation's four law schools in recent years. These data demonstrate the marked shift in enrollments at the University of Havana and in interior universities. In 1988–89, 42 percent of the nation's law students were enrolled at the University of Havana. By the next year, this figure had dropped to 35 percent due to the substantial increases in enrollments in the three secondary universities.

Table 4.2.
Law School Enrollments By University, 1988-89, 1989-90*

University	Students Enrollments			
	1988–89		1989–90	
Camagüey	530	(18.5)	850	(22.6)
Las Villas (Villa Clara)	510	(17.8)	700	(18.7)
Oriente (Santiago de Cuba)	620	(21.7)	900	(24.0)
Havana	1,202	(42.0)	1,300	(34.7)
Total	2,862 (100.0%)		3,750 (100.0%)	

* Source: University of Havana Law School Dean Julio Fernández Bulté, May 22, 1989; November 28, 1989. Numbers are approximate.

While the prerevolutionary legal profession was heavily dominated by males, the gender distribution of the profession has changed drastically in Cuba, as it has in much of the world (Abel, 1989:82, 100, 116–119; Neave, 1989:171–172; Menkel-Meadow, 1989a).

Table 4.3.
Gender Distribution of Enrollments at the University of Havana
Law School, 1987–88, 1988–89*

	1987–88		1988–89	
Women	737	(67.1)	835	(69.5)
Men	361	(32.9)	367	(30.5)
Total	1,098	(100.0%)	1,202	(100.0%)

* Source: University of Havana Law School Dean Julio
Fernández Bulté, November 28, 1989.

Three factors appear to differentiate the feminization of law in
Cuba from the 18 countries studied by Abel, Neave, and Menkel-
Meadow. First, the proportion of law students who are female is
higher in Cuba than in the other countries. As Table 4.3 shows, in
recent years slightly over two-thirds of the law students in Cuba's most
prestigious law school have been women.

The most current data available from the University of Havana
reaffirm this pattern: of the 200 first-year students entering the
University of Havana Law School in 1990–91, 125, or 62.5%, were
women. In contrast, Carrie Menkel-Meadow reports a maximum of
"close to half" of all law students being women in the mid- to late-
1980s in the 18 countries she studied (1989a:196). Second, because
the number of law graduates in recent years is so high compared to
prior years, and because many of the prerevolutionary lawyers left the
country before or shortly after the triumph of the Revolution, these
women have created a real presence for themselves in the profession.
Third, and in contrast to the situation in many countries, the increased
participation of women in Cuban law has occurred precisely at the
time when the legal profession has *gained* in prestige (see Evanson,
1990:63 for a similar conclusion).

Indicators of the increasing prestige of the legal profession in Cuba
coincidental with the rise in the number of female jurists include: (1) a
large number of new and modified laws as part of the institutionalization of the state; (2) the National Union of Cuban Jurists
(UNJC) and the National Organization of Law Collectives gaining
autonomous status in the mid-1970s; (3) a greater role for trial lawyers
as the criminal law moved increasingly toward an adversarial system
and away from the more inquisitorial system inherited from Spain (see
further discussion in Chapter Three); (4) an increasing number of top
students seeking to enter the legal profession; and (5) election in

February 1990 of the former Minister of Justice as President of the National Assembly.

Whether or not the increased number of women in the legal profession is transforming the practice of law cannot be assessed from quantitative data (Menkel-Meadow, 1989b). My observations and discussions with female jurists and representatives of the Federation of Cuban Women suggest that the profession as a whole is becoming more attentive to women's concerns and that the large presence of women is to at least some degree altering the perspectives brought to bear on jurists' practical, theoretical, and legislative work.

THE UNIVERSITY OF HAVANA AS THE GOVERNING CENTER FOR LEGAL EDUCATION

When Fidel Castro and the rebel army marched triumphantly into Havana in January 1959, two law schools existed in Cuba: the 200-year-old University of Havana and the University of Oriente in Santiago de Cuba. Since then, the University of Las Villas (in Villa Clara), the University of Camagüey and, for a limited period, the University of Pinar del Río, have established law schools. These additional programs helped alleviate the problem of training a sufficient number of jurists to meet the country's needs. However, most law professors at these newer universities and at the University of Oriente have very limited professional experience and "almost no" study materials (UNJC, 1987:21). Historically and contemporarily, the most important law school is the University of Havana because of its age, large number of students and professors, and location in the capital city (UNJC, 1987:22).

The historical importance of the University of Havana has been institutionalized by making it the *centro rectoral* (governing center) for all higher education in Cuba. Within the field of law, this means that the University of Havana Law School determines the curriculum, basic texts, and programs of study (which contain the objectives for each course as part of the Professional Plan of Studies) for all of the other law schools. Faculty in other universities can add material as they wish under the auspices of academic freedom, but any changes must fit within the general framework decided upon by the Faculty of Law at the University of Havana.

As the *centro rectoral*, the University of Havana also houses the *comisión de carreras* (career commission), established in the mid-1980s. This commission structures and periodically reanalyzes the Professional

Plan of Studies, and approves the course texts and programs of study for all of the law schools. Biannual meetings of commission members are usually, but not necessarily, held in Havana. In addition to the deans, senior representatives of the Ministries of Justice and of the Interior, the Office of the Attorney General, the Academy of Sciences, and the Central Committee of the Communist Party's Departments of State and Juridical Organs and of Higher Education attend these meetings (Fernández Bulté, November 28, 1989; Carreras y Cuevas, July 5, 1990; Fernández, November 14, 1989).

As part of his or her administrative responsibilities as dean of the school which is the *centro rectoral,* the dean of the University of Havana Law School also holds a seat on the Technical Council of the Ministry of Justice. The dean at the University of Havana is also responsible for drafting the Professional Plan of Studies and the five-year Programs for Scientific-Technical Progress in the Juridical Sector (Fernández Bulté, March 3, 1989; November 28, 1989). Because decisions made by the Law School at the University of Havana hold sway over the other schools, and the dean is the highest authority within the school, law professors and other deans joke that, "The dean of U-H [University of Havana] is the Dean of the Deans," although the dean was quick to tell me that the other deans are not *really* subservient to him (Fernández Bulté, November 28, 1989). Although he may not be able to tell the other deans what to do, the dean at the University of Havana's Law School during the period of data collection, Julio Fernández Bulté, is widely respected as a scholar and administrator. He encouraged all members of the faculty to conduct research and to publish, and provided time and an atmosphere conducive to research that was particularly beneficial to, and appreciated by, the junior faculty.

At the other end of the continuum from the University of Havana's Law School is the Law School at the University of Las Villas. Law at Las Villas was a department within the College of Economics until 1984, when it was made a separate Faculty. In his address to the Law School at Las Villas, Politburo member José Ramón Machado Ventura spoke of the assistance provided by colleagues from the University of Havana (1984:214). By 1990, the problems at Las Villas still had not been resolved. Major difficulties were the small size of the faculty and their limited practical and classroom experience. The problems at Las Villas were particularly acute in the area of criminal procedure, which University of Havana faculty described as "a mess." In the fall of 1989 the University of Havana, as the *centro rectoral,* was asked to help out. The head of the Criminal Sciences and Criminology Department went to Las Villas for 15 days to help prepare a new course on criminal procedure, bringing with him boxes of books for use by the faculty.

Nevertheless, some resources that have gone to the smaller universities have not flowed in equal or greater measure to the University of Havana. Particularly noteworthy is the presence of a computer in each of the provincial law schools, while the University of Havana Law School does not have a computer of its own.

ORGANIZATION OF THE LAW SCHOOL

Legal education in Cuba combines theoretical training with practical experience. In addition to lectures and discussion groups, students help faculty with their research and assist practicing jurists, returning to the classroom to discuss their experiences. Faculty are also expected to combine theoretical and practical work. Organizing teaching through faculty collectives facilitates these multiple pedagogical, ideological, and political goals.

All law schools in Cuba follow the same basic organizational structure, although it is most coherent at the University of Havana because of its larger faculty. This structure is displayed in Table 4.4.

Teaching Collectives

The law school is organized into four departments, each of which has an elected head. Within departments, professors are organized into teaching collectives, known as *consejos de asignaturas* or *colectivos de asignaturas*. Collectives include everyone teaching the same course (e.g., Roman Law, Criminal Procedure, Labor Law). Members meet to determine the basic course content, or *programas de asignaturas*. Beyond this joint determination of the minimal readings and lecture material, each professor is free to add other required readings for his or her discussion groups (*seminarios*).

Like department heads, the heads of the *consejos de asignaturas* are elected by the faculty. Department and *consejo* heads are usually professors with a large amount of experience and an impressive list of publications. While the opinion of the head tends to be widely respected and is generally followed, every faculty member has input into the decision-making process. It is possible, for instance, for junior faculty members to voice some course of action, and for others to go along with the junior scholar's ideas. Indeed, examples offered by the junior faculty at the University of Havana suggest that they are relatively comfortable expressing opinions that differ from those of their more senior colleagues, but they are also careful not to contradict

Table 4.4.
Organizational Structure of the School of Law,
University of Havana.*

Departments	Courses
Criminal Sciences and Criminology:	Criminal Procedure General Criminal Law Special Criminal Law Criminology Criminalistics Forensic Medicine
Civil Law:	Inheritance Law Property and Real Estate Law General Civil Law Civil Procedure Notary Law Obligations and Contracts Agrarian Law
Basic Juridical Studies:	Roman Law Theory of the State and Law Constitutional Law History of the State and Law History of the State and Law in Cuba
Economic and International Law:	Labor Law Financial Law Economic Law Administrative Law Public International Law Private International Law International Commercial Law Maritime Law

* Source: Miriam Laou (April 21, 1989).

older colleagues too often. My observations suggest that the situation is similar to that in U.S. universities, where senior faculty members are convinced that their junior colleagues speak up whenever they have something to say, while junior faculty members feel that it is best not to disagree with senior colleagues unless they have very strong views on an issue.

The *consejos de asignaturas* serve at least two purposes. First, law professors are often absent from the university for professional reasons. They travel abroad for advanced study, to attend conferences, and to offer courses of advanced study in less developed nations. Also, professors are often away from the classroom because they are needed in other capacities for extended periods of time, particularly to serve as judges or for maternity leaves. When professors are absent from the classroom, whether for a period of weeks, months, or years, colleagues in their *consejo de asignaturas* cover their courses.

Second, the *consejos de asignaturas* establish pedagogical consistency. In the United States, the bar exam system ensures that all lawyers have a consistent minimal level of juridical knowledge. In Cuba, students with grade point averages of 4.5 or above (on a five-point scale) write honors theses (*trabajos de diploma*) instead of taking the bar exam. Students with lower grade point averages must take the comprehensive state exam upon completion of their last year of law school. Accordingly, it is imperative that law students receive the same basic course content.[12]

In addition, collective efforts by the faculty are seen as pedagogically and ideologically desirable. As a result, what we see is a structure within which individual professors can teach as they wish, consistent with the general agreement (i.e., hegemonic ideological content) reached by the teaching collective of which they form a part.

Political Organization of the Law School: The Party Nucleus

Yet another dimension of the Law School is its organization along party lines. My sense is that it is both critically important and very difficult for persons from capitalist countries to understand how the Cuban Communist Party's leadership role actually operates. There are many points of intersection between the top positions in the party and leadership roles within the legal sphere (and other institutional arenas). Several members of the Politburo and Central Committee of the party are jurists. Top party appointments are made based on the person's abilities and character and are not dependent on whether the person holds a high governmental post. Of course, similar sorts of abilities and character traits are probably desirable for any position of authority, whether in government or the party. Nevertheless, the partial separation between party and government means, for example, that when Juan Escalona Reguera spoke as a member of the Central Committee he had to look beyond his specific interests as Minister of Justice, considering instead the more general needs and political direction of the society. The difficulty for outsiders rests both in how to untangle these dual responsibilities and, in the eyes of the Cubans, in the inappropriateness of doing so. This relationship may be easier to understand by examining the work of the University of Havana Law School's party nucleus and party recommendations for specific action by the Law School.

Every workplace has a Communist-Party nucleus. The nucleus is composed of all party members, known as *militantes*, within the workplace. It is responsible for the political governance of the workplace and provides a system of checks and balances on management's power. Membership in the Cuban Communist Party is neither imposed nor self-selected. Rather, party members are *elected* by their co-workers. Colleagues who are not party members offer their views on who deserves party membership during union meetings, but the vote itself is limited to members of the party nucleus. Most, but not all, *militantes* were previously members of the Young Communists (UJC), but membership within the UJC does not guarantee later election into the party. At least within the Law School, the decision of whether or not to admit a candidate into the party is taken very seriously. Meetings may go on for hours, as the candidate's level of maturity, responsibility, and behavior consistent with the ideological goals of the Revolution are assessed by her or his peers.

Until recently, candidates for party membership had to be at least 30 years old. This age requirement was relaxed slightly in recent years, and some persons in their late 20s joined the party. Prospective members take courses on the political economy and the ideological bases of the Revolution in special party-run schools, typically in the year prior to seeking membership. For the first year following election into the party, membership is provisional.

The party nucleus monitors the work of the administrator (in this case, the dean) and engages in collective self-criticism. As the dean at the time of the data collection told me, "The nucleus demands of me, as dean, that the teaching work is done regularly and is of high quality." For instance, it has asked him for progress reports on the new Professional Plan of Studies (Plan C). All members of the nucleus are equal, and the dean has no more power at those meetings than does anyone else. He is, as he told me, "just a *fulano*, just Julio." The term *fulano* is not exactly disrespectful, but neither is it particularly respectful. It means a fellow, a guy, and "*Eh, fulano*" translates roughly as "Hey, you!" Nucleus members, thus, may criticize the dean, saying "*Eh, fulano*, why are you doing this instead of that?" (Fernández Bulté, November 28, 1989).

Each party nucleus has a head (*jefe*). The workplace administrator cannot be the head of the nucleus, since that would negate the system of checks and balances provided by the party structure. The dean is answerable to the nucleus for his or her political actions but not for administrative decisions. As one member of the Law School faculty explained, "Neither the Dean nor any other faculty member is *required* to do what the *jefe* says. If the Dean does not follow the *jefe*'s suggestion, an explanation must be given. But as Dean, Julio is free to do what he wants without any sanction for not following the *jefe*'s suggestion" (Castanedo, July 4, 1990).

During its monthly meetings, the party nucleus addresses issues that are immediately relevant in the workplace. It may also discuss current political events as these relate to the workplace. In an effort to more fully understand the extent and boundaries of discussion, in the fall of 1989 I asked the Dean if the nucleus had discussed proposed modifications to the Family Code. The timing of revisions to this code was a particularly contentious issue at that time (see Chapter Three). He replied that it had not been discussed in the nucleus meetings, and further, that it would not be *appropriate* for such a technical matter to be discussed and debated in that forum. Similarly, the party nucleus does not evaluate specific pieces of research conducted by faculty members, saying that one study is better than another. Rather, it deals with pedagogical concerns, general suggestions for improving teaching, and political problems that may arise within the faculty. The nucleus also discusses specific political issues as instructed by the party leadership (e.g., the platform for party congresses).

Beyond running the monthly meetings of the party nucleus, the party head responds to any political difficulties that arise within the workplace and is responsible for answering any questions raised by nucleus members. If the *jefe* cannot answer a question, she or he brings it to the highest level of the party within the university, the *comité del partido* (party committee), for resolution. Each college's party head is a member of this university-wide committee (Castanedo, July 4, 1990). The same general organization is followed in other workplaces, as well.

An anecdote may help clarify further the role of the party head. In the spring of 1989, I gave a colloquium at the Law School in which I reported preliminary findings from this research. Most members of the audience were friends and/or sources of data for my research, but the party *jefe*, whom I had never previously met, also attended the colloquium. As a law school professor she was welcome at the talk, but I was surprised that she took the time to attend, since she worked in a different substantive area, and we had not interacted in the past.

Her attendance suggests two additional aspects of her role as *jefe*. First, so far as I am aware, she did not check on or attempt to control my research, nor did she speak with me about the theoretical, methodological, or ideological premises of my research. This was left entirely in the hands of those persons from whom I had specifically requested assistance in gathering or interpreting the data. The decision to offer me a visiting affiliation with the Law School was not discussed within the nucleus. That was strictly an administrative decision made by the dean in conjunction with the Ministry of Justice. Second, and perhaps contradicting the above, her presence at the colloquium suggests either a personal, professional interest in my research findings or that, as head of the party nucleus, she felt that she should take advantage of this opportunity to become aware of my conclusions, some of which bear directly on the work of the Law School.

At times, the upper hierarchy of the party will recommend certain administrative actions to the Rector of the University or its governing board (*consejo de dirección de la universidad*), and sometimes even to deans. Such suggestions are more likely to be sent to the Dean of the Law School at the University of Havana than to other deans because of the University of Havana's leading role in legal education. Theoretically, university officials are at liberty to accept or reject these recommendations, but in reality they tend to be followed whenever possible.

In our discussion of the relationship between the Central Committee and the Dean's office, Julio Fernández Bulté offered the following example. In late November 1989, he received a telephone call from the head of the Department of Revolutionary Orientation of the party suggesting that a workshop on the juridical legitimacy of *Telemartí* in terms of international public law be held prior to December 15. *Telemartí* is an anti-Cuba television station aimed at Cuba from the United States and funded by the U.S. government. At that time, the imminence of broadcasting by *Telemartí* had become a central and grave concern of the Cuban government. The head of Revolutionary Orientation suggested that the Law School hold a workshop and debate, perhaps concluding with an assessment of *Telemartí*'s legality. In relating this story, the Dean defined it as a "political request" to think about the idea, discuss it with students and professors, and reply to the caller by the end of the week. He assured me that it was not a directive and that he felt he could say no, that the professors have too much work to do and could not organize a workshop at that time. "As a political person myself," he said, "I know that this is a political exigency, and I will do everything I can to make a workshop possible, but I am *not obliged* to do so" (Fernández Bulté,

November 28, 1989, his emphasis). The symposium on television aggression did indeed take place at the Law School in December 1989.

PEDAGOGY

Education is never apolitical. Ideological, political, and societal demands influence the content and format of all studies. Far from being an exception, these beliefs and needs are at the forefront of legal education. For example, legal scholars and law professors played a central role in lending intellectual force and credibility to labor's efforts to create a workers' compensation system in the United States (Friedman and Ladinsky, 1967:68).

A critical pedagogy is often a key to political transformation, with universities in many societies providing not only a forum for debating new ideas but also the setting within which political confrontations and battles begin. In late eighteenth-century Colombia, the colonial Crown prohibited the teaching of constitutional law and the circulation of "The Rights of Man" or of the French Constitution. These prohibitions were, however, difficult to enforce, and the law schools continued to serve as focal points for informal debates over European political trends (Lynch, 1981:29).

It is interesting in this context to note that Fidel Castro's professional training was in law. This helped him prepare his eloquent self-defense following his arrest in 1953 for the rebel raid on the Moncada Barracks. Castro's self-defense, known popularly as *History Will Absolve Me,* laid out the major political, social, and economic tenets of the Cuban Revolution (see Chapter Three for further discussion of the Moncada Platform).

Following independence, throughout Latin America "legally trained men were prominent in the political organization of the new governments, and legal scholars contributed to the development of ideologies and values justifying the state's power" (Lynch, 1981:26). Yet the law schools continued to be centers of ideological struggle, with conflicts surfacing in controversies over their curriculums (Lynch, 1981:29–30).

According to Julio Fernández Bulté, Dean of the Law School at the University of Havana until late 1991, a basic premise of contemporary legal education in Cuba is that young people will influence the future content and practice of law. Students and their professors sometimes encounter contradictions between the law on the books and the law in action. Increasingly in recent years, students confronting such contradictions have been encouraged to express their own ideas about how laws should be written and enforced. As an example, Julio Fernández

Bulté mentioned the inconsistency between the 1975 Family Code's provisions concerning divorce and what the students see when they go to court. Divorce is generally a simple process handled with the aid of an attorney. The law stipulates that the president of the municipal court panel will meet with the couple and try to talk them out of the divorce. What students observe in court, however, is that often the couple simply goes to the court secretary and never sees a judge. The students, he concluded, often become justifiably upset by this clash between the law on the books and the law in action (Fernández Bulté, May 22, 1989). Through such experiences and discussions, students are taught to critically assess the need for changes in existing substantive and procedural legislation.

STRATEGIES FOR CHANGE: COMBINING THEORETICAL AND PRACTICAL TRAINING

Legal education in Cuba combines what in the United States would be considered undergraduate training with specialized professional training in law into a five-year course of study. From the perspective of the university system in the United States, what is missing from this more abbreviated program of study is the basic liberal arts (e.g., literature, world history, art, music appreciation).

Course Work

Most law school courses are required, but there are a few electives.[13] Some courses are completed in one semester while others continue into a second semester. All classes, including courses in other disciplines, are offered within the law school. Rather than a student going to another department on campus to take courses, as is common in U.S. colleges, professors from other faculties (e.g., philosophy, history, foreign languages, political science) come to the law school to teach their specialty courses. This pedagogical strategy is employed throughout the university system. Some students like this approach since it builds cohort solidarity and a sense of community within a large institution; others told me that they would prefer more structured interactions with students in other disciplines.

The requirement that students attend classes was a source of conflict between faculty and students throughout the Cuban university system during the late 1980s and into the 1990s. Many students and some faculty feel that class attendance should be voluntary, with students responsible for mastering the material by exam time. Mandatory class attendance makes the professor responsible for determining when an absence is justified. This has led to many jokes among the faculty. Since a common excuse for missing class is that an uncle died, a popular joke among faculty is, "When the professor comments on the large number of uncles who have died during the semester, the student replies, 'Oh yes, my family is very large. My father has 10 brothers! And my mother has eight more!'" (Rega, April 12, 1989; Hernández Ramírez, April 13, 1989).

This controversy is interesting, given the history of legal education in Cuba. In its 1982 and 1983 accords, the Politburo identified the limited number and availability of legal texts as a serious problem, with students forced to rely solely on lecture notes. As a consequence of that political definition of the problem, there has been a marked increase in legal texts written by Cuban scholars and of translations of foreign books (see Chapter Five). If class attendance becomes voluntary, the same problem may result in reverse. That is, if students do not attend class they will have to rely solely on the texts, without the benefit of lectures or class discussions. The problem arises from the more limited processing of information if students *only* hear lectures, or *only* read texts, rather than reading the texts, hearing the lectures, seeing key material written on blackboards, *and* writing notes from lectures and readings. This effort to be sensitive to student desires and to permit them a greater say in their education may thus have the unintended consequence of inhibiting critical thinking at the very time when such thinking has been identified as a pedagogical goal.

Honors Theses *(Trabajos de Diploma)*

Students with grade point averages of at least 4.5 write honors theses *(trabajos de diploma)*. Students work closely with a tutor (i.e., mentor) and other professors specializing in their subject area. Theses in law tend to be between 100 and 400 pages. They can be written individually or co-authored. They are defended in May of the fifth year at a ceremony known as a *tribunal de trabajo de diploma*.

While in many ways resembling a thesis defense in U.S. universities, the Cuban defense is more formal. Students dress in their finest professional attire including, for example, patterned hosiery for women even though it is so hot that members of the audience are fanning themselves in a fruitless effort to cool off. In addition to the student (or students if the thesis is co-authored), the other actors in this drama are the three members of the tribunal, the tutor, and the critic (known as the *oponente*).[14] The *oponente* and the president of the tribunal are generally senior professors in the department.

The defense begins with everyone standing as the president of the tribunal states the title of the thesis and names the student or students, the tutor, and the critic. The student then provides a brief summary of the theoretical bases for the work, major findings, policy recommendations, and conclusions. If there are co-authors, each speaks at some point, whether during the summary or later in response to the critic. Next, the tutor offers her or his opinion of the work and recommends a grade. The *oponente* offers what is typically a multipoint critique and raises a series of questions and suggestions. These range from broad philosophical questions that engage the students in critical thinking to detailed questions focusing on specifics of the research. A faculty joke is that the best students answer the *oponente*'s questions by referring back to the thesis and suggesting that the critic read it for the answer. Students often know or suspect the critic's questions in advance. In one defense I observed, the students had a full presentation prepared in advance, complete with the appropriate figure shown on an overhead projector! The *oponente* concludes by recommending a grade. The president of the tribunal then asks for any questions or comments from the floor. Members of the faculty tribunal consult privately, after which everyone reassembles to hear the decision and to congratulate the student. Grading is based on the quality of the theorizing and methodology, the originality of the research, and the quality and length of the bibliography. Where there are co-authors, each student receives the same grade.

Practical Training *(Práctica Preprofesional)*

The preprofessional practice is a strategy for combining theoretical classroom work with field experience. This "hands-on" training, according to the former Dean of the Law School at the University of Havana, is "a way of ensuring socialist legality in the teaching of law" (Fernández Bulté, May 22, 1989; see also Machado, 1984).

There are three forms of preprofessional practice. The first, known as *clases practicales,* or practical classes, is officially recorded as a class. Students discuss legal issues, write and edit draft legislation, and generally address juridical concerns suggested by the professor. The practical activities vary depending upon where the students are in their training and the substance of the course. In 1989 one law professor had first-year students assist in research she was conducting for the Ministry of Justice, while another had fourth-year students writing indictments (*actas de conclusiones*) in the provincial prosecutor's office (Arranz, May 2, 1989; Fernández Jiménez, May 9, 1989; Castanedo Abay, July 4, 1990).

Práctica de producción is a second form of preprofessional practice. It is required for the degree, but does not count as a formal class. The *práctica de producción* is roughly comparable to an internship in U.S. universities. In the past, internships began in the student's first year, but since the late 1980s they have begun in the second year. Following completion of their last exams for the spring semester, students spend a month working in law collectives or other juridical agencies (known as *entidades laborales,* or work sites). The *práctica de producción* becomes more complex and specialized in later years of study and is extended to 45 days in the final year.

Like the *clases practicales,* the *prácticas de producción* provide the student with practical experience while also meeting the needs of the legal community. Students generally seem to enjoy their practical work. As one student told me, "It is good experience and we learn a lot from it." From the faculty perspective, the value of the *prácticas de producción* varies. Seen as valuable in theory, in practice the quality of the training is uneven. Internships in the popular area of juridical advisement (*asesoria juridica*) and in the courts and law collectives are viewed by faculty as particularly problematic because jurists in these areas are usually too busy to work closely with the students (Fernández Jiménez, May 9, 1989; Castanedo Abay, July 4, 1990).

The third type of preprofessional practice, *actividad de unidades docentes,* is a part of regular class work. It is essentially a group internship. Students go to a law collective, courtroom, state arbitration agency, or another setting for juridical work to participate in and discuss their jobs. The *unidades docentes* provide students with a more active and realistic vision of what they are studying in the classroom.

While the professor is ultimately responsible for supervising the student's training, practicing attorneys also assist the students. The University of Havana Law School has formal *unidades docentes* relations with the prosecutor's office, the courts, the State Labor Committee, the Office of State Arbitration, the Housing Institute, and two law collectives. Students may work with other agencies, but the appropriate *unidad docentes* is still responsible for assisting them. For example, the law collective "J y 23" (the largest law collective in the country, located around the corner from the University of Havana at the intersection of J and 23 streets) is an *unidad docente* for the University of Havana Law School. Whether students are working at "J y 23" or at some other law collective, lawyers from "J y 23" help train the students.

Students engage in the same work as trained lawyers during their *unidades,* although they may be assigned the simplest cases. For instance, students assigned to the courts for their *unidades* join the judges in case deliberation, review indictments, and exchange technical ideas with criminal defense or civil attorneys. In their training in *asesoría* (juridical advisement), students attend to the clients' needs alongside the legal advisor. Similarly, in state arbitration offices, students participate in negotiations between workplaces (Fernández Jiménez, May 9, 1989; Castanedo Abay, July 4, 1990).

Postgraduate Social Service *(Servicio Social)*

Distinct from the *práctica preprofesional* is the *servicio social,* or social service. This is work that a new lawyer contributes in the three years immediately following graduation from law school, although exceptions are made for students with military careers. *Servicio social* began in medicine soon after the Castro government came to power and, as early as 1962, graduates in medicine were required to perform three years of clinical work in the countryside (Rodríguez, 1987a:504). The *servicio social* was designed to provide medical attention to the citizenry, especially in the countryside. Since all costs of a university education were paid by the society as a whole rather than the student, the graduating doctor was obliged to reimburse the citizenry by means of this service.

Plans for a *servicio social* for law graduates were developed in 1982, and it became a requirement in 1983 (UNJC, 1987:10; Castanedo Abay, July 4, 1990; Carreras y Cuevas, July 5, 1990). As in medicine, the social service requirement for law graduates helps meet the need for lawyers outside major urban centers (UNJC, 1987:13). The relative scarcity of lawyers in rural areas is a general feature of the legal profession globally. In his review of the legal profession in eighteen countries, Abel (1989:120–121; see also Lorey, 1988) notes two clearly visible geographic patterns. First, lawyers tend to cluster within the capital of a country, reflecting the historically close connection between lawyers and courts, and between courts and the executive power of the nation-state. The second tendency, although less pronounced, is for lawyers outside of the capital to be concentrated in cities and scarce in the countryside. Prerevolutionary Cuba was no exception to this general pattern. The ideological tenets of the revolution required that the countryside, which traditionally had been ignored, receive greater resources for development than the cities. Although Cuban lawyers still tend to concentrate in the capital city, sending some students into the rural areas for their *servicio social* is one way of augmenting the number of lawyers in the countryside.

During the spring of their fifth and final year of studies, law students are ranked according to their grades and any other relevant qualifications. Agencies, offices, and other work sites needing jurists submit requests, and students prioritize their *servicio social* placement preferences. A meeting of all of the fifth-year students and the Dean (or a Vice-Dean) is held in which these requests are matched, with highest preference going to the top students (Fernández, April 13, 1989; Arranz, May 2, 1989; personal observation). For example, if there are x slots for the prosecutor's office, y for the law collectives, and z for legal advisors in enterprises ranging from factories to the National Ballet, the best students get their choice. Students can, and do, trade with one another during this meeting. From my observations of these meetings over several years, the most striking aspect is the festive and excited atmosphere. The sounds of graduating students laughing, clapping, congratulating one another, and groaning carry widely, bringing a large number of professors and students to the doors of the meeting room to find out who received which assignment.

Top students are recruited by the law schools to do their *servicios sociales* at the school. There are two reasons for this practice. First, it provides useful experience for future professors (Laou, April 23, 1989). A second and historically specific reason is the paucity of law professors. The decision in the early 1980s to increase the number of law students created a severe shortage of adequately trained professors. One solution was for the law schools to hire their own top graduates for their *servicios sociales*, retaining the best on regular faculty lines following completion of their *servicios*. This practice was discontinued at the University of Havana in 1984 but still occurs at other universities (Fernández Jiménez, April 13, 1989; Arranz, May 2, 1989).[15]

PLAN OF STUDIES (*MODELO DEL PROFESIONAL: PLAN DE ESTUDIOS C*)

The programs of study agreed upon by the *consejos de asignatura* must be consistent with the broader goals and strategies laid out in Plans of Professional Study. Each college within the university develops its plan simultaneously, as called for by the Ministry of Higher Education. Work on Plan A was begun in 1975 and it went into effect in 1976. Preparation for Plan B began in 1980. It became effective with the 1982–83 entering class. In 1988, the first students graduated under Plan B, Plan B was modified, and work began on Plan C. Plan C became effective in the 1990–91 academic year.[16]

While Plans A and B were intended to last for about five years each, the universities and the Ministry of Higher Education expect that Plan C will be in effect for about 15 years, and it has built-in mechanisms for internal flexibility (Fernández Bulté, May 22, 1989). Plan C for the country's four law schools was initially drafted by the Dean of the Law College at the University of Havana, Julio Fernández Bulté, and clearly bears his imprint. Throughout 1989, the law schools worked feverishly to complete Plan C. Everyone involved with the training of law students offered suggestions and reviewed the multiple drafts, including the four law school faculties and deans, students, the Ministries of Justice and Interior, the Office of the Attorney General, the Cuban Communist Party, the Office of State Arbitration, and state enterprises employing jurists (Fernández Bulté, March 31, 1989). The Ministry of Higher Education is entitled to comment on new plans, but this appears to be a courtesy only, with major input coming from the faculty and those ministries and organizations most directly relevant to the profession.

Plan C was the major item on the agenda during the May 1989 and January 1990 Deans' Councils (Fernández Bulté, November 28, 1989). Minister of Justice Juan Escalona Reguera and Attorney General Ramón de la Cruz Ochoa personally attended the two meetings to discuss Plan C, as did representatives of other state, governmental, and party agencies.[17]

Premises and Objectives of Plan C

Plan C was founded on three major premises. The first was that students should receive greater practical training, increasing their responsibilities and authority each year. Under Plan B, students engaged in practical work for five weeks each year. With Plan C, this was expanded to nine weeks. The linkage between practical and classroom studies was strengthened by closer relations with the *unidades docentes* and comprehensive evaluations of students' work. Alternative methods of evaluation reduce reliance on final examinations, another desired outcome (Fernández Bulté, May 22, 1989).

The second premise of Plan C was clarification of the qualifications of law school graduates. As defined by Plan C, legal training does not prepare graduates to be judges or prosecutors. The 1990 Law of the Courts mandates eight years of postgraduate experience prior to serving as a Supreme Court judge, five years for provincial court, and three years for municipal court. These requirements are intended to ensure that judges are matured by their professional experience. This provision had existed under previous law, but had been relaxed due to the shortage of judges, particularly in the countryside. Indeed, in his address to the newly formed Law School in Las Villas in 1984, Politburo member José Ramón Machado Ventura spoke of the importance of preparing graduates to be judges and prosecutors (1984:219–220). The dramatic increase in the number of lawyers in the mid- to late-1980s, however, made it possible for the law schools to state explicitly in Plan C that they are no longer in the business of preparing judges and prosecutors.

The third premise of Plan C was a new emphasis on teaching students principles of law, rather than relying on lectures closely tied to existing legislation or memorization of statutes. A trend toward preparing students to be independent critical thinkers was already underway and was laid out explicitly as a pedagogical ideal in Plan C.[18] The hope was that by carefully building a theoretical basis of law, along with the historical, political, social, and economic principles necessary to make future jurists adequate users of law, they could be creative interpreters of law instead of simply relying on memorized facts. This requires a broad theoretical and philosophical education (e.g., theory of law and the state, historical materialism), learning how to express complex legal concepts in written and oral formats, and the elementary tools of legal research. Accordingly, under Plan C all students are taught how to conduct literature reviews, computer use, a foreign language, and research methods.

These three major premises of Plan C are related to its four objectives. The first and overarching objective was to create graduates with a broad understanding of the multifaceted practice of law. The working assumption was that training in the various branches of the legal profession would prepare students for future work in their specialty area and provide them with the ability to critique draft legislation "apart from small sectoral interests" (*Modelo del profesional: Plan de estudios C,* 1989b:19).

The second objective was to link theoretical and practical work with the study of research methods. Courses were grouped into larger disciplinary categories to more clearly define the areas of juridical activity. Research methods were incorporated into the plan of study through required term papers and by having students work in research teams with a professor. As was discussed earlier, the best students also write an honors thesis, which further hones their research skills.

The third objective was to better integrate practical and classroom training. Under Plan C, students learn jurisprudential basics (e.g., theory of law, philosophy, constitutional law) in their first three years of study. They then cycle through practical work in the three major areas of juridical activities: (1) civil law (including labor and administrative law) in the third year; (2) criminal law in the fourth year; and (3) legal advising in the fifth year. Practical training in each area is handled administratively through the *unidades docentes*. Students spend nine weeks each year in the *unidades*, under the supervision of their professors and adjunct professors who hold regular jobs in the *unidades*. The *unidades* where students work include the courts, prosecutor's office, law collectives, police stations, and state agencies and enterprises employing jurists. At the end of each nine-week cycle, students must pass a practical exam (e.g., in civil law they must demonstrate their ability to conduct a wedding, a divorce, a trial, and other basic civil-law responsibilities).

At the end of these three cycles, students have spent 27 weeks, or almost seven months, in practical work. This novel plan was a direct response to criticisms of Plan B, particularly that students "do too much sitting in chairs." In order to include this practical training without adding another year to legal studies, the number of electives was reduced, especially in later years of study. Students now go from having 30 hours per week in electives in the first year to 25 hours per week in the second year, to between 17 and 19 hours per week in the third and fourth years, and to 17 in the fifth year.

The fourth objective of Plan C brings us back to its underlying philosophy: to teach law, not legislation. Legal doctrines and values are taught with reference to legislation, but the law schools explicitly state in Plan C that they are no longer teaching legislation, per se. For example, in labor law courses students will be taught principles of contracts, but not the specifics of contract law. Ideologically, this redefinition of legal education to include critical evaluations of existing legislation is supportive of academic freedom.

The sweeping nature of the pedagogical changes in Plan C, and the expectation that they will remain in place for 15 years, meant that writing and approving Plan C proceeded slowly. Professors were able to gradually assimilate the new forms of teaching into their existing styles. As one law professor bemoaned, "This is not an easy task."

LAW PROFESSORS: WHO IS DOING THE TRAINING?

Professors in Cuba's law schools tend to be young women. They have the necessary academic training, but very limited practical experience (Hernández Ramírez, April 13, 1989; Machado Ventura, 1984:210). The National Union of Cuban Jurists (UNJC) reported that of the 61 law professors teaching full time at the University of Havana in 1986, 22 (33%) had less than five years of teaching experience, nine (15%) had five to 10 years of teaching experience, six (10%) had 10 to 15 years of teaching experience, seven (11%) had 15 to 20 years of experience, and only 17 (28%) had more than 20 years of teaching experience (UNJC, 1987:22). The UNJC's estimate of professors with more than 20 years of experience is probably inflated by including professors who had officially retired but continued to teach, since law school records in December 1989 listed only 50 full-time law professors at the University of Havana, including administrators but excluding retired persons who still teach an occasional course.

The youthfulness of law professors is particularly evident outside of Havana, and is most marked at the University of Las Villas. According to Politburo member José Ramón Machado Ventura, in 1982 the Law Department at Las Villas had 10 faculty members. When it became a Law School in 1984, it had grown to 22 full-time professors (i.e., not including adjuncts). Yet all 22 professors held the rank of Instructor; none had been promoted to Assistant Professor, Associate Professor, or Full Professor (Machado, 1984:214).

Qualifications and Internal Organization of the Faculty

The hierarchy of professorial rank (*categorías docentes*) in Cuba begins with Instructor (*instructor*) and goes up through Assistant Professor (*profesor asistente*) to Associate Professor (*profesor auxiliar*) to Full Professor (*profesor titular*). Honorary Professorships (*profesor de mérito*) are awarded to particularly deserving individuals (e.g., Blas Roca Calderío, Carlos Rafael Rodríguez), most of whom were full-time or adjunct professors at some point. The majority of law professors have not received degrees beyond the *licenciatura* (university graduate) and are Instructors or Assistant Professors.

Promotions from one faculty rank to another are determined by *tribunales de categorías*. These tribunals are composed of professors with more experience and higher rank than that held by the candidate. Candidates seeking promotion must pass written examinations in philosophy and a foreign language, a computer course, and an oral examination by the tribunal (Arranz, May 2, 1989). The key considerations for promotion to Associate Professor are the quantity and quality of the candidate's scholarly research. While uncommon, it is possible to jump from Assistant to Full Professor if, for example, the candidate completed a book-length monograph viewed as making an exceptional contribution to the field. As of 1988 there was no fixed term that must be spent in each rank prior to promotion, but previously the candidate had to be in rank for at least two years before becoming eligible for promotion (Arranz, May 2, 1989).

The degree of *Candidato Dr.*, (C. Dr.), essentially a Ph.D., seems to have become a requirement in recent years for promotion to Associate or Full Professor.[19] Very few law professors have this advanced degree. At the preeminent law school in the country, the University of Havana, only six professors had received their C. Dr. degrees as of the summer of 1990. A few of the C. Dr.'s are relatively young scholars who went abroad, mostly to the Soviet Union, for postgraduate studies. A doctoral dissertation was required for these foreign degrees. The other C. Dr.'s tend to be considerably older. Some of them received their *licenciaturas* in prerevolutionary days when lawyers, like medical doctors, used the title of Dr. A few older professors were granted their *Candidato Dr.* degrees by the government in recognition of their many scholarly contributions, even though they never formally completed the requisite doctoral studies. Each has written several books, any one of which would be acceptable as a doctoral dissertation in a Ph.D. program.

Following the European system, the highest scientific degree, Dr. in Juridical Sciences, is awarded to those persons who have earned what is essentially a second Ph.D., complete with a second dissertation. In 1990, there were only two Cuban legal scholars with the degree of Dr. in Juridical Science (Fernández Jiménez, April 7, 1989; Hernández Ramírez, April 13, 1989; Gómez Arias, May 2, 1989; Castanedo, July 4, 1990).

Whether or not there is a need for more jurists with postgraduate degrees is controversial. In 1987 the National Union of Cuban Jurists (UNJC) recommended against doctoral study abroad, concluding that advanced study in other countries distances the scholar from Cuban life and reality. The UNJC's fear is that scholars will forget the social reality that juridical doctrine is supposed to reference. According to the UNJC, of the 27 jurists who studied for advanced degrees in 1986, only nine selected topics that contributed to the development of the juridical science *in Cuba* (UNJC, 1987:22–23).

The UNJC further recommended against studying for the *Candidato Dr.* very soon after graduating from law school. It suggested that young scholars should practice law for several years prior to considering advanced scientific training. Finally, it concluded that postgraduate instruction has not been organized systematically and recommended that such studies be improved, particularly for the *Candidato Dr.*, if they are to become more than a mere formality (UNJC, 1987:23).

The salary scale for university professors is determined by the Ministry of Higher Education and the State Labor Committee. Professors holding the same rank throughout the university system receive the same salary, with the exception of those in the medical school. There is no merit system as such, but since the quantity of scientific publications is a key determinant of promotions, publications indirectly affect salaries (Arranz, May 2, 1989). In 1989, Assistant Professors earned in the low- to mid-300s of *pesos* per month, which affords a comfortable though not extravagant lifestyle (see Appendix A for comparisons to other economic sectors). In addition to salary, consumer amenities such as new cars and discount-priced color televisions, refrigerators, and fans are distributed within the university system, as in all other state agencies and enterprises, based on a combination of merit and need. An elected faculty committee decides who will receive these scarce resources. Adjunct professors earn a token salary of about 60 to 70 *pesos* per month, and on rare occasions have rejected this salary on the grounds that they earn a sufficient amount in their regular jobs and are teaching only for the pleasure and experience it affords them (Pérez, May 9, 1989).

Each professor has an area of specialization determined primarily by the individual's interests and secondarily by the needs of the law school when the person joined the faculty. For example, if two professors teach labor law and one teaches administrative law, and courses in both specialties attract the same number of students, then a new faculty member in the Department of Economic and International Law who wants to specialize in labor law may be nudged instead toward administrative law. Most new law professors were recruited by more senior colleagues for whom they worked as teaching assistants (*alumnos ayudantes*). This practice provides future professors with a mentor and teaching experience in a particular area. Typically, this remains their specialty when they are hired.

Practical Work by Law Professors *(Práctica Profesional)*

The combination of theoretical and practical training of students is replicated in the professional responsibilities of the faculty. The shortage of jurists means that the best lawyers cannot all be lost to the classroom, yet past history has shown that when the best jurists were out in the field, university teaching suffered. At the same time, professors who do not engage in some practical work within their fields of expertise might become isolated from the social context, needs, and problems they are studying. The result could be lesser quality and less interesting teaching, as well as the potential risk that professors could form a separate social strata (Machado, 1984:210, 215–216; UNJC, 1987:22). A balance, thus, was needed, in which professors would conduct some practical work in addition to their teaching, and some practicing jurists would teach courses on an adjunct basis. This was also the recommendation of the Communist Party in its 1982 and 1984 accords.

Currently, all university professors in Cuba regularly engage in some practical work in their specialty areas.[20] This is similar to the community service expected of professors in U.S. universities, but it is more organized in Cuba and forms a larger part of their job responsibilities than in the United States. As then-Minister of Justice Juan Escalona Reguera noted in his closing address to the Third Congress of the National Union of Cuban Jurists:

> We have old experiences that demonstrate that a true professor of Law is only formed when s/he adequately combines his/her teaching responsibilities with a professional practice as judge, prosecutor, [trial] lawyer, notary, arbitrator, or legal advisor to agencies or enterprises. It is in this way that we can set down the bases for development of the classroom teaching, by having professors combine the classroom with practice (1987:191–192; see also Machado Ventura, 1984:214).[21]

The selection of community service is made by the professor and other members of the faculty, based on a combination of the faculty member's area of specialization, interests, and the community's needs (Arranz, May 2, 1989). Advising the Ministry of Justice or a state enterprise is a particularly desirable and prestigious service post likely to result in data that can be used for publication. If too many professors want to work in this capacity, however, some will have to perform other tasks. Professors can decline service jobs if they prefer a different position. For instance, one law professor was asked if he was willing to be nominated as a judge. He responded that he would prefer to be a defense attorney, stating further that he liked murder cases, and his preference would be to assist a law collective by taking cases where a client had been accused of a violent crime.

Typically, professors devote about six months to community service every two years, but this varies depending on personal interests, the needs of the agency involved, and especially, the needs of the university. The extent to which other professors can cover the person's courses and administrative responsibilities is a key factor in this decision. For example, the standard of three semesters teaching and one semester of practical work must be revised for professors teaching year-long courses. In such cases, they typically teach and do professional service, often as legal advisors or judges, simultaneously. One example of this arrangement is the professor who chose to defend persons accused of violent offenses. He works with the law collective located around the corner from the law school, making it easy for him to stop into the law office as needed when he is not in class. Legal advisors to the Ministry of Justice and the National Assembly also typically combine their teaching and practical work into the same time frame, since the needs of the Ministry and the legislature cannot be delayed indefinitely. Several law professors are judges in Havana courts (see further Chapter Six). Some of them teach two or three days a week and work as judges the other two or three days. Others must devote larger blocks of time (e.g., six months) to their work as judges if, for example, they are presidents of judicial panels or of courts (Rega, April 12, 1989; Díaz Pinillo, May 9, 1989).

Occasionally, a professor is temporarily not involved in any practical work. One law professor confessed with some embarrassment that she was not doing any community service at the moment, explaining that she did not have any time since she was temporarily head of her department, spent part of a semester in Germany, was studying English, and was a union representative when she was not chairing her department.

University professors are also asked to serve as members of committees to revamp laws. Often persons charged with this assignment are temporary or permanent advisors to the Ministry of Justice, but they may also be appointed to working committees by the Attorney General's Office or other state entities. With a few exceptions, professors selected for these important committees are older faculty members who have demonstrated an in-depth knowledge of the subject matter under analysis. The most extreme case is that of Professor Renén Quirós Pírez, who is commonly referred to as the "father" of the most recent Cuban penal code. Professor Quirós spends most of his time working as a legal advisor for the Ministry of Justice, although he is a full-time professor of law and teaches on a regular basis.

CONCLUSIONS

Legal education in Cuba is a dynamic enterprise, with internal mechanisms for periodic assessments and major alterations, as well as ongoing minor adjustments. Changes in the mix of theoretical and practical aspects of legal education are strategies for resolving historically, structurally, and ideologically based conflicts and dilemmas within the legal arena.

For example, involving students in creating the popular tribunals of the 1960s was a strategy to meet the need for judges in the countryside, while also teaching law students the reality of life for peasant farmers. Recall that the law students of the early 1960s were teenagers or young adults at the time of the triumph, when higher education was only available to members of the bourgeoisie. Sending these young scholars into the countryside was a means of reducing the risk that they would remain an elite stratum, unaware of how most people lived.

The night-school era which followed was a strategy for teaching law to those already using it, again without creating a professional elite. The viability of this strategy became questionable, however, with the institutionalization process of the 1970s. Institutionalization of the Cuban state created a new set of conflicts and dilemmas in the legal arena. Greater numbers of trained jurists were needed to interpret existing legislation and to create new laws. Due initially to the personal interest that Blas Roca Calderío took in law, the profession once again became highly respected and prestigious.

The era of rectification came next. All aspects of Cuban life, and particularly the state bureaucracies, were reexamined to determine where there were problems and what midcourse changes were needed to correct them. While, generally, rectification is thought to have begun with the Third Party Congress in 1986, it could be seen in the legal sphere as early as 1983. Changes in key personnel in the Ministry of Justice and the Office of the Attorney General (see Table 3.2), coupled with attention by the Communist Party to legal education and professional continuing education, led to pedagogical revisions. Cuban legal education was redesigned to create jurists capable of carrying out innovative modifications of legal statutes—that is, of resolving conflicts and dilemmas through changes in the substantive content of law. It was hoped that combining professional service to the community with legal scholarship would circumvent the problem of an elite "ivory tower" which leaves scholars out of touch with the larger society and would also bring the latest theoretical ideas into the field. Moreover, this combination of scholarly and practical work is consistent with the Cuban commitment to resolving its historical problems in a manner consistent with its socialist ideology.

CHAPTER 5

LEGAL ADAPTATIONS FROM ABROAD

The slow, consensus-building process of law creation and the combined theoretical and practical approach to the teaching of law are two strategies used by the Cubans to resolve conflicts and dilemmas in the legal arena. A third general strategy is the examination and selective adaptation of foreign laws and legal philosophies consistent with the Cuban government's political and social agenda. This third strategy is closely related to the other two, since in evaluating their laws and legal education the Cubans look abroad to see what others are doing.

Selective adaptations are a response to the ideological and historical disjunctures between the legal tradition that Cuba inherited from Spain and the legal structures of socialist nations perceived by the leadership to be more applicable to Cuba's developmental path. Resolving the inconsistent features of these very different legal structures and philosophies to fit the reality of life in a small, Third World, Latin American island posed a serious dilemma for Cuban legal theorists and policy makers. A related dilemma concerned which models, or elements of models, should be prioritized where jurisprudential conflicts arose.

Research on legal pluralism has established that a multiplicity of legal forms, systems, and ideologies exist in most parts of today's world (e.g., Merry, 1988). Given the cultural overlaps in laws and legal philosophies, it is neither surprising nor particularly interesting that Cubans look at other legal models. What is interesting, however, is an examination of which foreign models the Cubans have chosen to study, how and why those systems were selected, and how they have been adapted to fit the Cuban reality. Each of these decisions constitutes a substrategy. The choices made reflect Cuba's past and present political, cultural, and economic experiences, its legal traditions, and the leadership's ideological goals.

Every legal order in the modern world adapts from other systems.[1] Roscoe Pound has said that the "[h]istory of a system of law is largely a history of borrowings of legal materials from other legal systems and of assimilation of materials from outside of the law" (cited in Watson, 1974:22). This is particularly evident in former colonies, such as Cuba, but it can also be seen in Europe. For example, the Spanish legal system derives from Roman civil law and was modified in the 1800s to reflect the influence of French law during the Napoleonic era. Justinian's *Institutes*, first issued as an elementary textbook in A.D. 533, still forms the basis for legal training in civil law in many parts of the world and provided an organizational framework for the Spanish Civil Code (Watson, 1974:36, 41).

The two major influences on Cuban laws and jurisprudence are the Spanish-speaking world and the socialist world. The foundation for Cuban jurisprudence is the transplanted Spanish system imposed upon it with colonization (see Chapter Three). Indeed, the Spanish Civil Code of 1889 was retained in Cuba, with some modifications, until 1987. Shared history, culture, and language have led the Cubans to look especially, although not solely, to Spain and Latin America in the areas of civil and administrative law. The socialist world provides examples of legal forms consistent with Cuba's socialist ideology. The influence of socialist models is evident in criminal law, most notably in the enhanced role of the prosecutor and the use of lay judges.

It is important to distinguish between copying or transplanting one system to another locale and selective adaptations. Cuba has indeed copied some Eastern European, and particularly Soviet, institutions. Examples of copying can easily be found in the economic realm and in the political-administrative structuring of the state apparatus. Some of these structures appear very cumbersome for the little island of Cuba, contributing to problems that the "rectification" process of the late 1980s sought to remedy (Couto, May 11, 1989; Guevara, May 29, 1991). Within the legal arena, however, adaptations seem to have been more carefully deliberated. My sources repeatedly emphasized that they review foreign legislation, published commentaries on laws, and legal theorizing from a wide range of sources—socialist and capitalist, First, Second, and Third World—looking for ideas that might fit Cuban circumstances, but they do not simply copy other juridical models in their entirety (e.g., Castaneda, May 3, 1989; Díaz, May 9, 1989; Quirós Pírez, May 15, 1989).

Legal scholars and consultants considering this strategy in other revolutionary contexts have reached differing conclusions about its efficacy. The contrast between Robert Seidman's recommendations for Zimbabwe and Albie Sachs's assessment of Mozambique's experiences is particularly informative. With certain caveats, Seidman (1984:333) sees value in examining other models and experiences. He writes:

No country can copy verbatim an institution from some other country, and expect it to work in its new environment precisely as it worked back home. Nevertheless, we can only learn through experience. To achieve development Robert Mugabe and his colleagues need reliable knowledge that will help them to create workable new institutions. *Lest they replicate the failures elsewhere, the lessons taught by analogous experience in other countries must inform that knowledge.* They require general heuristic propositions to guide their efforts to discover new versions of the legal order likely to change society in desirable ways (my emphasis).

Historical and cultural variations may reduce the usefulness of other models, however, as Sachs (1985:146) suggests:

I think one of the things we find is that the experience in other countries that have undergone revolutionary transformations *is interesting, it's valuable, it needs to be studied and evaluated, but in relation to concrete questions, it's not all that helpful.* You have to look to the guts of your own society, to the cultural modes, the historical traditions, the ways of saying and doing things that have emerged in the course of a long period of political struggle (my emphasis).

The Cubans appear to take a middle ground between these two positions. They carefully examine a wide range of foreign legal theories and laws, finding useful elements in many of them. These potentially valuable parts become incorporated into a whole, however, that is uniquely Cuban.

To better understand how and why Cuban legal scholars and policy makers consider particular foreign models, I address the following questions in this chapter: What are the mechanisms for locating alternative legal models? What are the foreign sources for Cuban ideas in the legal realm and why were they selected? How do the Cubans evaluate and adapt foreign models and theories?

MECHANISMS FOR LOCATING FOREIGN MODELS

Access to foreign publications, scholarly exchanges, and participation in international conferences held in Cuba and abroad are three major mechanisms, or substrategies, employed by Cuban scholars and policy makers seeking to learn about foreign legal systems, laws, and legal philosophies. The availability and usefulness of each is tempered by Cuba's political and economic ties and by language barriers.

Foreign Publications

If a book is not in a commonly known language, libraries tend not to purchase it. This practical economic consideration diminishes the book's potential usefulness, since even those who read the language do not have access to it. The importance of trade relations with Eastern European socialist nations made some knowledge of the Russian and German languages, in particular, a required research tool in many university programs. As a result, publications in these languages became more accessible to the Cubans. Translation of foreign scholarship into Spanish also became easier as more Cubans acquired foreign-language skills. Nevertheless, articles and books published originally in Spanish were still more readily, and more cheaply, available to the Cubans.

Publishing foreign laws, legal commentaries, and legal theories is the simplest route to enabling a large number of people to learn about foreign models and ideas. Once published in Cuba, scholars and policy makers can read and discuss these works. Throughout the 1960s and 1970s, the economic blockade imposed by the United States and its allies made it very difficult for information from nonsocialist countries to reach Cuba, although friends and solidarity organizations from around the world donated books to Cuban libraries (Quirós Pírez, May 15, 1989). By the early 1980s, most of Latin America had withdrawn from the blockade, and Cuba was able to purchase more books.[2]

The reduction in the number of countries engaged in the blockade was crucial for augmenting Cuba's juridical library holdings. At least as salient, though, was the Cuban leadership's political decision to allocate scarce resources to publishing legal texts. The Politburo's 1982 and 1984 accords, discussed in Chapter Four, were especially important. In these accords, the Communist Party called for increased publications by Cuban legal scholars, and for the acquisition and translation of foreign publications (UNJC, 1987:11; Kautzman, May 8, 1989). Analysis of Cuban publications, discussed later in this chapter, confirms that these recommendations were followed, with substantial increases in the mid-1980s in the number of articles and books published by Cubans and foreigners.

Scholarly Exchanges

The technical task of publishing the laws of other countries is relatively easy; determining which foreign articles and books warrant translation and outlays of scarce paper and ink is more difficult. Scholarly exchanges and international conferences gain added importance as a result, since it is through these channels that the most influential sources of ideas are often located.

During the 1970s and 1980s, Cuban universities, the Ministry of Justice, and the National Union of Cuban Jurists (UNJC) arranged numerous scholarly exchanges and sent Cuban jurists to Eastern European universities for postgraduate studies. By the late 1980s, however, advanced study abroad was losing its appeal to Cuban lawyers. As I discussed in Chapter Four, the UNJC recommended against postgraduate studies abroad that led to dissertations about other countries. Examining other models was viewed as helpful, but the focus, it urged, should be on conditions in Cuba (UNJC, 1987:22–23).

The UNJC has formal and informal relations with many foreign bar associations. According to its vice-president and chair of its international relations commission, Raudilio Martín, its primary function is to resolve domestic juridical problems. Ideas from abroad are useful in this endeavor. As Martín commented, "[K]nowing what is going on in the rest of the world helps in this. We seek information, we look for publications of an international character so that Cuban jurists can know of other experiences" (April 18, 1989).

Raudilio Martín defines the UNJC in part as a "channel" for connecting Cuban lawyers with foreign jurists, both in the socialist world and in the Americas. Involvement in international professional organizations is one means of linking Cubans and foreigners. As Martín emphasized,

> We cannot live isolated. We must live in contact with the entire world. And I believe that we have succeeded in this through our ties to international organizations. We belong to the International Association of Democratic Jurists, and to the American Association of Jurists. And many friends and jurists visit us who come with the expectation of knowing the Cuban reality. In this sense the organization [the UNJC] has met its objectives. But we still are not satisfied in the area of exchanges. We think that we must reach a greater exchange geographically and in specialized journals (April 18, 1989).

The UNJC collaborates with the International Association of Democratic Jurists and is represented in its Secretariat and Executive Committee. Regionally, it has close ties with the American Association of Jurists (AAJ). In 1989, a member of the UNJC was elected General

Secretary of the AAJ, and the UNJC was represented on the AAJ's Executive Council.

The UNJC has friendly exchange relations with organizations in socialist countries; maintains relationships with groups of lawyers, from a wide range of countries, who correspond with Cuban lawyers and send journals; has solidarity relations with human rights organizations in various countries; and has worked with TANA, the anti-imperialist court in the Americas. Jurists from all over the world visit Cuba. For example, Martín told me that in 1988 the UNJC hosted an important delegation of French lawyers. A prosecutor from Spain and professors from Spanish universities also visited Cuba in 1988. In the late 1980s the UNJC hosted visits from Libyan lawyers and from members of a bar association from Quebec, Canada, as well. Groups of progressive U.S. lawyers also travel to Cuba regularly.

These international exchanges tend to be mutually beneficial. For example, during Nicaragua's Sandinista era (1979 to 1989), the UNJC had:

> magnificent relations with the Association of Democratic Jurists of Nicaragua. We send jurists to Nicaragua to explain our juridical system, and Nicaraguan jurists come to Cuba to see our reality. In this sense there is an exchange— a collaboration between the two organizations (Martín, Guevara, and Fernández, April 18, 1989).[3]

Similar exchanges are organized through the universities. Law professors from the University of Havana, for example, have traveled to study or to teach in East Germany, the Soviet Union, Spain, Cape Verde, the United States, and Mexico.

The Ministry of Justice and the Office of the Attorney General have International Relations Departments headed by persons very knowledgeable in law and legal philosophies, both in Cuba and abroad. For instance, the Director of International Relations at the Ministry of Justice, María Luisa Arteaga Abreu, is one of only a handful of Cuban lawyers with doctorates. This important post requires stability of personnel so that both the Cubans and the foreigners know the person with whom they are working. In addition to overseeing delicate situations where Cubans need legal help abroad, they facilitate scholarly exchanges, organize international conferences, arrange travel (e.g., obtaining passports and visas) for Cuban legal scholars traveling abroad under collaboration agreements, and are officially responsible for foreigners coming to Cuba to study aspects of Cuban law and legality (e.g., requesting visas for them from Immigration).

Bilateral collaboration agreements (*acuerdos de colaboración*) cover exchanges of specialists between the Cuban Ministry of Justice and the Justice Ministries in other countries. Foreign scholars and policy makers come to Cuba, and Cubans travel abroad under these agreements, typically offering a series of lectures or similar types of collaboration. Exchanges of this sort cover a wide array of legal issues including criminal law and criminology, civil law, family law, administrative law, and economic law. The majority, but not all, of these accords are with other socialist nations.

The International Relations Department of the Ministry of Justice also attends to any Cuban responsibilities in international and regional juridical institutions. These include the humanitarian affairs institutes of the United Nations, the UN Congresses on the Prevention of Crime and Treatment of Delinquency, and what was, until 1990, the permanent commission for juridical affairs of the socialist bloc Council for Mutual Economic Assistance (CMEA). While the Cuban delegation to this and other commissions included representatives from a broad array of relevant institutions, the president of the Cuban delegation to the CMEA commission in 1989 was the Minister of Justice, the vice-president of the delegation was the first Vice-Minister of Justice, and the secretary of the delegation also held a position in the Ministry of Justice.

Language barriers are a major obstacle to successful exchanges with scholars outside of Latin America. I have been present on many occasions when Eastern European scholars were visiting, sometimes for an entire semester, but because they spoke little or no Spanish, an interpreter was needed whenever they spoke with Cubans. This seriously impeded the value of formal talks and discouraged informal dialogues. As the Director of International Relations at the Ministry of Justice commented in one of our conversations,

> You know that the language barrier is a tremendous thing. Unfortunately, when you bring a specialist who speaks another language what has to happen is that he or she talks through a translator, and many times you lose the real sense of what that person is saying. Because if the translation is not good there are difficulties. Perhaps the interpreter is a magnificent translator but does not have the technical legal vocabulary, and thus real difficulties are created. Right now we are a bit stagnated in this and are trying to establish some type of collaboration, principally with Latin American nations (Arteaga Abreu, April 19, 1989).

International Conferences

The economic blockade imposed by the United States (which bans travel to Cuba by most U.S. citizens), in combination with U.S. restrictions on visas for Cubans wishing to attend scholarly events in the United States, has seriously limited the amount of information reaching Cuba from the United States. A few sources of U.S. legal thought, such as the progressive National Lawyers Guild, have maintained intellectual ties with Cuban lawyers. Also, some European and Latin American nations, along with Canada, never participated in the blockade, and others resumed diplomatic and trade relations with Cuba in the late 1970s and the 1980s. Nevertheless, scholarly exchanges and receipt of publications were easiest with socialist nations. Furthermore, as Cuba sought to develop its own variant of socialist legality and to move away from some of the tenets of Spanish law, the ideas of legal scholars in other socialist societies became increasingly influential.

When it came to international conferences, however, geographic proximity and a shared language and history led Cuba to look toward its Latin American neighbors. Cubans attend conferences all over the world, but it is far cheaper and easier to attend, and to host, Latin American conferences. Transportation costs are lower within the region, and expensive simultaneous translations are unnecessary when most conference participants speak Spanish or Portuguese.

The value of attending and hosting international conferences was stressed by many of my sources. Of these, the most frequently cited were the United Nations Congresses on the Prevention of Crime and the Treatment of Delinquency, held in Milan, Italy in 1985 and then in Havana in 1990, and the American Association of Jurists (AAJ) meetings, hosted by Cuba in 1987. Renén Quirós Pírez underscored the significance of the 1985 Milan meetings, in combination with the 1987 AAJ meetings, for passage of the 1987 Criminal Code (see Chapter Three for a detailed analysis of this law):

> When the Cuban delegation went to Milan, ideas [for the new Criminal Code] were clear. We already knew what we wanted and where we had to go. But to our surprise, the ideas that drove the Milan Congress were the same as ours. Of course, the Milan Congress helped us in the sense that some ideas helped us refine the details of our plan. But the most fundamental contribution was to confirm that we were on the correct path (May 15, 1989).

Quirós's conclusion was reinforced two years later at the 1987

AAJ meetings, attended by more than 1,000 jurists from the Americas. In his words,

> There we announced the outline of our reform of the Criminal Code. Of course it wasn't known yet, but there we presented where we were going . . . we announced it and received a solid and open support for our positions. And again we saw that what we were doing was correct . . . and consistent with U.N. norms (May 15, 1989).

María Luisa Arteaga Abreu expressed a similar sentiment, noting that at these meetings,

> It became very clear to us that our Criminal Code had sanctions that were very high in comparison with other countries . . . . We knew the old code responded to a special situation in the first years of the revolution and that conditions were different by the time of the AAJ meeting, but in that meeting . . . we gained a tremendous understanding (April 19, 1989).

It is generally acknowledged by Cuban legal scholars and policy makers that these two international meetings were crucial for convincing Fidel Castro and other high-level Communist Party officials and legislators that the time had come for depenalization and decarceration. Indeed, Minister of Justice Juan Escalona Reguera referenced those two meetings in December 1987 when he presented the new Criminal Code to the National Assembly (Quirós, 1988; Escalona, 1988).

Speaking of Cuban participation in international conferences, Raudilio Martín, Vice-President of the UNJC, confided, "A few years ago we were not invited to a single event. Beginning in 1980 we have received many invitations to participate in events." Creation of the UNJC, Martín suggested, was a major reason for this surge of invitations. Previously, certain individuals would receive invitations. With establishment of the UNJC, they were given to the organization. As a result, a larger number of legal scholars gained access to these international forums and to the ideas presented in them. "Unfortunately," Martín noted, "due to economic problems we cannot attend all of the events to which we are invited."

International meetings offer Cubans an opportunity to inform foreigners of what life, including juridical life, is like in Cuba. The UNJC sent Julio Fernández Bulté (then Dean of the Law School at the University of Havana) to Spain as its delegate to a meeting on human rights in the Americas. Raudilio Martín and the President of the

Cuban Supreme Court, José Raúl Amaro Salup, represented the UNJC at a meeting of judges and magistrates in Colombia. After responding to numerous questions about the Cuban system, Amaro Salup went on to Peru, where 500 students at the National University of San Marcos questioned him for several hours about the Cuban legal order.

International conferences held in Cuba are desirable for political and economic reasons, but especially for scientific reasons since they "put our jurists in contact with foreign specialists. It is a success from the point of view of enabling comparisons between our country and the countries from which the participating scholars come" (Arteaga Abreu, April 19, 1989).

Hosting international conferences offers Cubans an opportunity to learn from foreign scholars and exposes foreigners to the reality of revolutionary Cuba and to Cuban scholarship, as well as bringing scarce foreign currency into the country. At least as important, more Cubans can attend conferences held in Cuba than conferences held abroad, augmenting the opportunity for Cuban jurists to learn about other legal policies and ideas.

THE FOREIGN INFLUENCES
ON CUBAN LEGAL THOUGHT

Latin America and Eastern Europe have been the most significant foreign influences on Cuban law and legal theorizing. Cuban scholars and policy makers listen carefully to ideas emanating from other parts of the world, as well. While there are multiple avenues by which foreign thought reaches Cuban legal scholars, the same countries are often represented.

According to María Luisa Arteaga Abreu, the Ministry of Justice has entered into collaborative agreements with "a whole series of countries that have given us this opportunity . . . . We are trying to open our radius of action and our collaboration with Latin American countries a little more." Exchanges within Latin America are very important because of the shared juridical and political history, culture and customs, geographic proximity, and common language. The socialist world is also very important, since Cuba shares its political structure and overarching ideology with these countries. The Ministry of Justice has collaborative exchange agreements with all of the socialist nations, including Viet Nam, Laos, and Kampuchea (Cambodia) in Indochina. It also has collaborative agreements with Mozambique, the Congo, Argentina, and Nicaragua. In December 1989, it was finalizing an agreement with Mexico.[4]

Throughout the 1980s, the UNJC had friendly relations with homologous organizations in the Soviet Union, East Germany, Bulgaria, Czechoslovakia, and other socialist countries. It also has close ties with groups of jurists in Spain, France, Angola, Libya, Canada, and the United States, and solidarity relations with human rights organizations in Chile, Guatemala, El Salvador, Honduras, and with the Palestinians (Martín, Guevara, and Fernández, April 18, 1989).

Members of commissions charged with modifying existing legislation or creating new laws stressed the importance of studying foreign models. I spoke with members of several commissions, and they all said that they examine legislation from all possible countries, review the literature available to them concerning foreign laws, and compare aspects of the different laws studied.

In criminal law, members of commissions to create or modify legislation noted that they analyzed all of the legislation and relevant scholarly works that they could acquire. Cuban criminal law is very much influenced by Spain, since Cuba inherited Spanish criminal codes and procedural laws (Quirós, May 15, 1989). The laws of socialist countries, especially East Germany, were also very important to commission members. Meshing these disparate systems was not an easy task. The enhanced role of the Cuban prosecutor (*fiscal*) in criminal procedure and as the protector of legality is attributed to the influence of the socialist systems studied (see also Markovits, 1989:389–400). In the Spanish tradition, the judiciary held far more power. As law professor and member of the commission to write a new law of criminal procedure Marcelino Díaz Pinillo remarked, "We try to maintain the equilibrium that the court is the center of justice, but it is good to elevate a little the role of the *fiscal* in this process, because in our judgment it was very poor" (May 9, 1989). In addition to the Spanish and socialist influences, specialists in criminal law cite the influence of Italian positivism and of Japan's legal system (Quirós, May 15, 1989).

As part of its preparation for writing a new Law of the *Fiscalía*, in 1988 the Office of the Attorney General (*la Fiscalía General*) published a compilation of laws of the *Fiscalía* in East Germany, Argentina, Bulgaria, Hungary, Mexico, Nicaragua, Poland, Venezuela, and the USSR (*Fiscalía General de la República de Cuba*, ed., 1988).

In the area of juridical institutions, Roman and Napoleonic laws form the bases for Cuban law. In administrative law, the Spaniards and Argentinians are considered by their Cuban peers to be especially advanced (Castaneda, May 3, 1989). Juan Escalona Reguera, who at the time was President of the National Assembly, reported that the commission writing the electoral law of 1992 studied 15 foreign electoral laws, naming specifically Spain, France, Mexico and Colombia (Molina, 1992:3).

The commission charged with codifying Cuba's 1984 labor law examined the experiences of other Council for Mutual Economic Assistance (CMEA) members, with particular attention placed on the laws of Bulgaria, Czechoslovakia, Poland, East Germany, and Rumania (Guillén Landrián, 1987:12, 229). The labor codes of Angola, Brazil, Ecuador, the Philippines, Mexico, Mongolia, Panama, and the Russian Republic were also helpful, as were legislative materials available through the International Labor Organization's office in Geneva (Guillén Landrián, 1987:229).

Foreign Articles and Books Published in Cuba

In its 1982 accords, the Politburo called for a program of acquisition, elaboration, and publication of juridical studies (UNJC, 1987:11). The plan included work by Cuban authors and translations of articles and books published elsewhere, particularly in European socialist countries.

Table 5.1 shows the number of books published between 1967 and 1989 by Cuba's major academic publishing house, *Editorial de Ciencias Sociales.*[5] Excluding 1986, for which information was not available, and excluding a reprinting, only 64 legal texts were published during this 23-year period. Table 5.1 also evidences the marked increase in the number of publications in the mid-1980s, in response to the Politburo's recommendations.

Of the 64 books published, 51 (80 percent) were by Cuban authors and 13 (20 percent) were written by foreigners. Half of the foreign authors were Soviets. Only one was from a non-socialist country, France.

Another measure of foreign influence is the number of books published about other legal systems and laws. Thirteen of the 64 books (20 percent) explicitly focused on other countries, mostly Eastern Europe but also the United States. The major Eastern European influences, measured both by the nationality of the author and the content of the book, were the Soviet Union, East Germany, and Rumania. *None* of the books, it is worth noting, are by non-Cuban Latin Americans or about other Latin American legal systems.

The abstracts to some of the books are informative, suggesting the Cubans' attention to particular models. For example, the Cuban abstract to a book about juridical rules for the Soviet Ministries, published in 1985 (first published in Russian in 1971), states that it has special importance for Cuba because the principles analyzed by the authors

Table 5.1.
Legal Texts and Laws Published by Editorial de Ciencias Sociales:
Cuban and Foreign Authors.*

Date	Cuban author	Foreign author	Explicitly about foreign country	Total
1967–76	3	1 (France)	0	4
1977–81	5	4 (USSR)	5 (USSR–4, CMEA–1) (a)	9
1982	5	0	0	5
1983	3	0	1 (USA)	3
1984	8	0	1 (CMEA) (a)	8
1985	7	3 (USSR–2, Rumania–1)	2 (USSR–1, Rumania–1)	10
1986 (b)				?
1987–88 (b)	9	3 (c)	1 (Cuba & 5 other socialist nations)	12
1989	11	2 (USSR–1, E. Germany–1)	3 (E. Germany–1, USA–1, USSR–1)	13

a. CMEA is the Council for Mutual Economic Assistance

b. No information was available for 1986 and only combined 1987–1988 data were available

c. Nationalities of authors are unclear, but not Cuban. These are translations of texts published elsewhere

* Sources: *Editorial de Ciencias Sociales* catalogs of published titles, 1967–1984, 1985, 1987–1988, 1989 preliminary catalog.

have guided Cuban thought in this area since 1976, when the organization of the central administration of the Cuban state was approved. Similarly, the abstract to a book by Cuban authors on contractual relations, published in 1987 or 1988, notes that the work is enriched by analyses of economic legislation in five other socialist countries.

Writing and publishing books is quite expensive and time consuming in comparison to journal articles. While some empirical studies and theoretic treatises require book-length manuscripts, journals are often a better outlet. Between 1983 and 1987, the Cubans started three new law journals, in addition to the already established *Revista Cubana de Derecho*. Many of the journal articles are translations of works by foreign authors and focus on other countries, as Tables 5.2 and 5.3 demonstrate.

Table 5.2 enumerates articles by foreign authors and texts of foreign laws published in the four Cuban law journals. By the end of 1988, a total of 498 articles had been published. Of these, 225 articles, or 45 percent, were by non-Cubans or were laws of other countries. About half of these, 119 (53 percent), were by Soviet authors. Another 56 (25 percent) were by Eastern European authors, mostly East Germans. The East German influence may appear slightly inflated, depending on whether one counts the number of distinct publications or the overall scholarly impact, because the text of a book published originally in East Germany was reproduced in five issues of *Divulgación Jurídica*. In addition to East Germany, scholars from Bulgaria, Czechoslovakia, Rumania, Poland, Hungary, and Yugoslavia also contributed articles. Latin America is represented in 23 articles (10 percent) by scholars from Peru, Chile, Puerto Rico, Argentina, Venezuela, Mexico, Costa Rica, Colombia and El Salvador. Another 27 articles (12 percent) were United Nations publications or by scholars from Spain, France, Japan, the United States, Sweden, Italy, West Germany, Viet Nam, and Norway.

Table 5.2:
Articles in Cuban Law Journals by Foreign Authors or Texts of Foreign Laws Published, by Journal through 1988.

Country or Region	Journal and Years Published			
	Revista Cubana de Derecho (1972–88)	*Revista Jurídica* (1983–88)	*Divulgación Jurídica* (1983–88)	*Cuadernos de Legalidad Socialista* (1987–88)
USSR	26	1	82	10
Eastern European Socialist Nations	5	1	46	4
Latin America	7	2	8	6
Other or United Nations	2	0	19	6
Subtotal and Percent of Total	40 (20.4%)	4 (4.0%)	155 (92.3%)	26 (74.3%)
Total Number of Articles	196	99	168	35

As Table 5.2 shows, *Divulgación Jurídica* is devoted almost entirely to articles by foreign authors (155 of 168 articles, or 92 percent), as is much of *Cuadernos de Legalidad Socialista* (26 of 35 articles, or 74 percent). *Revista Jurídica,* in contrast, rarely publishes articles by foreigners (only four percent of its publications), and two of the four articles by foreigners were by Latin Americans. *Revista Cubana de Derecho* falls in between, with 20 percent of its articles by foreigners. The foreign influence in *Revista Cubana de Derecho* varies over time. During the period from 1981 to 1987, neither *Revista Cubana de Derecho* nor *Revista Jurídica* published any articles by foreigners, focusing instead solely on studies by Cuban scholars. The majority of *Revista Cubana de Derecho*'s articles by foreigners, most of whom were Soviets or other Eastern Europeans, were published between 1972 and 1975. At that time Cuba was still very much isolated from Latin America due to the U.S.–initiated blockade. Also, the UNJC, which later took over publication of the journal, had not yet been created. In contrast, most of the Soviet contributions in *Divulgación Jurídica* were published later, in the period from 1986 to 1988.

Another measure of foreign legal influences on Cuban thought is articles published in Cuban law journals *about* other countries and their laws, regardless of whether they were written by Cuban or by foreign scholars. The Cubans publish articles and books about other countries so that jurists "are informed not only about our law but also about others, so that they can determine what the differences and similarities are" (Arteaga Abreu, April 19, 1989).

Using the conservative criterion that the name of another country must appear in the title to be counted, Table 5.3 shows that of the 498 articles published in the four law journals from their inception through 1988, 117 articles (23 percent) concerned other countries. Of these, the vast majority focused on the Soviet Union or other socialist Eastern European nations. Soviet law and the Soviet legal system were central to 43 articles (37 percent). Another 45 (38 percent) covered Eastern Europe, primarily East Germany and Bulgaria, but also Rumania, Czechoslovakia, and Poland. Four articles specifically addressed the socialist bloc Council for Mutual Economic Assistance (CMEA). In *Divulgación Jurídica* alone, the Soviet Union was represented in 29 articles and East Germany in 22 articles. Latin America was represented in 15 articles (13 percent) covering Chile, Puerto Rico, Argentina, Venezuela, Nicaragua, El Salvador, and Mexico. Fourteen articles (12 percent) were about the United Nations, the United States, Japan, Spain, Sweden, Viet Nam, or Angola.

Table 5.3:
**Articles about Other Countries and Laws of Other Countries
Published in Cuban Law Journals, by Journal through 1988.***

Country or Region	Journal and Years Published			
	Revista Cubana de Derecho (1972–88)	*Revista Jurídica* (1983–88)	*Divulgación Jurídica* (1983–88)	*Cuadernos de Legalidad Socialista* (1987–88)
USSR	12	1	29	1
Eastern European Socialist Nations	9	1	33	2
Latin America	11	1	2	1
Other or United Nations	8	0	4	2
Subtotal and Percent of Total	40 (20.4%)	3 (3.0%)	68 (40.5%)	6 (17.1%)
Total Number of Articles	196	99	168	35

a. Council for Mutual Economic Assistance

* The name of a country other than Cuba must be in the title to be included in this listing.

It is evident from Table 5.3 that most of the articles about other countries were published in *Divulgación Jurídica* and *Revista Cubana de Derecho*. Recall that older issues of *Revista Cubana de Derecho* were considerably more likely to have a foreign focus than recent issues. *Revista Jurídica,* especially, and *Cuadernos de Legalidad Socialista* published relatively few articles explicitly about foreign legal systems. Although *Divulgación Jurídica* had the greatest number of articles about other countries, 68, this is about half the number of articles it published by foreign authors, 155. Many of the articles in *Divulgación Jurídica* by non-Cubans are theoretical pieces not limited to a particular country's legal system.

In sum, Tables 5.1, 5.2, and 5.3 reflect the strong influence of the Soviet Union and East Germany, especially; plus Bulgaria, Rumania, Poland, and Czechoslovakia in Eastern Europe; Argentina, Peru, Mexico, and Venezuela in Latin America; and elsewhere Spain, Japan, the United States, France, Viet Nam, and the United Nations.

Representatives of the major juridical agencies (the Ministry of Justice, the *Fiscalía,* and the UNJC) mentioned these same countries when discussing their foreign connections. They also noted ties with Nicaragua, Laos, Kampuchea, Mozambique, the Congo, Angola, and Libya, and with nongovernmental solidarity groups in Chile, Guatemala, El Salvador, Honduras, and Palestine, but these countries and solidarity groups seem to look to Cuba for guidance, rather than representing countries to which Cubans look for ideas. Members of lawmaking commissions cited the same set of countries, also mentioning Angola, Brazil, Ecuador, Panama, the Philippines, and Mongolia.

Overall, the major influences were the Soviet Union and East Germany, followed by other Eastern European socialist nations. Latin American nations were named regularly by commission members and representatives of juridical agencies, but in terms of publications they represent between zero and 13 percent of the foreign influences on Cuban legal thought. Within Latin America, Argentina and Mexico were most important. In addition to these two spheres of influence, Spain and Japan were cited most frequently across data sources.

The primacy of socialist and Latin American influences on Cuba is readily understandable, since Cuba is ideologically close to the other socialist nations and culturally and historically tied to Latin America. Spain was Cuba's colonizer and retains its influence. Japan is generally acknowledged as the new global economic leader; it makes sense for scholars in any country to look to what the most powerful force is doing, even if only to understand it better.

I speculated further that trade in juridical ideas might be closely tied to economic trade. That is, you need to know the laws of countries with whom you trade, and to the extent that you have similar laws in at least some spheres, trade relations are facilitated. Also, if there are extensive economic interactions between Cuba and a given country, it is reasonable to assume that there would be sufficient numbers of people capable of translating publications. Accordingly, I examined Cuba's economic trade partners to assess whether its major economic ties were with the same countries that had the greatest influence on Cuba's juridical ideas.

Trade data, measured in thousands of *pesos,* are only complete through 1985. To provide a comparison with journal publications, I focus on trade in the 1980s. The import data reported in Appendix H indicate that most of Cuba's imports were from Western Europe, followed closely by Eastern Europe. Within Western Europe, Spain was the major source for imports, followed by the United Kingdom,

France, and West Germany, and then by Italy, the Netherlands, Sweden, Switzerland, and Austria. Within Eastern Europe, the Soviet Union was the major source for imports, followed by East Germany, and then by Bulgaria, Czechoslovakia, Hungary, and Rumania, and then by Poland and Yugoslavia.

As the data in Appendix H demonstrate, Asia came next, with China and Japan both very important sources, followed by Viet Nam. While, as a whole, fewer imports came from Asia than from Western or Eastern Europe, taken individually, imports from China and Japan surpassed every other country except the USSR and East Germany in 1984 and 1985. Finally came the Americas. Argentina led the rest of the Americas in imports, with tremendous increases during the 1980s that placed it, by 1985, on a par with Bulgaria and Czechoslovakia, exceeding even Spain. Substantial imports also came from Mexico and Canada.

Export data for the period from 1980 through 1985 show similar patterns, although exports to Eastern Europe exceeded those to Western Europe.[6] Most exports were to member nations of the Council for Mutual Economic Assistance (CMEA). The Soviet Union was the single largest purchaser of Cuban goods. It was followed within Eastern Europe by East Germany, then by Bulgaria, Czechoslovakia, and Hungary, and then by Rumania, Poland, and Yugoslavia. Western Europe followed, with Spain the largest Western European consumer of Cuban goods. France came next, and then Italy, West Germany, Switzerland, the Netherlands, and the United Kingdom. The principal Asian purchaser of Cuba's goods was China, followed by Japan and Viet Nam. There were also substantial exports to Egypt. Within the Americas, Canada was the greatest consumer of Cuban products, followed by Mexico, Venezuela, and Peru.

As these data indicate, Cuba's most important economic trade partners in the first half of the 1980s were the Soviet Union, East Germany, Spain, China, and Japan, followed by Argentina, West Germany, France, the United Kingdom, Canada, Mexico, and other Eastern European members of CMEA. While most of these countries influenced Cuban jurisprudence and legislation, their relative importance differed. That is, most of the Western European nations that were important trade partners were also represented occasionally in Cuban law journals and cited by members of lawmaking commissions, but far less frequently than Eastern European nations. China was also a very important trade partner, but was not represented in any Cuban juridical publications.

HOW FOREIGN MODELS
ARE EVALUATED AND USED

Comparative legal theorist Alan Watson (1974:92) has commented that commissions set up to reform law often begin

> not by trying to think [their] way through to [their] own solution based on local conditions and character but by examining external solutions. There is a conscious attempt to achieve the best possible rule. But the process is not entirely free from chance. Non-legal factors—library and linguistic deficiencies—reduce the role which might be played by certain systems.

Historical and political influences such as wars and colonization also affect the relative importance of particular foreign legal systems for domestic law reform efforts (Watson, 1974:50–51). Watson's critique is only partially true for the Cubans. Certainly, an array of nonlegal factors has had a bearing on the foreign legal influences on Cuba. Nevertheless, my interview data lead me to conclude that the Cubans truly do try "to think their way through to their own solution based on local conditions and character."

For example, Renén Quirós Pírez, generally considered to be the "father" of Cuba's recent criminal codes, commented that the laws of several countries were carefully studied when the criminal code was rewritten in the 1980s, but none were copied literally. Rather, those elements most consistent with Cuba's development in the area of criminal law were adopted (May 15, 1989). He went on to comment that, to the extent that the criminal codes of various countries have traits in common, this is due to a logical coincidence in the development of their social conditions and in how those conditions and possibilities for change have been interpreted. In other words, he was warning me not to mistake correlation for causation. Never, he asserted elsewhere, was the aim simply to transfer changes introduced elsewhere to Cuba (Quirós, 1988:4). Other members of commissions to write new laws have made the same point: models from many other countries were examined and compared, and conclusions about what might work best for Cuba were hammered out, with foreign laws serving as pieces of data but not as models to be copied wholesale.

Administrative law professor Armando Castanedo told me that when Cuban jurists began receiving more foreign legal references in the mid-1980s, they organized seminars and lectures to discuss and compare the foreign legislation. He said that the Cubans look to see the *results* of legal reforms elsewhere, arguing, "I think you must always look to see where a juridical institution was born, why it was born, and how it developed." From his perspective, "In the last couple of years we have been better able to make decisions without looking so much at other models" (May 3, 1989).

Castanedo went on to say that he introduces some comparative law in his classes

> to give students the opportunity to see legislation from other countries. . . . In our faculty we are trying to include comparative law because until now everything has been Cuban legislation. And when they analyze [our] legislation they can see what the deficiencies are. . . . I would say categorically that no model is good for another country, in total. There are aspects that can be taken from a system, you can take from that country with that experience and incorporate it into our system. Now, what I never personally do is to predispose myself. To say, here is what is good, here is what is bad. I am going to see what is out there . . . . The socialist legislation is very important because it is our system, but when I talk about juridical institutions it is at the base [where it arose] where I must look first, and then I compare it with other systems. What we think is that capitalism is not the ideal system for us, but not that it is all bad . . . *there might be something in it that would resolve some problem.* Why not? *To this we are open.* Science cannot be closed (May 3, 1989; my emphasis).

Cuban scholars often stressed their receptivity to foreign legal influences, including ideas from U.S. colleagues. Perhaps because I had spent a lot of time in Cuba and had become friends and acquaintances with a large number of Cuban law professors and policy makers, comments such as the following, by Raudilio Martín of the UNJC, were common: "You yourself, as a visitor and a specialist, acutely observe our reality. If you give us some recommendation, Marjorie, we will evaluate it and take it into account as something to think about and to consider" (April 18, 1989).

CONCLUSIONS

Every legal system in the modern world includes elements from abroad. Sometimes these are imposed, with little say by the receiving party. This is most readily seen in colonized nations, where the laws of the colonizer are transplanted. Once nations gain independence, however, we can conceive of legal adaptations as a *strategy* for resolving problems. Doing so turns our attention to conscious action by human beings making choices about which systems to study, and to how and why they were selected.

The data presented in this chapter demonstrate that the major foreign influences on Cuban jurisprudence and lawmaking were the Soviet Union and other Eastern European socialist nations, Spain and a few other Western European nations, and to a lesser extent Latin America. These were followed by a scattering of other countries, including especially Japan. Virtually the same list of countries is reached when we consider foreign authors of books and journal articles, books and articles about other countries and their laws, nations with which Cuban juridical agencies and organizations have established professional relations, and countries mentioned by members of law-writing commissions questioned about the significant foreign influences on their work.

Not surprisingly, we also see that these countries are major economic trade partners. There are some interesting exceptions. In particular, China has been a very important trade partner but was never listed as an important source of juridical ideas. Perhaps China's legal system is too different from Cuba's, or perhaps language has been too large a barrier. This appears to be changing as a result of the dissolution of socialism in Eastern Europe. Since 1991, China has become not only a major economic trade partner but also Cuba's major ideological ally. In 1991, very high-level visits and exchanges took place between Chinese and Cuban leaders in the juridical and legislative spheres, suggesting that we can expect closer ties in these areas in the future.

This part of the book has detailed strategies for resolving conflicts and dilemmas in the legal sphere. The strategies include the broad-based, consensus-building process of law creation (see Chapter Three), the mixture of theory and praxis leading to critical thinking among law students (see Chapter Four), and selective adaptations from abroad (this chapter). Each has a set of substrategies, which are the specific mechanisms by which Cuban-style socialist legality is produced. We now turn, in Part Three, to ways in which legality is produced and reproduced daily in the courts and on the job.

THE DAILY PRODUCTION AND REPRODUCTION OF LEGALITY

CHAPTER 6

LAY JUDGES
"BIDIRECTIONAL TRANSMITTERS" OF LEGALITY

People come here with their pain. It is like the doctor. If I go to the doctor because I am in pain, and this doctor with a face like an ogre who wants to eat me attends me badly, then I feel the pain more sharply . . . It is the same in the court . . . Why do you go to court? You go to court because someone in your family is in jail, or because a family member is going to be taken to jail, or is being judged. It is a serious thing. So, the people come to court with their pain."

—Elia Ester Rega
provincial court judge and law professor
April 12, 1989

The courts, along with the labor councils discussed in Chapter Seven, are sites for the daily production and reproduction of socialist legality. Beyond the tangible imparting of justice as judicial decisions are handed down, the courts also have an important symbolic content. It is here that people see their legal system in action, through their personal experiences with prosecutors, defense attorneys, and especially, judges, lay and professional. Who are the judges? How were they chosen? How do they perceive their roles as producers and conveyers of socialist legality? What is the nature of the interactions between lay and professional judges? These are some of the questions addressed in this chapter.

One of the themes of this analysis is that there is a dynamic mix of legal formalism and informalism in Cuba. While the use of lay judges does not make a legal system informal, a central component in most, if not all, analyses of informalism is the presence of ordinary people, who are not trained as jurists, imparting justice.

Not all judges who did not graduate from law school are what I would call "lay" judges. Sometimes they constitute themselves as professionals, whether or not they are accepted as such by those trained in law. Doris Marie Provine, for instance, examined decisionmaking by lawyer and nonlawyer judges in the United States, concluding that they act similarly in comparable court settings. She attributes this to the broad dissemination of the legal profession's version of the judicial process among nonlawyer judges and the general public (Provine, 1986). Similarly, I found that nonlawyer judges in Nicaragua behaved as legal professionals. They are knowledgeable about law, and they interpret cases and base decisions on the norms of formal law (McDonald and Zatz, 1992).

In contrast, I will show in this chapter that lay judges in Cuba do not conceive of themselves and are not perceived by others to be legal professionals. Their purpose is to bring a nontechnical view to legal proceedings. At the same time, Cuban lay judges are respected by lawyer judges (whom I call "professional" judges), and their opinions often hold sway over their professional colleagues. In municipal courts, and now in many provincial panels, lay judges form a majority. As I will show, they can and do outvote professional judges on occasion. Again, this is in marked contrast to what I saw in Nicaragua and what Provine reports for the United States, where lawyer judges in mixed-bench jurisdictions have considerable influence over their nonlawyer colleagues.

Nonlawyer judges in the United States may be remnants of more democratic periods in U.S. law, but in both the United States and in Nicaragua the overriding rationale for use of nonlawyer judges today is economic (Provine, 1986; McDonald and Zatz, 1992). Fiscal constraints are certainly a consideration in Cuba as well, but my interview data and observations suggest that the primary basis for retaining lay judgeships in Cuba is ideological.

Unlike nonlawyer judges in the United States who are generally restricted to lower courts, in Cuba they adjudicate cases at all levels of the court hierarchy, from municipal courts through the Supreme Court. Accordingly, I was attentive to the roles and responsibilities of lay judges throughout the judicial system. I conducted semistructured interviews with ten lay judges and nine professional judges. Interviews lasted an average of two hours each and were recorded on tape. Less structured interviews with another ten current or past judges were conducted in offices and private homes. They were not recorded, but I took copious notes afterwards, and sometimes during our conversations. I also observed judges during court proceedings. The interviews and observations are supplemented with national data on the composition of lay judges provided by the Ministry of Justice's Office of Preparation, Supervision, and Evaluation of Juridical Personnel (*Dirección de Cuadros y Capacitación*).

ROLE OF LAY JUDGES

Lay judges are a central feature of the Cuban judicial system. As a lay judge in the Supreme Court told me, the mixed bench is "a democratic forum for applying justice" (November 27, 1989). Lay judges are integral to the decisionmaking process; each judge, whether lay or professional, holds an equal vote. Rand (1991:41–42) found that in the Soviet Union lay judges simply rubber-stamp the decisions of their professional colleagues, even when they formed a majority on the panels. As is elaborated below, such acquiescent behavior does not appear to be commonplace in Cuba.

In municipal courts and, since 1990, in most provincial court cases, lay judges are in the majority, with panels consisting of two lay judges and one professional judge who presides as president.[1] In serious provincial court cases (i.e., potential criminal sanctions of eight years' incarceration or more, and complex civil, administrative, labor, or family law cases) and in the Supreme Court, a panel of two lay judges and three professional judges hears each case. Each level in the judicial hierarchy has first-instance jurisdiction over a range of cases, and the provincial courts and Supreme Court also hear appeals of lower-court decisions.[2]

The national distribution of lay and professional judges is presented in Table 6.1. Overall, 95 percent of the nation's judges are nonlawyers. The percentage of professionals increases as we move up the court hierarchy, from two percent of the municipal court judges to 13 percent of the judges in the provincial courts and the Supreme Court.[3]

What accounts for the widespread and institutionalized use of lay judges at all levels of the Cuban judiciary? Neither a shortage of professionally trained jurists nor fiscal constraints are adequate explanations. There was a severe shortage of lawyers in the era of the popular tribunals (1963–1973), but that is no longer the case and does not explain the institutionalized presence of lay judges since the 1973 reorganization of the judiciary. As María Luisa Arteaga Abreu, a high official in the Ministry of Justice, told me, "The incorporation of lay judges has nothing to do with the scarcity of professional judges." Economics is a factor, but only insofar as it influences the number of

Table 6.1.
Distribution of Lay and Professional Judges
Elected January 1988.*

	Supreme Court	Provincial Court	Municipal Court	National Total
Lay Judges	192 (87%)	1,632 (87%)	9,824 (98%)	11,648 (95%)
Professional Judges	29 (13%)	237 (13%)	229 (2%)	605 (5%)
Total	221 (100%)	1,869 (100%)	10,053 (100%)	12,253 (100%)

*Source: *Dirección de Cuadros y Capacitación*, Ministry of Justice.

months served by individual lay judges each year.

The institution of lay judges in Cuba is based fundamentally on the *ideological orientation* of the Cuban leadership, that is, the perception that lay judges add something unique to legal decisionmaking that enhances its popular and socialist character. This "popular sense, the human sense" may be lacking if only those trained in the technical aspects of law try cases (Arteaga Abreu, April 19, 1989).

Although lay judges receive some basic training in legal guidelines and procedures, they are neither expected nor intended to approach cases in a legalistic manner. They do not replace professional judges as, for example, I found to be the case in war-torn Nicaragua (see McDonald and Zatz, 1992). Rather, the dual intents behind their use are (1) to bring a *non*legalistic, popular sense of justice and the reality of everyday life into the proceedings; and (2) to educate others in their social circles about legal processes, what constitutes a crime, and the kinds of civil and labor problems that come up in court.

As one lay judge thoughtfully described his role, he is "an intermediary, or bidirectional transmitter, between the judicial system and the people" (June 28, 1990). Lay judges bring a view of everyday people to judicial proceedings and an insider's perspective on legal decisionmaking back to their workplaces and neighborhoods. They are well aware of their role as conveyers of socialist legality. One lay judge defined a "good" lay judge as "a healthy journalist, or propagandist for legality." They describe themselves, and are depicted by professional judges, as bringing "something fresh, something humane" to judicial decisionmaking, and as "representatives of the people" (July 5, 1990). One judge told me that when he is deciding a case, he tries to imagine what his friends, coworkers, and family would think about what he is hearing, and to let that image influence his decisionmaking (June 28, 1990). Every lay judge interviewed mentioned that coworkers, neighbors, and family members come to them for legal advice, and they can report on how the judicial system operates based on personal knowledge.

WHO ARE THE LAY JUDGES?

Legal Requirements

To be elected a lay judge, the candidate cannot be a practicing jurist.[4] She or he must maintain a good work attitude, have an adequate educational level, enjoy a good public reputation, and evidence good moral conduct (Article 42(1), 1990 Law of the Tribunals). According to the three Supreme Court lay judges I interviewed, these requirements translate into someone with a ninth-grade education who behaves her/himself well, is a good and disciplined worker, and is a revolutionary (November 27, 1989). Being a revolutionary is defined largely in terms of participation in one's local Committee for the Defense of the Revolution (CDR) and militia, rather than by Communist Party membership.

The candidate must have reached the age of 30 to serve on the Supreme Court, 25 to serve in the provincial courts, or 21 to serve in the municipal courts (Article 42(2), 1990 Law of the Tribunals). Persons who are physically or mentally incapable of the judicial function, who have been convicted of a crime and have not yet completed their sanction or rehabilitation, or who have been convicted of a crime that would cause the general public to lose respect for them (or who are subject to criminal-justice processing for such a crime) are ineligible for election as judges (Article 43, 1990 Law of the Tribunals; interviews with Supreme Court lay judges, November 27, 1989).[5]

At the municipal and provincial levels, judges are selected from within their local communities. In the Supreme Court, Havana is overrepresented and the interior and eastern parts of the country are underrepresented. The three Supreme Court lay judges I interviewed were all from greater Havana and reported that most of their colleagues were also from the City of Havana province, although some were from Havana province (a largely rural area outside the city proper) or Pinar del Río, a province bordering Havana on the west (November 27, 1989).

Whether lay or professional, judges must serve in municipal court prior to election to the provincial court and at both the municipal and provincial levels before becoming eligible for election to the Supreme Court. As a result, the lay judges in the Supreme Court tend to have the most extensive judicial experience, ranging from eight to 15 years or more. In addition, some older lay judges participated in the popular tribunals of the 1960s and early 1970s or in the base tribunals of the mid-1970s (see Chapter Three for the historical development of the court structure since the Revolution).

Nomination and Selection of Lay Judges

The nomination process begins with the mass organizations. Of these, the labor union (CTC) is the most important. The majority of candidates are proposed from within the workplaces during general assemblies held for this purpose. The union leadership typically brings a slate of names, with additional candidates nominated at the meeting. In rural areas, the National Association of Small Agricultural Producers (ANAP) proposes its members in a similar fashion. The neighborhood Committees for the Defense of the Revolution (CDR) also hold open meetings to nominate candidates, most of whom are housewives or retired persons.[6] Two or three times the number of judges needed are proposed in these open meetings.

These nominations are forwarded to the provincial offices of the Ministry of Justice for review. The review process ensures that the candidates meet the formal requirements of the job and, in particular, that they do not have criminal histories that would disqualify them (Fernández Guerra, April 26, 1989). The Ministry of Justice then interviews candidates to verify their interest in serving in this capacity and to assess the likelihood that they would make good judges (Rivero, March 22, 1989).

Prior to 1976, the Communist Party (and its counterpart for young people, the UJC) also examined the background of nominees. Since 1976, the party has not had any formal say in the nomination or election processes. The party nucleus in the workplace does not come to the meeting with a list of names nor can it veto nominations. A party member may nominate someone or be in a position to review the candidate's file, but only as a coworker or official of the Ministry of Justice, not in the name of the Communist Party (Díaz Pinillo, November 17, 1989).

The names of all candidates approved by the provincial offices of the Ministry of Justice are then forwarded to the appropriate legislative body, where the election takes place. Municipal court judges are elected by the Municipal Assemblies of Popular Power, provincial court judges by the Provincial Assemblies, and Supreme Court judges by the National Assembly. Judges are responsible to the legislative body that elected them and may be recalled.

According to the lay judges I interviewed, who of course have a vested interest in the answer, those persons chosen to be lay judges are "meritorious citizens who sacrifice a lot for others." They "work hard, and do voluntary labor" (June 28, 1990; July 5, 1990). Some judges suggested that more careful attention be paid to less political selection criteria, such as the ability to form an opinion fairly quickly and not being so timid that they would censor themselves in the presence of professionally trained judges. A panel president in municipal court added that it is important that the people who are selected want to be judges (Dujarrez, July 5, 1990).

Composition

Table 6.2 presents selected characteristics of the 11,648 persons elected to lay judgeships in 1988. Cuba's lay judges are very heterogeneous. "There are men, women, young people, old people, laborers, nonlaborers, farmers, blue-collar workers, intellectuals, doctors" (Fernández Guerra, December 1, 1989).

In the aggregate, the youngest judges are in municipal courts, and the oldest in the Supreme Court. Forty-four percent of municipal court judges are age 30 or younger, compared to 25 percent of the provincial court judges and four percent of the Supreme Court judges. Conversely, 40 percent of the Supreme Court judges are over 50 years of age, as compared to 18 percent of the provincial court judges and ten percent of the municipal court judges. This difference can be explained by the increasing age requirements for the three levels of the court hierarchy and the requirement that higher court judges have prior experience in the lower courts.[7]

A provincial court judge told me that the Ministry of Justice has expressed a desire for more young people to serve as lay and professional judges (Rega, April 12, 1989). In the case of professional judges, this may be a reflection of improved legal education in recent years, and younger people are more likely to be recent law-school graduates. In the case of lay judges, it may be an effort to make judges reflective of larger population demographics, where the number of young people is quite large. Yet there is also a desire for some older, retired persons to serve as lay judges. This is a socially useful role for older people, and it allows the judiciary to draw on their extensive knowledge of human relations gained by virtue of having lived for a long time.

The educational achievements of lay judges are varied. This is particularly evident in the Supreme Court, which has the largest

Table 6.2.
Selected Characteristics of Lay Judges Elected January 1988.*

	Supreme Court (N=192) %	Provincial Courts (N=1,632) %	Municipal Courts (N=9,824) %	National Total (N=11,648) %
Age in Years:				
30 or less	4	25	44	41
31–40	14	34	28	29
41–50	42	23	18	19
51–60	28	12	7	8
61 or more	12	6	3	3
Total	100	100	100	100
Educational level completed:				
University	16	9	6	6
Pre-university & technical	37	53	54	54
9th Grade	42	35	38	38
6th Grade	5	3	2	2
Total	100	100	100	100
Party Membership:				
Communist Party (PCC)	79	40	28	30
Young Communists (UJC)	3	17	49	44
Not affiliated	18	43	23	26
Total	100	100	100	100
Sex:				
Male	69	55	49	51
Female	31	45	51	49
Total	100	100	100	100
Race:				
White	58	66	63	63
Black	30	17	18	18
Mulatto	14	17	19	19
Total	102(a)	100	100	100
Occupation:				
Laborer	28	23	25	24
Service	5	7	9	9
Technician	19	35	27	28
Administrator	20	20	23	23
Manager	1	8	5	5
Other	27	7	11	11
Total	100	100	100	100

* Source: *Dirección de Cuadros y Capacitación*, Ministry of Justice.

(a) Does not equal 100% due to rounding error.

percentage both of university graduates (16 percent) and of persons who did not finish high school (47 percent). The percentage of lay judges with a university degree decreases as we move down the court hierarchy, but most have a high-school degree (53 percent at the Supreme Court where judges tend to be older, 62 percent at the provincial court, and 60 percent in the municipal court). While by law judges must have at least a ninth-grade education, this requirement has been waived for those few older judges who began serving as lay judges before this condition was added and for some retired persons with extensive experience in the earlier popular tribunals (Fernández Guerra, December 1, 1989).

Most lay judges belong to the Cuban Communist Party (PPC) or the Young Communists (UJC), with a national average of 74 percent (82 percent in the Supreme Court; 57 percent in provincial courts, 77 percent in municipal courts). These are generally not persons in leadership positions within the party since, like the workplace managers discussed below, it is difficult to replace them. The percentage of Cuban judges who are party members is noticably lower than in many other socialist countries. For example, Ginsburgs (1985:300) states that in the Soviet Union all judges were party members, and in Yugoslavia 85 percent of the professional judges in 1979–80 were party members (Cohen, 1985:336). The percentage in East Germany was closest to Cuba, with 70 to 75 percent of the East German judges belonging to the party (Meador, 1986:136, cited in Markovits, 1989:424).

Two points are worth noting here. First, it is the most diligent and most respected workers who are invited to join the party, and these same characteristics are desirable in selecting judges. Second, some judicial autonomy from the Communist Party is evidenced by the 26 percent of lay judges nationally, and especially the 43 percent at the provincial level, who are *not* affiliated with the party. Indeed, combining PCC and UJC members overrepresents party membership, since some members of the UJC are not admitted into the PCC when they turn 30 or choose not to join it.

Among lay judges, men hold a slight majority nationally (51 percent). The gender difference is most pronounced in the Supreme Court, where 69 percent of the lay judges are male. In the more numerous municipal courts there are slightly more women than men (51 percent female). Overall, women have a larger presence in civil and labor judicial panels than in criminal panels.

Most judges are racially classified as white. Contrary to what one might expect, the white majority is *smallest* in the Supreme Court, where 30 percent of the lay judges are black and 14 percent are mulatto. The racial composition of the judicial panels differs geographically, depending on the demographic characteristics of each province. The need for racial and gender diversity and representativeness is a factor in the Ministry of Justice's recommendations of which nominees should be placed on the final electoral slate submitted to the legislative bodies, although there are no set quotas (Fernández, April 26, 1989; December 1, 1989). Indeed, I was surprised to learn that the Ministry of Justice kept records of the racial composition of the judiciary since these demographic statistics are not recorded in other spheres, including the population census.

The occupational composition of the lay judges is diverse. Overall, laborers and technicians predominate. In comparison to the national occupational distribution (see Appendix J), technicians and administrators are overrepresented as lay judges, and persons with service jobs are substantially underrepresented. Nationally, about ten percent of the lay judges are members of farm cooperatives. Farmers can be found throughout the occupational categories. For example, a technician working on a farm cooperative would be included in the category "technician." Managers are relatively rare because it is difficult to temporarily replace them in the work force. Again reflecting the age differentials across the courts, many Supreme Court lay judges are retired, accounting in large part for the many Supreme Court judges classified occupationally as "other" (Fernández, December 1, 1989).

Who Wants to Be a Lay Judge?

One of my more interesting findings was the variety of reasons given by lay judges for seeking or accepting their nominations. They ranged from personal goals to a fascination with judicial proceedings to a belief that this was an important public service.

One of the judges I interviewed, a young man in his early twenties, had begun his first term of office a month prior to our conversation. He was a judge in a municipal court just east of Havana and held a regular job as an engineer in a truck factory. When I asked him why he wanted to be a lay judge he smiled, looking a bit sheepish, and confessed, "I always wanted to be a lawyer, but I didn't do well enough in high school to get into law school." He went on to say that he hopes to become a lay judge in a provincial court, and eventually in the Supreme Court (June 28, 1990). For him, the lay judgeship is a means of reaching his personal goal of becoming a legal expert, without having to complete law school.

A municipal court judge in his fifties who worked as a planner in the Ministry of Transportation exemplifies the public-service dimension of the job. He reported that his family is very proud that he is a judge. Based on his three-year experience as a lay judge, he can tell youths "what happens to bad kids." He went on to note that because much of his judicial work involves labor disputes (see Chapter Seven), his coworkers turn to him for legal advice when they have problems in the workplace (July 5, 1990).

TRAINING

The Ministry of Justice is responsible for the training of lay judges and the advanced training of professional judges. This task was greatly facilitated by the Ministry's acquisition of a video camera in 1987. One of the first uses of the camera was home production of an instructional video for lay judges, copies of which were distributed throughout the country.[8] Reminiscent of the old U.S. television show "Candid Camera," it includes interviews with pedestrians walking past the busy intersection outside the Ministry of Justice in downtown Havana, asking if they know what a lay judge is. It also includes an interview with the President of the Supreme Court, José Raúl Amaro Salup, in which Amaro Salup stresses that the goal is *not* to turn lay judges into professionals, but simply to acquaint them with legal terminology. Amaro Salup also affirms in the videotaped interview that lay judges can supervise neighbors and coworkers on probation and help resolve conflicts in their workplaces during the 11 months each year when they are not in court.

The Ministry of Justice's Office of Preparation, Supervision, and Evaluation of Juridical Personnel (*Dirección de Cuadros y Capacitación*) also compiles manuals about criminal and civil law for lay judges. These are organized thematically, and typically include speeches by top officials in the juridical arena (e.g., the Minister and Vice-Minister of Justice, the Minister of the Interior, and the Attorney General). The speeches are discussed, in conjunction with major laws and sometimes a videotaped lecture by a renowned Cuban or foreign jurist, in five weekly seminars of two hours each. The seminars are led by professional judges, who then evaluate the quality of each lay judge's participation and assign grades based on responses to two or three questions. The questions do not have correct answers; evaluation is based on the judge's ability to discuss and analyze the case and to express a reasoned opinion (Ministry of Justice, Dirección de Cuadros y Capacitación, 1987; Fernández Guerra, April 26, 1989).

Most lay judges confirmed that they were trained in this manner. There are, however, some lay judges who did not participate in this training. Persons excused from all or part of the training typically have substantial responsibilities in their workplaces, making it difficult for them to attend the preparatory sessions. They also include some of the best educated of the lay judges, since as one lay judge told me, "You cannot compare an engineer and a factory worker."

The training of lay judges differs from that of professional judges for two reasons. First, like jurors in the United States, they are voluntary participants in judicial activities. Most work full time and simply cannot be available for extensive training sessions. Second, extensive legal instruction of lay judges would be contrary to the ideological rationale for having them in the first place, which is:

> to bring the social lens, the popular lens, the critique of the people to the court. If we technify the lay judge, then we have incorporated one more professional judge who brings to the analysis of the event a technical juridical focus, when what we need is for her or him to analyze it with a popular lens, with the sentiment of the people, of the worker, of the housewife, the mother, the son, the father, the brother (Fernández Guerra, April 26, 1989).

For these reasons, the training of lay judges is limited to teaching them the rudiments of the law, especially procedural law, and basic juridical terms that defense attorneys and prosecutors will use in presenting their cases.

Special Training of Professional Judges

The Ministry of Justice also trains professional judges. Recall from Chapter Four that in 1982 the Politburo called for a critical analysis of the preparation of jurists, and in 1983 and 1984 for greater attention to their training and continuing legal education. In response, programs of postgraduate legal education have been developed under the joint auspices of the Ministry of Justice, the nation's law schools, and the National Union of Cuban Jurists. These include continuing education for judges, with an emphasis on instructing judges and other jurists about major changes in civil, criminal, and housing laws passed in the 1980s. They also include seminars with foreign scholars, experts in the area of mental illness, and other technical aspects of legal decisionmaking.

These postgraduate seminars are generally held on working Saturdays.[9] When they are held during the week, typically only one judge from a panel attends and she or he later informs the other judges of what was covered in the seminar (Rega, April 12, 1989). The only professional judges exempted from this advanced training are those who are also law professors. As one professor/judge told me, "I teach criminal law. I have to know about anything new in the area; that is my responsibility. It does not make sense for me to take a course in what I teach" (Rega, April 12, 1989).

Professional judges are evaluated periodically by the Ministry of Justice's Office of Preparation, Supervision and Evaluation of Juridical Personnel. Individualized plans for retooling are then developed wherever there is evidence of deficiencies (Fernández Guerra, April 26, 1989). The most serious problems have arisen with judges who graduated from law school when there were shortages of books and of well-trained professors, especially if they attended regional law schools (see Chapter Four for a more detailed assessment of legal education).

INTERACTIONS BETWEEN LAY AND PROFESSIONAL JUDGES

Knowing who becomes a lay judge and how they are trained is informative, but to make sense of the institution of lay judges, we need to know the nature of their interactions with their professional colleagues. The discussion which follows elaborates these interactions, from the perspectives of both lay and professional judges.

From the Perspective of Lay Judges

Lay judges describe their relations with professional judges in such terms as "cooperative," "very good," and "friendly." I wondered at the start of my research if they would be reticent to speak up and just be a popular "rubber stamp" on decisions made by professionals. Cowed by the greater legal training of professional judges, they might be reluctant to participate fully in decisionmaking. Accordingly, I made it a point to interview lay judges when professional judges were not present. Some of these interviews took place in the courts, others in my home.

I found a basis for my concern in a few cases, but I was more frequently chastised by lay judges for assuming that they could be intimidated by their legally trained colleagues. They reminded me that persons nominated by their coworkers and neighbors to be judges tend to be known for speaking up on behalf of their beliefs. Indeed, they stressed that a good lay judge cannot be pressured by professional judges and presents her or his opinions in such a way that they will be taken seriously by colleagues. If the lay judge is not very assertive, they acknowledged, professionally trained peers may succeed in moving cases in the direction they desire.

Lay judges tend to respect the expertise of professional judges but are also willing to argue with them. For example, a municipal court judge told me that he does not like the ambiguous law against "dangerous" activities and has taken a stance against its application, contrary to the opinion of the professional judge who presides over his panel. Another municipal court lay judge reported that the professional judge with whom she works is dedicated and knowledgeable about law. She said that the professionals generally prevail in complex cases with important legal ramifications, but in minor cases the lay and professional judges are equal, and lay judges may dominate the discussion and vote. According to lay judges, while agreements can usually be reached without much pressure, where there is pressure its source is as likely to be a lay judge as a professional.[10]

Lay judges describe themselves as responsible first to themselves and to their own consciences, and second to their electorate. Although I probed for it so explicitly that I sometimes feared I was becoming obnoxious, none of the lay judges described themselves as in any way responsible to their professional colleagues.

As I discuss below, professional judges often ask lay judges to begin the panel discussions. Based on their experience at all levels of the court hierarchy, Supreme Court lay judges added that when lay judges are not asked to speak first some will wait until the professional judge(s) finish before speaking, while others will jump in and immediately voice their opinions.

From the Perspective of Professional Judges

Having heard from the President of a provincial criminal court that perhaps the historical need for lay judges in the provincial courts and Supreme Court had passed, I asked lay and professional judges, as well as Ministry of Justice officials, whether they saw a continuing need for lay judges. The response was overwhelmingly and emphatically affirmative.

Professional judges tend to be quite respectful of the knowledge that lay judges bring to the court. As one professional judge recounted,

> Professional judges do not have the vision of a worker, a doctor, et cetera. They shop in the same places, but don't know of the problems in the factories, of problems raised in the workers' assemblies. Lay judges have this viewpoint and can bring it to the professional judges. They also bring a

freshness to the trial since they serve only for a month [at a time]. They also do preventive work in the factories and other workplaces; they are transmitters, divulgers, of all these issues. They give lectures in their workplaces, people ask them legal questions, and they become legal activists in their workplaces.

Another professional judge added that lay judges bring valuable technical knowledge resulting from their work experiences. For instance, a butcher knows how clients can be cheated if meat is cut a certain way, or if salt water is added to butter to make it heavier, because he or she has seen this happen. Similarly, a store manager serving as a lay judge knows more about shoplifting than a lawyer would, because awareness of shoplifting techniques is necessary for her or his regular job. Engineer, construction worker, teacher, doctor, farmer, demographer, cook, secretary . . . each offers a different perspective and knowledge base. Furthermore, some lay judges may understand the street language used by defendants better than jurists would. Thus, in addition to bringing a popular sentiment to the case, lay judges often contribute specialized insights that professional judges probably will not have (Rega, April 12, 1989).

Nevertheless, the differential in technical juridical knowledge can create a power imbalance. This concern was raised far more often by professional judges than by their lay colleagues. In an effort to lessen any intimidation, many professional judges ask the lay judges to speak first. One judge thought asking lay judges to express their views first was a national policy. He reported that the Ministry of Justice and the Supreme Court have urged all panel presidents to take this approach. Once the lay judges have spoken, he, as president, responds to their analyses of the case (Hernández Sosa, November 24, 1989). Another judge recalled that the president will turn to the lay judges and say, "OK, what do you think? What do you believe? What has been proven? What has not been proven? Was it this way or wasn't it?"

Another professional judge pointed out that every judge, whether lay or professional, must explain her or his position, drawing on the evidence available to the entire panel. Individual judges may disagree as to which witness they find more credible, but he has not seen evidence of one judge being unduly influenced by another. Some professionals acknowledged that they prefer to work with younger lay judges, especially in comparison with elderly, retired persons. The general sense expressed was that young people are more likely to stand up for their views in the face of opposition. Also, professional and lay judges repeatedly told me that the best lay judges are well educated (which correlates inversely with age) and highly motivated.

The professional judges concurred that a consensus can usually be reached. They relished telling stories of situations in which their votes were overruled by the lay judges who form a majority in municipal court and in most provincial court panels since 1990. They also generally agreed that while lay judges speak freely in case deliberations, they tend to defer to the professional judges when it comes to legal concepts, particularly when hearing appeals or rulings likely to be subject to appeal.

Professional judges observed that their relations with lay judges are closest in municipal court. Relations are not as tight in the provincial courts and the Supreme Court because of the larger number of persons interacting on the panels. Yet a professional judge in a provincial court commented that professional and lay judges get to know one another well, and they stay in contact in the months when the lay judge is not working at the court. During their off months, lay judges will stop by the courtroom when in the vicinity to say hello, and they often must come to court to sign papers filed after a case they heard was completed. These ongoing interactions help maintain smooth working relations.

One of my sources was President of a regional criminal court from 1975 to 1978, President of an entire municipal court from 1978 to 1983, and provincial court judge since 1987 (serving in this capacity one year out of five, and as a law professor the other four years of his judicial mandate). He concurred with the other professional judges in viewing lay judges as especially important in municipal court, since they are likely to know the other inhabitants of the municipality. As he said, "the lay [judge] was born with them, went to school with them" (Díaz Pinillo, May 9, 1989). Another professional judge, who also has experience as President of a provincial criminal court, commented that the institution of lay judges "has an incredible force" in municipal courts (Rivero, March 22, 1989).

At the provincial courts and the Supreme Court, there is some concern that professional judges may become so embroiled in the intricacies of judicial procedure and legal technicalities that they forget the everyday concerns of the populace. Lay judges help mitigate this risk. For example, robberies are acts that everyone understands. Specialized legal education is not necessary to be able to say, "He couldn't have stolen all of those things himself because some of them are too big for one person to move. He must have been working with someone else." Even in the Supreme Court, where much of the work is very technical, "there is always a part of the process that is not necessarily technical . . . . Also, death penalty cases must be retried in the Supreme Court, and the participation of the lay judge is very evident in such cases" (Díaz Pinillo, May 9, 1989).

Lay judges, professional judges, and Ministry of Justice officials all noted that lay and professional judges sometimes cast differing votes. There does not appear to be a consistent pattern in who is more lenient; sometimes lay judges are harsher than their professional colleagues, and sometimes more lenient. An important point brought to my attention by a Ministry of Justice official is that the minority position is recorded and is a factor that is taken into account by higher courts when cases are appealed.

COURT PROCEEDINGS

In this section, I present a brief overview of provincial criminal court proceedings in the late 1980s and early 1990s. The description fits most provincial and municipal courts, except that in municipal court cases the defense attorney and prosecutor are not required to participate. Consistent with my discussion of lawmaking in Chapter Three, I emphasize criminal courts.

Appearance of the Court and Courtroom Actors

The physical structure of the courtroom is marked by some formality. The judges sit on a raised podium behind a long table, with the Cuban flag to one side. The president of the panel sits in the middle, flanked by the other judges. The prosecutor and defense attorney(s) sit behind desks on opposite sides of the room, at right angles to the judges. The court recorder's desk is in the center of the room, facing the judges. The defendant sits alone on a bench facing the judges. Behind the defendant sit witnesses and observers, on rows of wooden benches.

As mandated by Article 59 of the 1990 Law of the Courts and earlier law, all judges, prosecutor, and attorneys wear judicial robes. Male judges, prosecutors, and attorneys are required to wear shirts with closed collars and ties. The male dress code is somewhat of a joke, however, since the top few buttons on shirts are typically open due to the sweltering heat. Ties seem to have permanent homes in the men's briefcases, with the same loosely knotted tie worn whenever they have a trial, whether it matches or clashes with the shirt. Female judicial actors wear nice but comfortable outfits. The defendant, victim, other witnesses, and court recorder all dress casually.

The Defense Attorney

Criminal defense attorneys, civil trial attorneys, and notaries work in *bufetes colectivos* (law collectives) located in each municipality. The law collectives provide services for persons with cases in municipal and provincial courts. They also may handle Supreme Court cases, but one *bufete* in Havana specializes in such cases and is reputed to have the best attorneys in the country on its staff. The law collectives are autonomous entities organized administratively under an elected National Directorate and, within each *bufete,* under a director (Decree-Law 81, June 8, 1984).

Clients pay nationally set fees to the *bufete,* rather than to the individual lawyer. The fees increase with the complexity of the case, the level of the court hierarchy, and for appeals. The average person can readily afford these charges, but if a criminal defendant cannot afford them, the case is handled for free by a public defender. Lawyers receive a flat salary from the collectives, plus a percentage of the fee.

Clients can request a particular attorney, but if that attorney is too busy, the director of the *bufete* will appoint a substitute. If the substitute is not acceptable to clients, they may request someone else. Quite often, a family member will hire a lawyer as soon as a person is arrested. Even though the lawyer cannot officially initiate work on the case for a period that may extend to ten days, in reality she or he begins some of the work right away, including going to jail to meet with defendants who were not released on their own recognizance or on bail (see Chapter Three for discussion of proposed changes allowing the attorney to enter the case at a much earlier date).

Criminal defense attorneys work for their clients, not for the state. Yet unlike their colleagues in the United States, they are explicitly responsible to society as a whole and to seeking truth, even above the defense of their clients. In the Constitutive Congress of the National Organization of *Bufetes Colectivos* (ONBC) in 1974, Blas Roca Calderío stated:

> It is clear that the lawyer has to defend, in the civil process, the interests of the party s/he represents, and in criminal cases, the accused with whose defense s/he is charged . . . [Criminal defense attorneys must be] loyal to the defendant, and loyal, at the same time, to the society (quoted in Lagunilla Martínez and Yanes Sosa, 1989:78–79).[11]

The potential for contradictory loyalties to the defendant and to the society was recognized at the General Assembly of the ONBC in June of 1985, when Politburo member José Ramón Machado Ventura said:

> In exercising his/her defense, the lawyer has to demand that the process incorporate all of the elements, propose whatever evidence would favor the interests of the defendant, but above all help reveal the truth and clarify the facts. The success of his or her function is not in winning absolution, but

in establishing the truth . . . . (quoted in Lagunilla Martínez and Yanes Sosa, 1989:79).[12]

This clear statement of responsibility to society as well as to one's client is a distinguishing feature of socialist legality. Yet socialist societies differ in the extent to which court proceedings favor the prosecution or defense. Defense attorneys in the largest *bufete colectivo* in Cuba gain acquittals in 22 to 31 percent of their cases, depending on the type of crime charged (Michalowski, 1989). In contrast, Robert Rand reports a sharp accusatorial bias in the Soviet Union, lessening somewhat under Gorbachev (1991). The major organizational factor expected to alter this bias was creation of the Soviet equivalent of the Cuban ONBC in the late 1980s, when "for the first time in Soviet history there is a sanctioned group of individuals whose political agenda reflects the interests of the accused and not those of the prosecution" (Rand, 1991:108–109). In this endeavor the Soviets were far behind the Cubans, whose ONBC was established in 1974.

The Proceedings

Criminal court begins with the court reporter reading the case number, charge, and names of parties to the case. The president of the judicial panel, rather than the defense attorney or prosecutor, calls witnesses and directs questioning. Other judges can pose questions during the trial, but they generally pass their queries to the president, rather than voicing them themselves. A professional judge explained this deferential behavior as a means of maintaining the president's authority and control over the courtroom, including the opposing parties or defendant, witnesses, attorneys, and prosecutor. The defendant is typically called for questioning first, followed by witnesses. The victim does not usually speak; more frequently, the prosecutor speaks for him or her.

The presiding judge begins by asking the defendant if he or she wishes to speak. Defendants and witnesses come forward to stand facing the judges. They tell their stories, sometimes in very somber tones, sometimes in a very animated manner that has observers, and on occasion even the judges, laughing. Presentations by defense attorneys and prosecutors also differ in style. I have observed calm, oratorical, and very theatrical opening and closing arguments. The contrast to the somber trials in the U.S. is striking. In the United States such animated behavior by witnesses and court officials, as well as the lengthy stories told without interruption, would appear inappropriately informal. While this may be a characteristic of informalism, it also reflects a difference in cultural norms, as the Cubans are far more expressive than the staid North Americans.

Once all of the evidence has been presented, judges have asked all of their questions, and closing arguments have been made, the judges retire to chambers to deliberate privately. At this point all judges are free to speak. The president may lead the discussion, or she or he may ask lay judges to present their views first. They analyze the evidence presented before them, including the extent to which witnesses corroborated one another's stories and any physical evidence to determine whether a crime has indeed occurred and if the person charged is culpable. This is decided by majority vote, although generally a consensus is reached.

I have, however, observed a trial in which the judges went into chambers to deliberate, returning soon after with the conclusion that the police did not gather sufficient information in their investigation, and thus, they voted to continue the case. That particular case involved a traffic accident in which logs fell off a truck, seriously injuring a pedestrian. The truck driver was accused of being drunk, which made the incident a crime rather than an accident. The defense argued that he had consumed two beers at lunch but was not drunk. The judges called for the police to conduct a more complete investigation by asking neighbors and coworkers how the man typically drove and how he drove when he was drunk. Without such information, they did not think they could reach a fair decision. When I recounted this incident to lay and professional judges, they said that while this situation was not unique, they generally had sufficient information at the time of the trial to reach a verdict.

If the judges decide that the defendant is guilty, they look at the circumstances of the offense and the offender (e.g., age, if there are any priors, if the person appears amenable to rehabilitation) and discuss the appropriate sanction from within the range mandated by law. Often the sentence is determined at the same time guilt or innocence is adjudicated, but the judges may delay sentencing until additional information is available.

CONCLUSIONS

Popular participation is a cornerstone of socialist legality in Cuba. It is most visible in the judicial system, where the use of lay judges has been institutionalized. Lay judges describe themselves as "bidirectional transmitters," bringing the view of the people into judicial decisionmaking and knowledge of legal procedure and juridical norms back to the workplaces and neighborhoods that nominated them.

Popular and informal justice are often confused in the literature. Judicial procedure in Cuba is in some ways less formal than its counterpart in the United States, but decisionmaking is still bounded by statute. The popular component enters into determinations of guilt or innocence and the appropriate sanction from within a legislated range. From the perspective of Cuban legal scholars, and particularly in contrast to the earlier period of popular tribunals when sanctions were less restricted, this means that the contemporary legal order is *not* informal.

The Cuban legal order is not fully formal, either. Incorporation of lay judges into judicial panels is central to the prevailing ideology in Cuba. They bring a popular, democratic element into decisionmaking, reminiscent of more democratic periods in U.S. legal history (see Provine, 1986). They do not and are not intended to substitute for legally trained professionals; instead, they supplement professional jurists to provide a more encompassing perspective on decisionmaking. This intermingling of professional and lay perspectives in case adjudication supports my contention that there is a mix of formalism and informalism in the Cuban legal order. The Cuban case also contributes more generally to a broader understanding of the role lay judges play in the formation of legality.

Some lay judges are subservient to their legally trained colleagues, others are not. Both lay and professional judges agree that the best lay judges are willing to state and defend their opinions without fear of disagreeing with the professional judges. They view themselves as having a valid role in the process, with views worthy of being considered.

As I suggested in Chapter Three, Cuban legal procedure is becoming increasingly adversarial. Cuba appears to be moving away from many of its Latin American neighbors, which still follow the more inquisitorial Spanish system. Yet this trend cannot simply be explained by the influence of other socialist nations since, in comparison with Rand's (1991) depiction of the prosecutorial bias in the Soviet system, the Cuban judicial system appears far more adversarial. Cuban defense attorneys work for and are paid by the client, not the state.

In comparison with the U.S. legal system, however, the Cuban system is much less adversarial. Beyond the Spanish influence, this can be explained by the Cuban defense attorney's responsibilities to the society as a whole, in addition to their clients. This characteristic of Cuban-style socialist legality means that they must seek the truth in every case. This is in sharp contrast to the individualistic, bourgeois legality in the United States in which lawyers, as officers of the court, cannot lie but are not otherwise constrained to seeking the truth.

The system of lay judges which has been expanded and institution-alized in Cuba is based on an ideological commitment to popular participation. During the era of the popular tribunals, the creation of lay judgeships rested on economic necessity, a shortage of lawyers, and ideology. Today, however, no other consideration is as important as ideology in explaining the strength and persistence of popular partici-pation in judicial decisionmaking.

CHAPTER 7

DISPUTE RESOLUTION
IN THE WORKPLACE

In the preceding chapter we saw the centrality of lay judges to the Cuban legal order. All court cases in Cuba are adjudicated by mixed panels of lay and professional judges. Lay judges are not intended to replace legal professionals, as sometimes happens when there is a shortage of trained jurists or when jurists do not want to be judges because of the low pay or risk of injury during war (cf. McDonald and Zatz, 1992). Nor do they clamor for advanced technical training in law as a means of establishing their credentials (cf. Provine, 1986). Their purpose is to supplement the technical skills professionals possess with a humanistic, popular perspective. They also bring knowledge of the legal system back to their families, neighbors, and coworkers. Through their actions in the courtroom and their daily interactions with professional judges, lay judges are integrally involved in the ideological and practical production and reproduction of legality.

We now turn in this chapter to the only forum in which decisions with legal force are made *solely* by lay people. Labor councils (*consejos del trabajo*) constitute a nonjudicial forum for resolving disputes between workers and management. As we have heard Cuban legal scholars, policy makers, and judges say throughout this analysis, "The closer to the base, the greater the justice." Is there greater justice in the workplace councils than in the courts? As the evidence presented in this chapter indicates, the answer depends on the power labor councils have to adjudicate different types of grievances, the extent to which their decisions are respected by the workplace management, and the composition of the councils. As we will see, these factors have varied across different historical moments, leading to changes in the relative mix of formalism and informalism in the application of labor law.

I use a combination of interview, documentary, and court data to better understand (1) the historical development, operation, and composition (i.e., whether they are staffed solely by workers or include management) of the *consejos;* (2) appeals to the courts; and (3) changes

over time in whether or not the *consejos* hear cases involving disciplinary actions.

Robert Hayden (1986:231) has characterized worker and other
social courts as:

1. staffed by nonprofessional judges who serve only part time;
2. using procedures meant to be informal and nonlegalistic, with
   lawyers often not permitted to attend proceedings;
3. holding hearings within the relevant social context (e.g., factory,
   commune, apartment block);
4. having the aim of educating offenders and the community and
   of correcting errant behavior rather than punishing offenders;
   and
5. use of social pressure for sanctioning (e.g., mandated apologies
   to victims, public or private censures and reprimands, small
   fines, assignments to socially useful labor, and, as an ultimate
   sanction, eviction from housing or dismissal from employment).

As we shall see, many but not all of these characteristics can be found
in the Cuban labor councils.

The *consejos* have jurisdiction only over work-related disputes.
They hear allegations of violations of workers' rights and, in some
historical moments, of workers' complaints concerning disciplinary
actions by management. The findings of the *consejos* are not legally
binding and are often ignored by administrators. In that case, the only
recourse available to dissatisfied workers is appeal to the formal court
system. Sometimes, though, administrators do concede to decisions
reached by the *consejos,* and workers are spared the difficulties
inherent in bringing their complaints to judicial authorities who are
unfamiliar with the disputants and the social context within which the
conflict arose.

At every level, from the workplace to the Supreme Court, parties to
labor cases may represent themselves or may be represented by a
coworker, union official, or family member. They also may be represented by a lawyer in court if they so desire (del Junco Allayón, May
22, 1991; Castro Cabrera, May 22, 1991; Article 697 of the 1977
Law of Civil, Administrative, and Labor Procedure).

The primary goal of the *consejos* is to facilitate conciliation between
the parties to the dispute (Laou, April 21, 1989). Stated somewhat
differently:

> [T]he Councils came to represent the last opportunity to
> resolve a labor-management dispute before the matter
> spilled over into the formal legal arena. As a result,
> according to one informant, Council members tried very

hard to get both parties in a dispute to agree to their decision (Fuller, 1987:143).

Are the *consejos* and the ideology underlying them helpful to workers? Do they promote the rights of workers? These are difficult questions. Vacillations in the composition, authority, and jurisdiction of labor councils reflect a series of contradictions, conflicts, and dilemmas. The most marked contradiction is between the protection of workers' rights and the assurance of productivity in a society described in its Constitution as composed of workers, peasants, and other manual and intellectual laborers (Article 1, *Constitución de la República de Cuba,* 1976; see also García Hernández, 1989). The fundamental contradiction in capitalist societies between workers and owners as sellers and buyers of labor power has long been recognized. The contradiction between workers' rights and productivity in a socialist society such as Cuba is similar, in that any profit depends on workers not receiving full payment for the value of their labor. Yet it is also different, because the factories and other workplaces are owned by the state, and the state is defined constitutionally as operating for the benefit of the workers.

The ideological contradiction between the desire for consensually driven, accessible, and *informal* avenues for redressing grievances on the one hand, and the desire for rights and guarantees *formally* backed by the authority of the state on the other, is another basis for the historical vacillation evidenced in Cuban labor law. The relatively informal *consejos* can be viewed from one perspective as equalizing the power of labor and management. Yet from another perspective, this power is not equalized, because management can simply ignore the *consejo*'s rulings and because for much of their history the *consejos* have not held jurisdiction over disciplinary actions by management.

In April 1992, first-instance authority to resolve disputes over disciplinary actions was returned to the workplace. At the same time, a representative of the workplace management was added to the labor councils, and most decisions concerning worker discipline can no longer be appealed to the courts. Do these changes represent a net gain or loss for Cuban workers? How does it alter the mix of formalism and informalism in labor law? As this chapter demonstrates, Cuban labor relations are complex and fluid.

HISTORY OF THE *CONSEJOS* PRIOR TO 1977

Between 1959 and 1965, four separate pieces of legislation addressed conflict resolution in the workplace. The 1962 Law of the Administration of Labor Justice had the greatest longevity, lasting until 1965. It established grievance commissions (*comisiones de reclamación*) in the workplaces. These commissions were composed of a worker delegate, a management delegate, and a chair representing the Ministry of Labor. They held jurisdiction over alleged violations of some workers' rights, including contested dismissals and sanctions for absenteeism. They could not, however, mediate conflicts surrounding hiring, promotion, and placement decisions; nor could they review all wage disputes. Commission decisions were made by majority vote, with appeals to five-person boards representing the Cuban Labor Confederation (CTC), management, and the Ministry of Labor (Fuller, 1987).

In 1965, labor councils (*consejos del trabajo*) were established and the grievance commissions disbanded. Unlike the grievance commissions, in which workers controlled only one of three votes, the *consejos* were staffed by five workers elected by their peers. *Consejo* members served three-year terms, although many were re-elected, testifying both to appreciation of their contributions as judges and to the general unwillingness of the work force to serve on the *consejos* because they were so time consuming. Continuing the tradition established in 1962, until 1980 the *consejos* heard conflicts over disciplinary actions as well as allegations that workers' rights were violated. In response to complaints that *consejo* members were not adequately versed in labor law, beginning in the early 1970s they received some legal training at a school run by the Ministry of Labor (Fuller, 1987).

Appeals of *consejo* decisions could be brought to Regional Appeal Councils or to the National Review Council. Regional councils were staffed by representatives of the Ministry of Labor, management, and the union (the CTC). The National Review Council consisted of two members each from the Ministry of Labor and management, and one union representative. Thus, at both appellate levels workers held only a minority vote (Laou, April 21, 1989, November 10, 1989). Moreover, broad powers were retained by the Ministry of Labor, which could dismiss any member of a *consejo*, overturn any *consejo* decision, and take responsibility for cases at any point, issuing nonappealable verdicts (Fuller, 1987:141).

CHANGES IN 1977 AND 1980

Oversight of the *consejos* by the Ministry of Labor ended in 1977 with passage of Law No. 7, the Law of Administrative, Civil and Labor Procedure, and Law No. 8, the Law of the Organization and

Functioning of the *Consejos del Trabajo*. Oversight passed to the union (CTC), and appeals moved to the courts. With some modifications, these laws continue to govern workplace disputes.

Composition of the Consejos

Law No. 8 established *consejos* in every work site with 25 or more workers. Smaller workplaces are integrated into *consejos* in larger work sites nearby, with a coworker from the workplace where the conflict arose representing the disputant (Laou, April 21, 1989). The composition of the *consejos* was not altered with passage of Law No. 8. Consejo members and alternates are elected by majority vote from within the workplace and are trained by the CTC. Qualifications for serving on the *consejos* include a good work record (i.e., good attitude and work discipline); adequate educational level to fulfill *consejo* functions; good moral conduct; never having been sanctioned for infractions of labor discipline or being clearly rehabilitated if previously sanctioned; and active incorporation into the Revolution, usually defined as involvement with one's neighborhood Committee for the Defense of the Revolution (Fuller, 1987:142; Laou, April 21, 1989; Article 8 of Law No. 8, 1977).

Administrators and union officials are prohibited from serving on the *consejos*. According to Miriam Laou, a law professor specializing in labor law, this prohibition was designed to avoid compromising situations in which *consejo* members might have conflicting loyalties and, as a result, favor management or union interests (April 21, 1989). Linda Fuller (1987) offers an additional, historically based rationale for excluding union officials—the close identification of prerevolutionary unions with the Batista government. Given the continued close ties between the union leadership and both the Castro government and the workplace administration in the 1960s, it is reasonable to speculate that some lingering distrust on the part of workers might have remained well into the 1970s.

Types of Cases and Caseloads

Throughout the 1970s, discipline cases fell under the jurisdiction of the *consejos*. About 85 percent of the cases brought to the *consejos* in the 1970s involved disciplinary actions (Fuller, 1987). The vast majority of these concerned sanctions for absenteeism without justification or for tardiness. They also included sanctions for failure to meet work quotas or time schedules, insubordination or disobedience of management orders, disrespect or abuse of superiors or fellow workers, physical offenses, fraud, robbery, worker violations of health and safety legislation, appropriation of work-center property for personal use, damaging or wasting work-center equipment, property or materials, and negligence, carelessness or mistreatment in production or service delivery (Fuller, 1987:140–141, 144). Typical sanctions in discipline cases were temporary transfers to lower-paying jobs and postponement of vacations, but a range of more severe sanctions could be applied, including firing, which the *consejos* upheld in cases of repeated and serious violations (Fuller, 1987:144).

The remaining 15 percent of the *consejos'* caseloads during the 1970s involved alleged violations of workers' rights. These included disputes over wage levels, working conditions, transfers, demotions and failures to promote, temporary or permanent layoffs, scheduling of vacations, and workers' rights to disability, retirement, and death pensions (Fuller, 1987:141).[1] Of these, salary disputes were the most frequent, followed by complaints concerning transfers from one work site to another. Salary determinations in Cuba are based on very detailed job classifications. They are also affected by regulations governing difficult or unsafe working conditions, illnesses and accidents, interruptions in production, and what is called "historical wages" for persons who have continued to hold certain jobs (e.g., airplane pilot) from a time, generally prior to the Revolution, when wages for that job were above the current level. Thus, salary decisions are quite complex and "fairness" in a particular case may be open to multiple interpretations.

While the *consejos* address conflicts between workers as well as between workers and administrators, the former are interpreted as being between the administration and one of the workers, since an administrator favored one employee over another. The second worker sits as an interested party at hearings (del Junco Allayón, May 22, 1991; Castro Cabrera, May 22, 1991).

The number of cases brought to the *consejos* increased throughout the 1970s. Fuller (1987:146) reports that 161 cases were heard by the *consejos* for every 10,000 Cuban workers in 1972. This rate increased to 270 per 10,000 workers in 1974, to 280 per 10,000 workers in 1976, and to 306 per 10,000 workers in 1978. In comparison with other countries, these rates are quite high. For instance, Hayden (1986:233) found that in the Serbian Republic of Yugoslavia in 1981, 87.1 worker-initiated cases were brought to workers' courts for every 10,000 workers. Markovits (1987:553–554) reports that only 17 of every 10,000 workers brought cases to workers' courts in East Germany in 1977, and in West Germany the rate was 143 per 10,000 workers.

The high caseload in Cuba relative to other countries is partially attributable to the requirement that cases go the *consejos* prior to court. That explanation is incomplete, however, because it does not account for the *increasing* use of the *consejos* over time, particularly since workers could simply give up, not bothering to contest decisions by management if they felt that complaints would be a waste of time or harmful to them.

Two additional factors help explain the increased use of the *consejos* by Cuban workers. First, the unions became increasingly aggressive as they became more independent of management and of the state. This gave workers a sense that their complaints would be taken seriously and that, as a collectivity, they had some real control over actions by management. Second, measures taken in the 1970s by the System of Economic Direction and Planning placed additional imperatives on managers and workers. These new demands exacerbated conflicts between workers and managers as they contested the value of labor and the rights of workers (Fuller, 1987).

In an effort to resolve the problems created by the backlog of cases, Law No. 32, passed in 1980, removed the authority of the *consejos* to adjudicate conflicts over workplace discipline. Under Law No. 32, management is required only to inform the worker and the union of disciplinary sanctions in a timely manner (i.e., within 30 days). Workers can appeal these cases only to the courts, not within the workplace (Laou, November 10, 1989). Based on interviews with Cuban workers, Fuller (1987:147) concludes:

> [W]ith Law No. 32 an impressive and longstanding revolutionary tradition which granted Cuban workers a great deal of control over workplace discipline was nullified by a single decree. It is not hard to imagine how, by removing the arbitration of disputes over discipline from the shop floor and from the hands of fellow workers, Law No. 32 might make it more complicated, more intimidating, more time consuming, and less profitable for workers to counter unjust disciplinary measures imposed by administrators.

Consejo cases since passage of Law No. 32 concern: (1) workers' rights; (2) short-term social security; and (3) maternity. All cases alleging violations of workers' rights *must* go to a *consejo* before going to court. Workers' rights issues include salary, workplace transfers, work hours, timing or lack of vacation, and the right to occupy a particular job. The latter refers primarily to promotions and job titles, but it also includes lateral moves where a person wishes, for instance, to work closer to home or in an air-conditioned section of the workplace (Laou, April 21, 1989, November 10, 1989; Garrido Lugo, December 3, 1989; Article 11 of the Law of the Organization and Functioning of the *Consejos del Trabajo* (Law No. 8), 1977).

Some examples may help clarify the types of workers' rights cases brought to the *consejos*. A common grievance is one worker receiving a higher evaluation than another but the administrator giving the lower-ranked person a raise or award instead of the higher-ranked person. The timing of vacations is another common source of grievances. For example, university professors are entitled to a month's vacation after the semester ends. If a professor wants to take her vacation in July, but the administrator decides she must wait another month for her vacation because so many people will be gone in July, she can bring the case to the *consejo*, arguing that she is entitled to a vacation once the semester ends and should not have to wait (Laou, April 21, 1989). Failure to receive a salary consistent with one's job title is also a commonly alleged violation of workers' rights. Because the Cuban salary scale is so complex, it is often interpreted differently by workers and administrators (Guevara, May 29, 1991; Garrido Lugo, December 3, 1989).

A final example which surfaced in my interviews is probably not very common, but it is interesting. A worker was accused and convicted of robbery. Upon appeal, the court determined that he was innocent. In the meantime, he lost his job and was not paid for three years. The appellate court ruled that he be reinstated and receive back pay. The workplace administration refused, saying that the court should pay these costs because it was the judicial system that had initially charged, tried, and convicted him. The worker brought his case to the *consejo*, which found in his favor. The administration refuted this decision, and the case went back to court. The court found in the worker's favor—or, interpreted differently, in its own favor since the workplace, not the courts, was deemed responsible for providing the back pay (Garrido Lugo, December 3, 1989).

The most common social-security complaints brought to the *consejos* concern accidents and illnesses. Consider, for example, a worker who claims a work-related injury after falling down a stairway in her apartment complex and breaking a leg en route to work, and an administrator who argues that it was a common accident. The distinction between work-related and nonwork injuries is important, because the social-security payment for missed work due to employment-related accidents or illnesses is higher than that for common accidents or illnesses (Laou, April 21, 1989).

Disputes over maternity leaves are the third type of case that can be brought to the *consejos*. Such cases are rare, however, since women's rights to paid maternity leaves for six weeks during pregnancy and for 12 weeks following birth are explicitly stated in the Maternity Law of 1974 (Law No. 1263).

As I indicated earlier, *consejo* decisions are not binding (del Junco Allayón, May 22, 1991; Castro Cabrera, May 22, 1991). The administration has ten days to formally declare that it does not accept the decision. More frequently, however, administrators simply ignore the rulings. Consequently, a number of complaints have been raised, including inadequate training of *consejo* members and managers in labor and social welfare legislation, lengthy delays in settling cases, too much paperwork, the perception that many *consejos* immediately side with the administration, lack of knowledge among workers as to how the *consejos* work and the time limits for bringing cases to them, overly mechanistic use of grievance procedures by administrators, and management misuse or abuse of the *consejos*. The latter set of complaints include the failure of administrators to appear at *consejo* hearings when a complaint has been filed against them, sending a replacement who is unaware of the details of the incident, bypassing the *consejos* or missing deadlines for informing them of sanctions, and most commonly, ignoring the rulings of the *consejos* (Fuller, 1987:145–146; del Junco Allayón, May 22, 1991; Castro Cabrera, May 22, 1991; Garrido Lugo, December 3, 1989).

APPEALS TO COURT

Workers are often intimidated by the appellate procedure, which is far more complicated and formal than bringing cases to the *consejos*. Appeals must be in written form and they necessitate braving the court bureaucracy. Union backing is often a critical factor in workers' decisions to appeal disciplinary sanctions or *consejo* decisions that they view as unfair.

Despite these difficulties, it is in the municipal courts that workers can obtain binding decisions when they feel their rights have been trampled and where they can appeal disciplinary actions. Management ignores the verdicts of the *consejos* so frequently, according to Ministry of Justice officials, that most workers' rights cases go to court (del Junco Allayón, May 22, 1991; Castro Cabrera, May 22, 1991). As Hayden (1986:247) concluded from his study of Yugoslav labor courts, "Given a choice between easy access to an institution that has little to offer and more difficult access to one that does afford some means of effecting one's wishes, the second appears to be more often likely to be chosen than the first."

If either party is dissatisfied with the municipal court decision a final appeal can be made to provincial court. The provincial court typically limits itself to reviewing the municipal court record rather than agreeing to a time-consuming hearing that would repeat declarations made earlier. Labor law specialist Dolores Castro Cabrera told me, "People always ask for a meeting in court, and the [provincial] court typically denies it" (May 22, 1991). The Supreme Court hears labor cases only when new facts or evidence surface or when it can be demonstrated that the earlier decision was inappropriate, illegal, arbitrary, or unjust (Article 734 of the Law of Civil, Administrative and Labor Procedure, 1977). As is the case in every other realm of Cuban law, the judicial panels at each level are composed of a mixture of lay and professional judges (see Chapter Six).

Infringements on workers' rights constituted an increasing proportion of the appeals during the 1970s: 11 percent of the cases appealed in 1969, 17 percent in 1972–73, 25 percent in 1974, and 78 percent in at least one province in 1977 (Fuller, 1987:141). These numbers skyrocketed after 1980, when the court became the only recourse for appealing disciplinary actions. Almost 85,000 cases were appealed each year between 1980 and 1983, nearly tripling the figure for 1976 (Fuller, 1987:149).

In general, the courts tend to side with management in disciplinary cases, although judges may reduce penalties they think are unduly harsh (del Junco Allayón, May 22, 1991; Castro Cabrera, May 22, 1991). For instance, the Cuban Labor Confederation (CTC) announced in 1981 that the nation's courts upheld the maximum sanction, firing, in only 47 percent of the cases appealed by workers (Fuller, 1987:147).

Tables 7.1, 7.2, and 7.3 present national-level data on labor cases heard in 1990 by the municipal courts, provincial courts, and the Supreme Court. The data are broken down by type of case, which party appealed, and how the case was resolved.[2]

As Table 7.1 indicates, 32,516 labor cases were brought to the nation's municipal courts in 1990. Of these, 88.7 percent involved labor discipline. The most common complaints concerned negligence (20 percent), followed by crimes in the workplace (16 percent) and absenteeism (15 percent).[3] The municipal court may accept the administration's position, reject it, or reduce the sanction. The courts found overwhelmingly in favor of the administration in discipline cases. The most common sanction was a job transfer—temporary in 33 percent of the cases and permanent in another ten percent. Work transfers are often demotions. Three- to six-month suspensions were handed down in another eight percent of the cases sanctioned by the municipal courts. The most severe penalty, firing, was upheld in 20 percent of the cases.

Table 7.1.
Labor Cases Brought to Cuba's Municipal Courts in 1990 (a).

Type of Case	Number	Percent
Discipline Cases	28,855	88.7
Absenteeism	4,272	14.8
Negligence	5,921	20.5
Crimes	4,642	16.1
All Other	14,020	48.6
Total	28,855	100.0
Resolved by courts	27,877	
Resolved in favor of management	26,448	
Court-ordered sanctions for discipline cases found in favor of management:		
Temporary work transfer	8,738	33.0
Permanent work transfer	2,659	10.0
Suspension (3–6 months)	2,160	8.2
Firing	5,281	20.0
All Other	7,610	28.8
Total	26,448	100.0
Workers' Rights Cases Appealed		
From Consejos	3,661	11.3
Mejor derecho ("better right")	2,110	57.6
Economic issues	1,200	32.8
Short term social security and other	351	9.6
Total	3,661	100.0
Grand Total	32,516	100.0

(a) Some inaccuracies arise due to pending cases and computational errors in aggregating from the 169 municipal courts to the national level.

Source: *Comité Estatal de Trabajo y Seguridad Social* records compiled by Lydia Guevara, May 29, 1991.

Table 7.2.
Labor Cases Appealed to Cuba's Provincial Courts in 1990 (a).

Type of Case	Number	Percent
Discipline Cases	8,560	84.1
Appeal by administrator	1,752	20.5
Appeal valid	945	53.9
Appeal not valid	597	34.1
Pending or unknown	210	12.0
Appeal by worker	6,808	79.5
Appeal valid	324	4.8
Appeal not valid	5,859	86.1
Pending or unknown	625	9.2
Workers' Rights Cases	1,624	15.9
Appeal by administrator	344	21.2
Appeal valid	150	43.6
Appeal not valid	177	51.5
Pending or unknown	17	4.9
Appeal by worker	1,275	78.5
Appeal valid	129	10.1
Appeal not valid	1,057	82.9
Pending or unknown	89	7.0
Unclear who appealed	5	
Grand Total	10,184	100.0

(a) Some inaccuracies arise due to pending cases and computational errors in aggregating from the 14 provincial courts to the national level.

Source: *Comité Estatal de Trabajo y Seguridad Social* records compiled by Lydia Guevara, May 29, 1991.

The remaining 11.3 percent of the municipal courts' labor caseloads consisted of appeals of *consejo* decisions. Over half of these, 58 percent, involved what is known as *"mejor derecho,"* where one employee claims that she or he has a "better right" to some benefit than another employee who was granted it by the administrator. *Mejor derecho* cases typically concern promotions, lateral moves to a work area with better conditions (e.g., air conditioning), evaluation of qualifications and placement on the salary scale, and timing of vacations. Another 33 percent of the workers' rights appeals involved explicitly economic concerns, usually salary disputes associated with job changes or merit pay. Finally, just under ten percent of the appeals were for short-term social-security claims.

Table 7.2 shows that 10,184 appeals of municipal-court decisions were brought to the labor sections of the nation's provincial courts in 1990. Of these, 84.1 percent were appeals of disciplinary decisions, and 15.9 percent were appeals of workers' rights. It is usually the worker who appeals (in 79.5 percent of the discipline cases and 78.5 percent of the workers' rights cases), and the court typically rules that the appeal is not valid. As was found at the municipal level, provincial court decisions strongly favor management, but workers win sufficiently often—in five percent of the discipline cases and ten percent of the workers' rights cases brought by workers—that appeal is a reasonable avenue for persons who feel that they were wronged.

Table 7.3.
Labor Cases Appealed to Cuba's Supreme Court in 1990 (a).

Type of Case	Number	Percent
Discipline Cases Found in Favor of Administration:		
Appeals by administrator	3	6.1
Appeals by worker	46	93.9
Court-ordered sanctions:		
Fines	4	8.2
Temporary work transfer	6	12.2
Permanent work transfer	12	24.5
Firing	27	55.1
Total	49	100.0
Social Security Appeals		
Appeals valid	2	
Appeals not valid	37	
All Appeals		
Appeals valid	212	12.8
Appeals not valid	140	8.4
Under investigation	1,188	71.4
Still pending	s123	7.4
Grand Total	**1,663**	**100.0**

(a) Some inaccuracies arise due to pending cases, cases under investigation, and computational errors in aggregation. Appeals of workers'-rights cases (e.g., vacations, promotions, right to a given position) are not included.

Source: Supreme Court records compiled by Lydia Guevara, May 29, 1991.

At the Supreme Court, Table 7.3 demonstrates that once again, it is workers who generally bring appeals, and they usually lose. The Supreme Court tends to hear the most serious discipline cases, typically involving firings or permanent job transfers. More than half (55 percent) of the discipline cases in which the Supreme Court found in favor of the administration resulted in the worker being fired. In another 37 percent of the cases, the worker was temporarily or permanently demoted.

THE VILLA CLARA EXPERIMENT AND DECREE-LAW NO. 132 OF APRIL 9, 1992

Under the auspices of Decree-Law No. 121 of July 19, 1990, an experimental mode of resolving labor disputes was initiated in Villa Clara province in November of 1990. It established a new dispute-resolution body known as the Base Level Organs of Labor Justice (*Organos de Justicia Laboral de Base,* OJLB). Three characteristics of the OJLB are particularly salient for our purposes. First, they include a representative of the workplace administration. Second, they are empowered to hear discipline cases as well as alleged violations of workers' rights. Third, their verdicts in most discipline cases cannot be appealed.

Like the *consejo*s, the OJLB are composed of five members. While union officials and workplace administrators were explicitly prohibited by Law No. 8 from serving on the *consejo*s, each OJLB includes a union representative and a management representative, along with three persons elected from within the workforce. Each member of the panel is supposed to act as an impartial judge and not represent the specific interests of management, the union, or workers (del Junco Allayón, May 22, 1991; Castro Cabrera, May 22, 1991). Nevertheless, inclusion of management on the panel makes some Cuban labor lawyers nervous. These labor advocates interpret this move as a step backwards to the grievance commissions of the early 1960s.

The return of discipline cases to the workplace as the initial site for conflict resolution can be viewed as a gain for workers, countering any potential loss due to management gaining a seat on the panel. However, this too may ultimately be detrimental to workers. When the grievance commissions and the pre-1980 *consejos* heard discipline cases, their decisions were always subject to appeal. In contrast, the decision of the OJLB is definitive if the sanction is not too severe, with "too severe" defined operationally as permanent or long-term transfer or firing. Only when these latter two sanctions are used to discipline laborers is the decision open to appeal (del Junco Allayón, May 22,

1991; Castro Cabrera, May 22, 1991; Point 1.3 of Joint Resolution No. 1/90). Labor's concern, as expressed by labor lawyer Lydia Guevara Ramírez, is that "the administrators know their decisions are definitive if they don't fire someone or order a long-term transfer. So they'll give sanctions of a shorter time, and then the worker cannot appeal" (May 29, 1991).

In addition, the authority of management to invoke disciplinary actions is in no way restricted by the new legislation. The fourth "Whereas" to the preamble of Decree-Law No. 121 states, "Administration's license to directly impose disciplinary measures with an immediate effect *must be maintained* but it is *convenient* to give greater participation to the workplace collective . . ." (my emphasis).[4] This wording, in combination with the removal of the right to appeal sanctions that either do not change one's job status or alter it only temporarily, suggests that the return of disciplinary cases to *consejo*-like bodies is neither expected nor intended to benefit workers, either individually or collectively. As of the summer of 1991, the general expectation among labor lawyers was that the Villa Clara experiment would be expanded throughout the country. A second and related expectation was, "the workers will lose out."

On April 9, 1992, the Villa Clara experiment was officially defined as a success and was extended to all Cuban workplaces under Decree-Law No. 132. The first "whereas" to the new law praises the experimental OJLB for strengthening labor discipline and reducing and simplifying the appellate process. From the perspective of labor advocates, however, the new law is "nothing else than a means of freeing the courts from appeals of sanctions of small amounts, resolving grievances through an administrative route within the same workplace" (Lydia Guevara, personal communication, November 6, 1992).

Like the experimental OJLB in Villa Clara, the new nationwide OJLB consist of a representative of the workplace administration, a union representative, and three workers elected in a general assembly. Workplaces with fewer than 25 employees have three-member boards, only one of whom is an elected worker. As in the *consejos*, the employee members cannot simultaneously hold union or management posts.

The OJLB resolve cases quickly, generally within ten days of filing a written or oral complaint with a board member. Three additional days can be granted as needed for a full investigation and gathering of evidence (Articles 28 through 36 of Joint Resolution No. 1 of the State Committee for Work and Social Security, Ministry of Justice, and Supreme Court, April 11, 1992). The OJLB are required to hold public hearings, but these are to be held during nonworking hours. Finally, as in the Villa Clara experiment, the OJLB's decisions cannot be appealed unless the sanction includes firing or permanent transfer (Article 41 of the Joint Resolution). Workers' rights cases are the sole exception. Claims that one's rights as a worker were violated can still be brought to municipal court by workers or administrators (Article 39 of the Joint Resolution).

RATIONALES FOR CREATION OF THE OJLB

Given the openly articulated reservations about the new OJLB, why were they created and expanded throughout the country? Cuban labor law experts suggest two major reasons: economic necessity and, secondarily, ideological goals.

Economic Necessity

Individually and in combination, the rectification process (officially launched in 1986), the awareness of continued low productivity that emerged from the 1990 Call for Discussion (*Llamamiento*) prior to the Fourth Communist Party Congress, and the devastating economic plight of the country following the collapse of socialism in Eastern Europe and the economic and political changes within the Soviet Union in 1990 and 1991, required that every effort be made to enhance productivity and efficiency in Cuban workplaces.

Resolving additional disputes within the workplace was one means of increasing workplace efficiency (Guevara, May 29, 1991, personal communication November 6, 1992; del Junco Allayón, May 22, 1991; Castro Cabrera, May 22, 1991). Going to court over every grievance was very time consuming. It meant disruptions in the labor process and a consequent loss in productivity as the disputants and witnesses took time from work to travel to court, wait for their case to be called, and have their hearings. In contrast, resolving more conflicts within the workplace offered considerable savings in time and productivity. Adjudicating conflicts over disciplinary actions in the workplace also reduced transportation costs, since fewer people must travel to court. Transportation became an especially serious consideration in 1990, when bus service was cut drastically in response to petroleum shortages.

Lowering the court caseloads was also an economic necessity. As Tables 7.1 through 7.3 indicate, and as I was more forcefully told whenever I asked, "The courts are full of labor cases." Reducing the number of labor cases meant attention could be given to other cases more quickly, and by fewer judges and other court personnel.

Ideological Goals

A secondary reason offered for moving disputes over disciplinary actions back to the workplaces was ideological in nature. Coworkers are more knowledgeable about the parties to a dispute and the conditions surrounding the conflict than are judges who are meeting the disputants for the first time. For this reason, decisions are viewed as "more just" when made at the most local level possible (del Junco Allayón, May 22, 1991; Castro Cabrera, May 22, 1991). As we have seen throughout this analysis of the Cuban legal system, "The closer to the base, the greater the justice" is one of the central tenets of Cuban socialist legality.

ARBITRATION

At the same time that more disputes between workers and managers are moving out of the courts and into the work sites, conflicts between workplaces are moving into the courts. I suggested in Chapter Five that the Cubans carefully adapted foreign legal structures to their own specific needs rather than copying other systems wholesale. An exception to this, as Cubans now say with the wisdom of hindsight, was in the area of state arbitration (*arbitraje estatal*). The state structure that Cuba established in 1976 and refined in 1983 was modeled closely after the Soviet Union (Couto, May 11, 1989). Some aspects of this complex structure may be necessary in a large country, but not in tiny Cuba. State arbitration was one such feature.

Since 1991, minor disagreements between workplaces are arbitrated within the corresponding Ministries (e.g., of Construction, Sugar, Agriculture, Light Industry, etc.). More serious disputes go a new economic section of the provincial courts and to the Supreme Court. Collapsing arbitration into the court structure reduces the number of persons and offices needed to resolve disputes between work sites, reaping immediate economic benefits. It also further unifies the judicial system, which is one element of formal, bureaucratic legal structures.

CONCLUSIONS

Vacillation between the workplace and the courts as the site for deciding contested disciplinary sanctions is an example of how a resolution to a particular dilemma is often a temporary measure. Whether discipline cases are heard in labor councils or in the formal court system, the underlying contradiction between labor rights and productivity needs remains. This contradiction, which is the basis for labor-business conflicts in capitalist societies, does not disappear in the socialist context, even though the workplaces are owned by the state, and the state is supposed to exist for the benefit of the workers.

A second contradiction which has been a theme throughout this book concerns the ideological disjuncture between the desire for informal, local avenues for redressing grievances as a means of enhancing justice, and the desire for rights and guarantees formally backed by the authority of the state through its courts. This is particularly apparent in labor law. The Cuban response to the conflicts and dilemmas engendered by this contradiction has been to resolve as many conflicts as possible within the workplace where they arose, while also allowing for appeals to the courts. Historical fluctuations in whether disciplinary cases can be decided within the workplace, and whether these decisions can be appealed to the courts, are indicative of the tentative and temporary nature of the resolutions the Cubans have reached. Similarly, labor rights cases have generally had to be heard first in the labor councils before they could be appealed to court, yet many workers do not feel that their grievances are adequately redressed in the *consejos*.

The dilemmas discussed in this chapter go to the heart of debates over legal formalism and informalism. Just as popular participation has sometimes been confounded in the literature with informalism, so too "close to the base" can be confounded with both informalism and a popular perspective. As I have endeavored to show through my discussions of the courts (in Chapter Six) and labor councils, decision makers do, indeed, better understand the circumstances of the case when they come from the same communities (in municipal court) and workplaces. The power that lay adjudicators wield over disputants, however, is quite different in the two contexts. In the courts, lay judges have as much say as professional judges. Judicial decisions may be appealed, but they are respected by all of the participants. Depending upon the historical era, however, worker members of the *consejos* can often be outvoted, and administrators do not always take their decisions seriously.

Are labor councils beneficial to workers? Many Cubans feel that they are, since case resolution in the workplace is easier and less intimidating. At the same time, because management often ignored the verdict reached by the *consejos,* many Cuban workers brought their cases to the courts for review and for binding decisions. Good reasons exist for having *both* labor councils and courts hear labor cases, with the presence of these dual forums providing workers and management with alternative means of conflict resolution.

CHAPTER 8

CONCLUSIONS

The production of legality in Cuba is a story of human actors seeking to steer the country through the shoals of contradictory demands, pressures, and goals. As both an economic form and an ideology, socialism is a product of social, political, and economic forces originating in Cuba's history as a colony of Spain and as a neocolony of the United States. Cuban socialism has been shaped by its Latin American culture, and over time, by growing ties with other socialist nations and progressive political movements in the Third World. Similarly, the legality that has developed since the revolutionary triumph in 1959 has its roots in Cuba's Spanish inheritance and in the legal traditions of Eastern European socialist nations.

Throughout this analysis I have focused on the dynamic process of producing and reproducing legality in a context of rapid social change. Taking as my starting point some basic contradictions inherent in building socialism in a tiny Third World nation with a colonial legacy, I have explored the resulting conflicts and dilemmas within the legal order. I then traced the strategies devised by policy makers in their efforts to resolve these tensions through changes in the form and content of law. To be viable, the strategies and resolutions must be consistent with the socialist and nationalist ideological orientation of the political leadership. Nationalism as I have used it implies a focus on what is best for the Cuban people, not isolationism. Indeed, Cuba's global ties and the importance of respect in the eyes of the international community are quite evident in the legal arena.

Changes in the Cuban legal order both reflect social transformations that have already occurred and are catalysts for desired social and cultural change. The dialectical nature of social and legal change is most apparent in the areas of criminal law, where modifications largely followed social transformations, and family law, where legal innovations were intended to promote social and cultural changes in gender relations. Yet the scope of proposed legal reforms is constrained by a wide range of economic considerations, including the cost of courtrooms, imperatives of meeting production plans, the need for professionals in various technical positions, the price of paper, and military defense.

This research has explored how law and legality are understood by Cuban legal scholars and policy makers. It is primarily a view from above, from the juridical elite. While other voices are heard, I have relied extensively on how those persons responsible for writing the laws explained their decisions, in their own words. The conceptions of law, legality, and the legal order held by these powerful men and women are central to the ways in which socialist legality has been produced in revolutionary Cuba. Their legal ideologies, including the tension between desires for a centralized legal structure with uniform laws and for localized dispute resolution, framed their selection of strategies for promoting legal and social change.

The three principal strategies I have analyzed are the broad-based, consensus-building process of law creation; the combination of practical and theoretical training of law students, intended to make them critical thinkers while also addressing urgent societal needs; and the careful examination and adaptation of legal models and theories from abroad. As each strategy unfolds, a series of substrategies is produced. Examples are the popular tribunals of the 1960s and early 1970s and night-school courses for those whose jobs required some knowledge of the law. Substrategies are useful in their historical moment, but must be replaced by alternative mechanisms when the conflicts and dilemmas they were intended to resolve pass and new problems surface.

From another perspective, distinct from that of top-echelon policy makers, socialist legality is produced and reproduced daily by the actions of jurists and nonjurists in the courts and workplaces. Here we see lay and professional judges and workplace dispute mediators interpreting and shaping legality. Popular participation in these functions is, in the words of one lay judge, "bidirectional." It brings the views of the average person into decisionmaking and also educates the citizenry about Cuban-style socialist legality.

POPULAR JUSTICE AND INFORMALISM

Popular participation is a cornerstone of Cuban socialist legality. Policy makers in the legal realm repeatedly asserted, "The closer to the base, the greater the justice." In addition to lay judges and employee involvement in workplace councils, the role of the mass organizations in debating prospective laws and in nominating lay judges is another means of ensuring popular participation in the legal sphere.

Popular justice initiatives emerged in a context in which the pre-existing legal system and legal actors were seen as corrupt and held little legitimacy. They developed initially in response to wartime exigencies and reflected a desire for visible changes in the form and content of law. At first, popular justice was restricted to resolving fairly minor disputes. Over time, elements of popular justice have become fully institutionalized in Cuba, as the ideological bases for it moved increasingly to the core of the Cuban legal order.

One of the themes of this analysis has been the relationship between popular participation and informalism—and the danger of confounding the two. Some First World legal scholars and community activists have called for greater informalism in legal decisionmaking. Their interest in informalism is based in large part on appreciation of popular participation in socialist legal systems. Others have criticized informalism, at least as it is now used in the United States and other First World capitalist nations. There are two major sets of criticisms. First, some scholars charge informalism with expanding the social control powers of the state, neutralizing disputes, disorganizing opposition, and undermining collective action before it can organize. Second, critical race theorists in the United States warn that informalism undermines the rhetoric and reality of rights, thereby opening the door to further disempowerment of subordinate groups.

The tensions between popular access to legal forums, the risk of expanded social control by the state, and the state as the guarantor of individual rights are also evident in Cuba. They can be seen, for example, in the experimental popular tribunals of the 1960s. These tribunals were dismantled because they were perceived by legal scholars as *too* informal, thus weakening the rule of law. Yet they were not completely tossed aside. Some aspects of the popular tribunals were not only retained but further institutionalized within formal guidelines in the unified court system that emerged in the 1970s. The most prominent example is the use of lay judges throughout the judicial structure. The tension between popular participation and protecting individual rights is also visible in the vacillating relations between workplace labor councils and the courts, particularly in the extent to which disciplinary actions by management can be appealed.

Another theme of the analysis was the relationship between the form and content of law. As I have used it, the form of law refers to the relative mix of legal formalism and informalism, and the content refers to the substantive intent of the law, whether this precedes or solidifies normative changes in the society. A simple mapping of form and content within a given area of law (e.g., criminal, family, labor) does not do justice to the complex interplays of formalism and informalism. As the extensive debate in the scholarly literature demonstrates, we never see a pure form of legality. Whether we depict formalism and informalism as distinct yet mutually influential, relating dialectically, having homologous configurations of power, or see one as subordinate to the other, we can expect to find a mix of forms operating in each substantive area. I have suggested that the specific mix varies, depending on the substantive content of law and the historical and international concerns influencing individual legal policy makers. Thus, for example, the mix of formalism and informalism in criminal law at a particular historical moment differs from that of family law, and both are distinct from what we see in labor law.

The relationship between the legal sphere and other state institutions and mass organizations has been a third underlying theme. The Cuban Communist Party guides much of the planning in the legal arena. Yet, since many top officials in the legal order are also party members, and some hold posts in the Politburo or Central Committee, the relationship is not simply one of the party directing the actions of policy makers and implementers. What we see instead is an interwoven set of relations between top actors in the legal arena, other state agencies, the party bureaucracy, and the mass organizations. In many instances their views and priorities conflict, with resolution often a slow process of conciliation.

THE FUTURE

By the late 1980s the Cuban legal system was well respected at home and abroad. The Cuban people felt that they had a voice in determining what the laws would say and how they would be interpreted in the courts. Internationally, Cuba was a leader in the depenalization movement and in using the law to promote gender equality. The choice of Cuba as the site for the 1987 meetings of the American Association of Jurists and the 1990 United Nations Congress on the Prevention of Crime and the Treatment of Delinquency were clear indicators of this international esteem. Cuba seemed to have found a balance between popular involvement in legal decisionmaking and protection of the rights of individuals.

Some of the reforms enacted in the 1980s appear fragile in light of recent global transformations. The Cuban people face tremendous economic hardships and political uncertainty as a consequence of the breakup of the Soviet Union, the dismantling of the Council for

Mutual Economic Assistance, the disintegration of socialism in Eastern Europe, and renewed pressure by the United States for international support of its blockade against the island (e.g., the Torricelli bill), all in the context of a global debt crisis affecting Cuba and its trade partners. Imports plummeted by 75 percent between 1989 and 1992 (Castro, 1992a:8), the standard of living has dropped precipitously, and unemployment is a reality previously unknown to Cuban youth.

These structural dislocations pose tremendous challenges to the political leadership. It is important, therefore, to remember that the Cubans are adept at making policy changes swiftly. In the words of one Cuban legal scholar, "One year for us is like 100 years for you."

The history of socialist legality in Cuba as I have traced it suggests three principles that will underlie any changes in the legal order in the near future: they will include popular participation, they will be economically expedient, and they will be sensitive to international opinion.

In 1989, when the global scene underwent abrupt disjunctures, we saw a temporary pause in legislative activity while the implications of these transformations for Cuba were assessed and the most pressing needs (e.g., a new food plan) addressed, most of which fell outside the juridical arena. This was followed by the 1990 Law of the Courts, the 1990 experiment in labor law in Villa Clara province and its nation-wide extension in 1992, and passage in 1992 of a revised Constitution and a new electoral law. Work has continued on a new Law of Criminal Procedure, but it is not expected to reach the floor of the National Assembly until 1994 or 1995. Also, satellite municipal courts have been established in Havana neighborhoods. These branch courts operate according to the same rules as the regular courts. Each of these changes was designed, at least in part, to enhance popular partici-pation in decisionmaking.

Recent and proposed changes in the legal order are also expected to conserve scarce economic resources. At a minimum, they will not require additional financial outlays. Consider, for example, the new satellite municipal courts, establishment of workplace labor boards to hear grievances about disciplinary actions, and changes in the compo-sition of provincial court panels and in the jurisdiction of municipal courts. Each of these measures lowers transportation costs since fewer people must travel to court. They also reduce court backlogs by allowing more cases to be handled concurrently without increasing the number of judges, clerks, and other court personnel needed, and they lessen the physical strain on delapidating courthouses. Furthermore, they result in fewer interruptions of the production process because the parties to the disputes and the witnesses do not have to leave work to go to court. The sharp reduction in bus service since 1990 led to missed court appearances, and thus, continuances for many cases. By moving municipal courts into the neighborhoods, the interested parties no longer need to be transported to court. Although court personnel must be brought to the satellite courts, they are comparatively few in number.

In contrast, legislation such as proposed changes in criminal procedure that would require additional infusions of financial resources into the judicial sphere or increased transportation costs are not expected in the immediate future. If the shortage of fuel for buses becomes more severe, and bus schedules are further reduced, law school enrollments may decrease, and universities may be forced to offer classes only a few days each week. Limited resources also mean that the plan for increased publications relevant to the legal profession will not be met. Such changes suggest a slowing of growth in the juridical sector but do not portend any serious alteration in its direction.

Economic travails often sharpen political discontent. Throughout Latin American history, the leadership's response to political and economic pressures has been repression, generally by means of extralegal tactics. Ironically, the reforms of the 1980s that led to greater respect for the legal order may now be viewed by the political leadership as too lenient, particularly those involving political protests and economic crimes, such as black marketeering, that throw an already devastated economy into further disarray. Whether or not Cuba's progressive legal order will be able to sustain itself in these difficult times remains to be seen and is, perhaps, the ultimate test of the prestige and power of the legal sphere within the governmental bureaucracy.

Dire predictions about needing to resort to extralegal means of maintaining social order must be tempered by the stability of personnel within the legal sphere and by the close attention that these individuals have demonstrated to international opinion. Juan Escalona Reguera, Ramón de la Cruz Ochoa, and José Raúl Amaro Salup, among others, were key actors in the reforms of the 1980s, and they have continued to maintain positions of authority within the government. Recall, for example, how Juan Escalona Reguera and his colleagues used the force of international opinion to convince Fidel Castro of the need for a more lenient criminal code. While these individuals have taken a hard line in some cases, none are likely to endorse any action that would seriously harm Cuba's standing in the eyes of the international community.

Passage of a new electoral law in 1992 that included direct election of representatives to the Provincial Assemblies and the National

Assembly is further evidence of the leadership's attention to the international community. Fidel Castro explicitly referred to the importance of international respect when he said that the new electoral law "was an unavoidable commitment to the Cuban people and international opinion" (Castro, 1992b:4).

The international community is not a single entity, and shifts can be seen in Cuba's primary international audiences. In the past, these were the Soviet Union and Eastern European socialist nations, along with Latin America and the rest of the Third World. Today, Cuba aligns itself most closely with Latin America. Constitutional changes in 1992 explicitly acknowledge this connection to Latin America, with references to the socialist world deleted and unity with Third World nations and Latin American integration emphasized. The Cuban government is also increasing its ties to China, its remaining powerful socialist ally, and has won some important battles in the United Nations. On November 24, 1992, the United Nations voted overwhelmingly on Cuba's side against attempts by the United States to thwart trade with Cuba by other countries, with only Israel and Rumania supporting the United States.

As these examples demonstrate, the Cubans are showing considerable ingenuity in responding to the changing global economic and political situation. Moreover, the strategies employed are largely consistent with the path they had been following previously—a path that has garnered them considerable international respect.

Finally, the theoretic framework that guided my analysis of socialist legality explains not only the history of changes in the Cuban legal order, but also the nature of legality during the current, tumultuous period. Hopefully, it will prove useful as a general framework for studying law and legality in other contexts as well.

EPILOGUE

In August 1990 Cuba entered into a "special period in times of peace." This term references the indefinite period of economic hardship during which resources must be conserved. The special period is the immediate consequence of the breakup of socialism in Eastern Europe, economic difficulties and political unrest within the former Soviet Union, and the more general worldwide economic crisis. The effect of these changes on daily life in Cuba has been devastating.

Economic planning has been totally disrupted. The disintegration of the socialist Council for Mutual Economic Assistance (CMEA) means that fewer goods can be imported, since most imports must be purchased with hard currency. The extent of Cuba's structural dependence on Eastern Europe and the former Soviet Union as cheap sources of primary goods is only now becoming generally recognized. Shortages affect every aspect of the economy, from egg production, because the feed for hens is imported, to insufficient paper for students. Factories sit idle, awaiting imported parts. Some have closed or reduced their hours of operation. The result is real unemployment, virtually unknown to Cubans since the 1959 Revolution.

Petroleum, which in the past Cuba imported from the Soviet Union in large enough quantities that some could be resold on the world market for dollars, is now in very short supply. This means that there is less fuel for public transportation, for private cars, for transporting food products from the countryside to the cities, and for electricity.

No one knows when, how, or if this special period will end. Political jokes abound, expressing the general public's preoccupation with food shortages. A favorite in the summer of 1991 was: During the first phase of the special period the sign in the zoo says, "Don't feed the animals." During the second phase, the sign is changed to "Don't eat the animals' food." And in the third phase, "Don't eat the animals."

I was in Havana when monthly "special days" for the "special period" began, on May 23, 1991. There was no water, except what people had stored in their tanks. Nonessential electrical services, such as elevators, were also shut off. Yet contrary to the public's fears, buses ran and electricity was available.

The stores where one could buy nonrationed goods or rationed goods in excess of the rationed amount, known as "parallel markets," no longer exist. Everything is now rationed. Rationing has the general support of the populace. It means that your share, if available at all, will be held for you if you do not get to the store the day the product arrives. Nevertheless, many foods and other commodities are not consistently available, and there are shortages of such basic goods as soap, detergent, milk, meat, chicken, and cooking gas. Workplaces no longer supply lunches. Restaurants have limited selections, excepting those catering to the tourist trade where meals are purchased in dollars. Schools still provide children with lunches and snacks, but these are neither as large nor as nutritious as in the past. Obtaining sufficient food for one's family has become a daily struggle for the Cuban people.

There were never enough buses to meet the needs of the population. Between 1990 and 1991, the number of buses was reduced by approximately one-third, and I have been told that there are even fewer buses today. Taxis can rarely be found, except those designated for tourism. Bicycles imported from China are increasingly visible in the streets. Bicycles seem to be viewed simultaneously as symbolic of greater difficulties and as new toys. They cost 130 *pesos* (60 *pesos* for students), payable in installments. By the end of 1992, over one million bicycles had been distributed through the workplaces and schools to those persons living between two and 12 kilometers from their workplaces or schools. But the shift to bicycles as a primary mode of transportation may not be adequate. If transportation difficulties become more aggravated, as is generally expected, offices, factories, and the universities may operate for longer hours, fewer days per week.

Paper is in extremely short supply. There is less toilet paper, and fewer newspapers, schoolbooks, and cartons for breakable goods. In the summer of 1991, the national newspaper, *Granma,* was sold only Tuesday through Saturday, instead of Monday through Saturday. Fewer copies are printed, the price doubled from 10 to 20 *centavos,* and papers are no longer sold by streetcorner vendors. If you do not have home delivery, you must join long lines to purchase your copy of the morning newspaper before it runs out. *Juventud Rebelde,* another popular national daily paper, is now published only on Sundays. The third most popular national newspaper, *Trabajadores,* is not being published. Academic journals are not being printed. Fewer books are being published, and the number of copies printed is markedly lower than in the past.

Construction of housing continues, but at a slower pace due to shortages of building materials. In 1990 and 1991, construction efforts focused on building the Pan American City, just outside the city of Havana, in preparation for the Pan American Games. Hosting these games was a political success for the Cuban government, and most Cubans are proud of this opportunity to show off their athletes and their country, particularly as the Games were expected to boost tourism. At the same time, there was widespread resentment of the scarce resources being channeled into hosting them at this time.

The greater tension caused by economic hardship and uncertainty is visible in the streets. How to acquire food is the primary topic of conversation in workplaces, at bus stops, and in private living rooms. People do not laugh as much as they used to, and everyone is a little thinner. Such conditions are conducive to increasing crime rates. Crime has not increased to anything near the level in the United States, but by Cuban standards it is significantly higher. Black marketeering, robberies, and thefts are especially problematic, but fighting, assaults, and rapes also have increased.

The word on the streets in the summer of 1991 was that approximately 17 to 20 percent of the food supply operated through the black market. If gasoline and clothes are included, about 35 percent of the domestic economy was regulated by the black market. These estimates were unofficially confirmed by sources within the Attorney General's office. Since then, the black market has garnered even more control of the economy, selling basic foods and goods at exorbitant prices, such as 40 *pesos* for a chicken. In an effort to curb black marketeering and to move additional dollars into the formal economy, in mid-1993 it became legal for Cubans to have dollars and to purchase scarce goods in special dollar stores. While this decision has reduced some tensions and has brought more of the underground economy under government control, it has exacerbated tensions between those Cubans with access to dollars (most of whom have relatives in the United States) and those who lack this resource.

Nonetheless, the hospitals, clinics, and family doctors continue to provide services for all Cubans free of charge. Some imported medicines are not readily available, but health care for the average Cuban remains far superior to that in the rest of Latin America. Also, the children still go to school, and they all have their school uniforms and free bus transportation to and from school.

With severe economic difficulties comes political unrest. Politically it is a time of uncertainty and instability. Jokes are more clearly pointed at Fidel's persona than ever before. There is a growing sense that economic and political changes are needed, yet the Cuban people are also firm in their desire to maintain the benefits of socialism,

including especially free and excellent health care and education. At
this moment of global upheaval, the future path of this tiny Third
World country and its proud people is unclear. The citizenry is united
and adamant, however, in their determination that any political or
economic changes must come from within Cuba, and they will resist
any external efforts to impose a new social order.

NOTES

NOTES TO CHAPTER I

1. Tom Miller's (1992) recent journalistic account of his travels through Cuba provides a refreshing exception.

2. I use the present tense in this chapter because it reflects the Cuban reality for the historical period analyzed. The political and economic changes since 1989 in Eastern Europe and in the former Soviet Union have had devastating consequences for the Cuban people, as is discussed in my epilogue.

3. The population in 1989 was 10,577,000, reflecting a monotonic increase from 6,977,229 in 1959 (Comité Estatal de Estadísticas, 1990: Table 1.1, page 9; Comité Estatal de Estadísticas, 1978: Chapter Two, Table 1, page 28).

4. The term "*radio bemba*" dates from the 1950s, when the rebel army controlled the eastern part of the country, *Oriente*. It was an important means of passing information about the rebel army's plans and successes in those days.

5. Until mid-1990, milk could be purchased both from the ration system and at higher prices off-ration at government run parallel markets. Since that time, milk has been sold only through the rationing system. The rationing system ensures that everyone receives a minimum quantity of milk at very low prices. Pregnant women and children are allotted additional quantities of milk, and pregnant women also receive extra meat.

6. There is a wide array of other "diplo" facilities and services, ranging from grocery stores to beauty parlors to auto parts and service stations.

7. In contrast to beer bottles, which are manufactured in Cuba, soft drink bottles are imported. As of the summer of 1990, construction of an additional plant for manufacturing beer bottles was nearing completion. Ironically, at the very time that the shortage of beer bottles was being relieved, the supply of soft-drink bottles was reduced. Soft-drink bottles had been imported at low prices from Eastern European countries. When the disintegration of the socialist trading bloc made it necessary to pay for soft-drink bottles in dollars, the Cubans eliminated this nonessential import. By the summer of 1991, beer and soft drinks in bottles could only be purchased in "diplo" dollar stores or through the black market.

8. Bus transportation clearly deteriorated in the spring and summer of 1990. Fewer buses were on the roads due to a lack of parts and to an effort to conserve petroleum. These factors can be attributed directly to the effects on Cuba of political and economic changes in Eastern Europe and in the former Soviet Union.

9. From late fall through the spring, Cuban beaches and cities fill with throngs of tourists. The greatest numbers come from Canada, Italy, Spain, and Germany. Prior to the disintegration of the socialist economic community, elites from Eastern Europe and the Soviet Union also vacationed in Cuba. Within Latin America, most tourists are from Argentina, Mexico, Chile, Colombia, and Venezuela. Joint ventures in tourism exist between Cuba and businesses in several countries, with Spain taking the lead (see further *Granma International*, 1993:13).

NOTES TO CHAPTER 2

1. See Santos (1980, 1982a), Abel (1981, 1982a, 1982b), Spitzer (1982), Cain (1985), Cohen (1985), Harrington (1985), Henry (1985), O'Malley (1987), Fitzpatrick (1988, 1992), and Merry (1990).

2. See Chambliss (1979, 1988), Chambliss and Seidman (1982), Chambliss and Zatz (1993).

3. See Greenberg (1980), del Olmo (1981), Sumner (1982), Fitzpatrick (1983), Seidman (1984), Huggins (1985), Aniyar de Castro (1987), Smith (1983, 1984, 1986), Burawoy (1985), McDonald and Zatz (1992).

4. While Gramsci's work provides a useful starting point for a discussion of nonhegemonic ideology, his approach is hampered by its emphasis on the Communist Party as the central source for alternative ideological constructions. This is an overly narrow view of the potential for counterhegemonic forces to emerge. People may be generally ambivalent to hegemonic explanations of reality until the gap between representation and reality becomes too acute to deny the dissonances that have been created. A political party or some other organization may help catalyze resistance to structures of domination and creation of alternative ideological spaces. But people also have the ability to be very creative with the dominant institutional myths and symbols, reinterpreting and recontextualizing them in ways that the leadership did not intend (see McDonald, 1993).

5. Researchers rarely look for pure examples of formalism, seemingly taking it for granted. This omission makes sense once we remember that theorizing about informalism first developed when First World researchers in the Third World came face to face with very different customs and institutions from those to which they were accustomed. In trying to make theoretical sense of foreign cultures and social relations, the distinctions between formalism and informalism of law and social control were created (see further Zatz and Zhu [1991], and Merry [1992]).

6. This perspective has emerged into critical race theory (Matsuda et al., 1993). I am primarily concerned here with the 1987 articulation of the perspective as a critique of the informalism component of Critical Legal Studies.

7. The question of representation refers both to the demographic composition of judicial actors and to the relationship between the political and cultural heterogeneity in the population and in the legal/normative arena.

8. See, for example, Santos (1982c), Isaacman and Isaacman (1982), Brady (1982), Sachs (1985), van der Plas (1987).

9. See Brady (1977, 1982), Salas (1979, 1983), Pepinsky (1982), Isaacman and Isaacman (1982), Tiruchelvam (1984), Azicri (1985), Hirst (1985).

NOTES TO CHAPTER 3

1. Speech at special session of the National Assembly of People's Power held February 20, 1990, concerning the Assembly's appointment of two extra people to the election commission in violation of the electoral law (Castro Ruz, 1990:2).

2. *"Nadie en particular, por sí solo, puede concebir acertadamente un proyecto legislativo. El trabajo colectivo es imprescindible; especialmente cuando no se cuenta con un fondo sociológico acabado, ni medios tecnológicos modernos para una prospección de las posibles conductas futuras. En esos casos, es necesaria la contribución de todos, la discusión pública y honesta, lo más amplia posible"* (Gómez Treto, 1988:71).

3. Fernández-Rubio Legra (1985) suggests that the decade of the 1970s initiated the *perfection* of the process of institutionalization, a process which began on January 1, 1959. For Fernández-Rubio Legra, institutionalization encompassed two stages. The first, from January 1959 through the mid-1960s, was the democratic-popular, agrarian, and anti-imperialist stage. The second stage began in the mid-1960s and continued until the inception of "rectification" in the mid-1980s. Others see institutionalization as beginning in the early 1970s following Cuba's failure to achieve the famous ten-million-ton sugar harvest (e.g., Azicri, 1985). Although the 1970 harvest was far larger than in previous years, the failure to meet the planned goal led to serious economic reassessments. I see 1969 as the inception of the process of institutionalization, since that is when the Commission for Legal Studies began its work of writing the new constitution and other key pieces of legislation affecting not only the economic structures (as a limited focus on the 1970 harvest risks), but also the political, legal, and social ordering of the state.

4. The membership list of the Committee on Legal Studies reads like a "who's who" of Cuban legal scholars and officials. The members are (or were in the case of deaths) individually and collectively extremely influential in Cuban legal affairs: Blas Roca Calderío (President of the Commission), Armando Torres Santrayll and José Raúl Amaro Salup (Secretaries), Enrique Hart Ramírez, Fernando Alvarez Tabío, Nicasio Hernández Armas, José García Alvarez, Francisco Varona y Duque de Estrada, Raúl Ruíz Monteagudo, Gregorio Valdés de Pedros. Alfredo Yabúr and Sergio del Valle (then Ministers of Justice and of the Interior, respectively) also participated in these discussions (Prieto Morales, 1982:13,35).

5. A jurist (*jurista*) is someone formally trained in law. A lawyer (*abogado*) is a jurist who represents clients in civil or criminal trials or as a notary.

6. The Central Administration of the State is composed of the following (Article 28, Law of the Organization of the Central Administration of the State, 1983):

State Committees
National Planning
Technical-Material Goods
Economic Collaboration
Statistics
Finance
Standardization
Prices

Labor and Social Security
Academy of Sciences

Ministries
Sugar
Agriculture
Foreign Trade
Domestic Trade
Communications
Construction
Culture
Education
Higher Education
Revolutionary Armed Forces
Food Industry
Basic Industry
Light Industry
Construction Materials Industry (since 1987)
Fishing Industry
Iron and Steel Machine Industry
Interior
Justice
Foreign Relations
Public Health
Transportation

National Institutes
Civil Aeronautics (since 1985)
Research and Orientation of Internal Demand
Radio and Television
Sports, Physical Education and Recreation
Automated Systems and Computer Technology
Tourism
Housing (since 1984)

7. In order of legal authority, the Constitution has highest priority, followed by laws (*leyes*) passed by the National Assembly of People's Power, decree-laws (*decreto-leyes*) passed by the Council of State and decrees (*decretos*) promulgated by the Council of Ministers. Decree-laws and decrees must be ratified by the National Assembly, although my legislative sources could not recall a decree-law that was not ratified.

Following these are resolutions (*resoluciones*) of the various ministries. Directors of state enterprises, rectors and deans of universities, the Party's Central Committee, and other directorships can also enact resolutions. Instructions (*instrucciones*) by the Governing Council of the Supreme Court, the Attorney General's office, and the national leadership of other multitiered institutions follow. Finally the Municipal Assemblies of People's Power pass ordinances (*circulares*) that direct service activities at the municipal level (e.g., transportation, education, health). Accords (*acuerdos*) are agreements, generally from the National Assembly, the Council of State, the Council of Ministers, or the Politburo, covering a range of issues including the number of ambassadors, revocations or substitutions of heads of ministries, and other plans of action.

In addition, explanatory regulations (*reglamentos*) generally accompany laws, decree-laws, decrees, and resolutions (Hernández, March 30, 1989).

8. If the legislation was initiated by the Supreme Court or the Office of the Attorney General it does not go to any other legislative commissions except the CACJ.

9. In reality, the Ministry of Justice, as the agency charged with assisting in the elaboration of laws, decree-laws, and decrees, shoulders most of the responsibility for ascertaining that these conditions are met. Under Article 79 b) and c) of the 1983 Organization of the Central Administration of the State (*Organización de la Administración Central del Estado,* Decree-law No. 67), the Ministry of Justice is charged with studying, proposing, and directing the systematization and codification of laws, as well as advising the National Assembly, Council of State, and Council of Ministers in the elaboration of laws, decree-laws, decrees, and other legal dispositions.

10. For example, when the Accord to Regulate the Process of Elaboration and Presentation of Legislative Bills (*Acuerdo para Regular el Proceso de Elaboración y Presentación de Proyectos de Leyes*) went to the National Assembly in December 1988, it included a report detailing the changes in the *proyecto.* This was in response to the National Assembly's decision to postpone a vote on an earlier version of the accord until all of the critiques had been evaluated. The report states that 26 agencies sent critiques to the Office of the Secretary of the Council of Ministers. Of these, 18 agencies did not raise any objections, 11 commented on various points, six offered suggestions, and one questioned the necessity of the *anteproyecto.* Twenty-three suggestions were accepted and incorporated into the *proyecto* and 13 points were discussed, analyzed, and where possible reconciled by a work group of specialists from the National Assembly, the Ministry of Justice, and the CACJ (National Assembly of People's Power, December, 1988:1–2).

11. *"Ya no se corresponden con la realidad de nuestro desarrollo económico, social y político, ni tienen la coherencia requerida por los cuerpos jurídicos de este carácter. La aprobación de un nuevo Código Penal se halla incluida entre las tareas básicas del plan legislativo destinado a crear los cuerpos jurídicos fundamentales que, en sustitución de los antiguos, requiere nuestro Estado socialista"* (*Código Penal,* 1979:1)

12. *"En aquellos tiempos nosotros intuíamos que la política penal que se venía aplicando en el país no estaba en correspondencia con las condiciones sociales, políticas, y económicas alcanzadas . . . y que la respuesta penal con que veníamos actuando ante esta problemática [del delito en Cuba], sobre la base única de la represión, no nos permitiría superarla"* (Escalona, 1988:30,32).

13. See further Quirós (1985, 1987, 1988), Escasena (1988), Viera (1986, 1987), Vega Vega (1987), Escalona (1985, 1987), Amaro Salup (1989).

14. The Law of Civil, Administrative, and Labor Procedure (*Ley de Procedimiento Civil, Administrativo y Laboral*) is also generally revised alongside the LOSJ, since it is affected by changes in the court structure as well as by changes in the Civil, Labor, and Administrative Codes. Modifications of these codes have not been as rapid as in criminal law, however, lessening the need for frequent changes in the Law of Civil, Administrative, and Labor Procedure. The corresponding 1973 law was Law No. 1261, enacted January 4, 1974, and the corresponding 1977 law was Law No. 7. In the summer of 1990, a commission to modify the Law of Civil, Administrative, and Labor Procedure was being formed. The primary

impetus for this modification is the new Civil Code, however, rather than changes in the Law of the Courts.

15. The 1987 Criminal Code increased the jurisdiction of municipal courts to sanctions of one year's incarceration or 300 *cuotas*.

16. See Brady (1977, 1982), Salas (1979, 1983), Pepinsky (1982), Isaacman and Isaacman (1982), Tiruchelvam (1984), Leng and Chiu (1985), Azicri (1985), Hirst (1985).

17. Work on all legislation that does not focus explicitly on the country's grave economic needs was halted in late 1990. The new LPP will be an expensive law since it will require major changes in institutions. The *anteproyecto* for a new LPP was submitted to the Council of State in the fall of 1992, but a final version of these reforms is not expected to be passed until 1994 or 1995.

18. A different source, also a member of this commission, told me that each agency has two representatives. The difference between these two sources can be explained by the fact that each agency *formally* has two representatives to the commission, but due to other responsibilities, sometimes only one agency representative attends the meetings. The Ministry of Justice and the Supreme Court, like other agencies, have the right to assign two members to the commission but chose to send only one representative each. Theoretically it is possible for law professors from other universities to serve on commissions instead of University of Havana professors, but this is difficult in practice due to problems internal to these other universities (see Chapter Four) and geographic distance from the capital city.

19. Since the new LPP is not likely to be passed until 1994 or 1995, this cannot be viewed as conclusive. Nevertheless, it provides further evidence that the defense will enter case processing considerably earlier than in the past.

20. It should be noted that this is my own interpretation. No Cuban legal scholars or policy makers offered or explicitly corroborated this opinion, although neither did they dispute the potential validity of my interpretation. And, the Ministry of the Interior remains a very powerful force in Cuba. Nevertheless, I suggest that the Ministry of the Interior, and in particular its police department, is losing power to the substantially more professional Ministry of Justice and Office of the Attorney General.

21. This assumes that lay judges perceive themselves as acting on behalf of the average citizen and apply humanistic principles in their deliberations. As I demonstrate in Chapter Six, this assumption is valid in contemporary Cuba, but not necessarily in other contexts. For instance, in Nicaragua during the Sandinista era there was a severe shortage of lawyers willing to serve as judges. Lay judges adjudicated many cases, but they were acting as legal professionals rather than as conveyers of popular sentiment (see McDonald and Zatz, 1992).

22. See Gundersen (1990, 1992) for an interesting analysis of the use of popular tribunals in Mozambique to increase women's access to law, thereby potentially enhancing gender equality.

23. "... *demanda la objetiva interpretación del nivel alcanzado por las condiciones sociales imperantes en un momento histórico específico ... [y] tiene que ser elaborado y reelaborado con sentido histórico y subordinado al curso fluyente de los acontecimientos, sin propósitos o finalidades de extensa durabilidad*" (Quirós, 1988:5).

24. "*Debemos erradicar de nuestras concepciones que las leyes se dictan para toda la vida o para un espacio muy largo de tiempo. Esto es imposible en la etapa actual de construcción de una nueva sociedad*" (de la Cruz Ochoa, 1985:50).

NOTES TO CHAPTER 4

1. This sentiment may have been particularly strong in Cuba, but it also arises in other revolutionary settings, such as Nicaragua (see McDonald and Zatz, 1992), South Africa (see Sachs, 1992), and Mozambique (see Sachs and Welch, 1990).

2. Students enrolled in *cursos libres* study on their own, coming to the university only to take exams based upon their assigned readings. Although rarely mentioned in any discussions of legal education in Cuba, this program still exists, with 1,512 students enrolled in *cursos libres* in the 1989–90 academic year (Castanedo Abay, July 4, 1990).

3. *"Es conocido que durante muchos años la enseñanza del Derecho no recibió la mejor atención y ello tuvo su consecuencia inmediata principalmente en el debilitamiento de la docencia en las Facultades de Derecho, en la ausencia de textos, materiales, programa de estudios adecuados, cuyos resultados se reflejaban ostensiblemente en la preparación deficiente con que egresaban los graduados de esta especialidad de las aulas universitarias"* (Machado Ventura, 1984:210).

4. *". . . la sensible ausencia de asignaturas en las que se expliquen algunos aspectos del Derecho y el Estado en nuestros planes de enseñanza media e incluso universitaria, lo que determina que con frecuencia encontremos en nuestros graduados universitarios y técnicos medios, una gran ignorancia jurídica, lo que afecta también a determinado número de dirigentes estatales que no son capaces de distinguir entre una ley, un decreto-ley y un decreto, ni conocen suficientemente la legislación laboral que están obligados a aplicar o a exigir que se aplique"* (Escalona, 1987:187–188; see also UNJC, 1987:6–7).

5. *"Continuar fortaleciendo la legalidad socialista y la lucha contra el delito. Elevar la calidad del trabajo judicial, enfatizando las tareas relacionadas con la preparación y formación de los cuadros jurídicos y exigiendo el cumplimiento de las normas del trabajo de jueces, fiscales, instructores y abogados"* (Central Committee of the Communist Party of Cuba, 1983:10, punto 25).

6. *"Incrementar los esfuerzos encaminados al fortalecimiento de la Legalidad Socialista. Mejorar el trabajo de educación jurídica y de divulgación de las leyes y demás normas jurídicas entre las masas. Ejecutar y controlar adecuadamente el programa de superación político-ideológica de los juristas. Trabajar en la elaboracion de nuevas legislaciones acordes con el carácter y los objetivos de nuestra sociedad . . . elevando la eficiencia y calidad de la actividad de los órganos e instituciones correspondientes"* (Central Committee of the Communist Party of Cuba, 1984:18, punto 24).

7. *"Nadie duda que en estos momentos se perciben avances positivos en esa dirección, pero todos estamos conscientes que nos falta un largo camino que recorrer. En ese empeño se trabaja, para elaborar un nuevo plan de estudios de dichas Facultades, que debe conducirnos a una preparación más integral, que abandone la enseñanza memorística y normativista de las leyes y que arribe, oportunamente, al conocimiento de las instituciones jurídicas socialistas y logre dar a conocer a sus alumnos las bases filosóficas y políticas que explican la necesidad de su existencia . . ."* (Escalona, 1987:191).

8. *"Sólo así será posible alcanzar el desarrollo cultural y técnico imprescindible para dar respuesta a la demanda que nos formulara en 1982, la Dirección del Partido"* (Escalona, 1987:192).

9. University students receive a military deferral, and upon graduation they serve in the army reserve, rather than in active duty. Since 1986, the military has called a portion of the student reserve to serve for six months of active duty. This responsibility generally applies only to men, with women reserve members only called into active duty if they attended a military high school in preparation for a career in the military.

10. Interviews typically last about twenty minutes and cover the applicant's motivation, conception of justice, inclination to defend "what is just and true," and moral conduct. Although in reality very few students are turned away as a result of this interview, it is perceived to be an important step in the selection process (Castanedo Abay, July 4, 1990; Escalona, 1987:192; Fernández Jiménez, April 13, 1989).

11. Reported estimates of the number of Cuban law students are not always internally consistent. Some estimates are based on the number of students *enrolled* in a given year, others on the number of students *entering* the law schools in a given year, and others on the number of students *graduating* in a given year. Also, some estimates include day and night students, while others count only day students, and some include students at the University of Pinar del Río during the five years in the 1970s when it offered a law degree. In addition, until recently systematic admissions records were not kept. I have presented all of the published estimates to provide readers the opportunity, where possible, to examine each of the several indicators of the number of law students. In my estimation, the most accurate estimates are those reported by the UNJC, reprinted here in Table 4.1, and recent enrollment figures from the records of the Dean of the Law School at the University of Havana (Tables 4.2 and 4.3).

12. I was told in the summer of 1990 that the law schools were discussing the requirements of the state exam and honors thesis with the Ministry of Higher Education. It was unclear at that point whether (1) the current system (of top students writing honors theses and all others taking the state exam) would be maintained; (2) all students would be required to take the state exam; (3) all students would be required to write theses; or (4) all students would be required to take the state exam but those who wished could also write theses. The dilemma is similar to that of many U.S. master's programs vacillating between comprehensive exams and theses, except that the number of graduates in law is greater than in most U.S. master's programs. Requiring all students to write theses would tremendously increase the work of the supervising faculty, since theses in law tend to run well over 100 pages. It is unreasonable to expect that many students would choose to write theses *in addition* to taking the state exam. Thus, maintenance of the current system or requiring all students to take the state exam are the more likely outcomes.

13. Grading is based on a four-point scale ranging from five (excellent) through four (good) and three (average) to two (poor). Any student receiving a course grade of two is placed on suspension. Midterm and final essay exams written by the teaching collective are given in each course. Faculty, in turn, are evaluated by the students. The University Student Federation (FEU) conducts the evaluations with assistance from the Union of Young Communists (UJC). Representatives of the FEU meet with students, and later with the head of the department and the professors involved, to discuss these student evaluations (Hernández Ramírez, April 13, 1989; Fernández, April 13, 1989).

14. On two occasions I served as a second critic for theses concerning political-juridical matters in the United States. There was not a second *opo-*

nente in the other three defenses I observed, but I cannot say with any certainty how common it is to have a second critic.

15. During one's *servicio social* the government pays a small stipend and living expenses, but not a regular salary. Sometimes, the best workers receive a salary, during their third year of *servicio social,* comparable to that earned by jurists who have already completed their social service.

16. Sources for this section include two preliminary drafts of Plan C, the final version of Plan C, personal interviews with the Dean and a Vice-Dean of the University of Havana Law School at the time Plan C was developed (Julio Fernández Bulté and Omar Fernández Jiménez), and conversations about Plan C with approximately 20 professors as well as the head of the Federation of University Students at the University of Havana Law School during the spring and fall of 1989. Preliminary assessments of the plan at the end of its first year were provided by some of the same sources in the summer of 1991.

17. While the deans, the Attorney General, and the Minister and Vice-Minister of Justice are all party members, they do not represent the Communist Party at the Dean's Council. Rather, they represent their respective law schools, the Office of the Attorney General, and the Ministry of Justice. Only the official party representative formally represents the Cuban Communist Party's position at these meetings.

18. The intellectual space for critical thinking that emerged during the 1980s may become smaller in the 1990s. There has been some tightening of the political hard line in response to economic difficulties and a sense on the part of Fidel Castro and other top party officials that Cuba is under siege politically as a consequence of the move toward capitalism in much of Eastern Europe and the former Soviet Union. In this light, the resignation in late 1991 of Julio Fernández Bulté as Dean of the University of Havana Law School does not bode well, as he provided considerable intellectual and administrative support for critical thinking among faculty and students.

19. This is a bit unclear, since one source, a Vice-Dean, told me that the degree of *Candidato Dr.* is required for Associate or Full Professorships but two other sources said that it is not formally required but "weighs heavily" in promotion decisions and most Associate Professors have their C. Dr. degrees.

20. University professors do not receive extra pay for their practical work since it is defined as part of their job responsibilities. Rather, the organization which the professor serves pays the university (Machado Ventura, 1984:215). This appears to operate in a similar fashion to the practice in the United States of "buying out" a faculty member's time.

21. *"Poseemos viejas experiencias que muestran que un verdadero profesor de Derecho, solo se forma cuando se combina adecuadamente su docencia con la práctica profesional como juez, fiscal, abogado, notario, arbitro o asesor de organismos o empresas. Es de esta forma que debemos sentar las bases de desarrollo de los docentes, haciéndoles compartir su cátedra con la práctica . . ."* (Escalona, 1987:191–192).

NOTES TO CHAPTER 5

1. "Legal borrowing," while a common term in the literature, is not used here because it implies a noncritical transplantation. Adaptation is more suggestive of a spirit of assessment and selective modeling following careful

review. Also, as a Cuban colleague pointed out after I used the term "borrow-ing" (*prestando*), to borrow suggests that you will return something after you are done with it, like a neighbor's garden tool. That is clearly not what hap-pens in the realm of ideas.

2. The U.S. blockade against Cuba began in 1961 and continues to this date. As part of its effort to stop dollars from reaching Cuba, the U.S. govern-ment prohibits not only trade in goods, but also travel to Cuba by most of its citizens. The United States is isolated in its maintenance of the blockade, with most of its close allies (e.g., Great Britain, France, Canada) trading freely with Cuba (see Appendix H).

The United States attempted to strengthen the blockade further in 1992 when it passed the Cuban Democracy Act (better known as the Torricelli bill), which tries to restrict foreign governments from trade with Cuba. Other nations have not accepted this limitation on their economic and political sov-ereignty, as was evidenced by the November 24, 1992 vote on the international repercussions of the Torricelli bill in the United Nations. Only Israel and Rumania sided with the U.S., with all other nations voting in oppo-sition or abstaining.

The Clinton Administration supports a continuation of the blockade, including the Torricelli bill. It may, however, be willing to negotiate certain points. The U.S. Treasury Department took the unprecedented step of approv-ing a license for a humanitarian agency to send food and medicine to Cuba following the devastating March 1993 "storm of the century." This delegation was led by former U.S. Attorney General Ramsey Clark. Also, in July 1993 Clinton indicated some willingness to negotiate expanded telephone service with the Cubans, with the Cuban government receiving its share of the rev-enues. A major contingency in any such negotiation will be release of the $80 million in escrow already owed Cuba for past telephone service. Thus far, the United States has not been willing to release these funds, and the Cuban gov-ernment is not likely to agree to any arrangement that ignores this debt.

As is evidenced by U.S. trade relations with China, and most recently with North Korea and Viet Nam, economic considerations may ultimately pre-vail over cold-war politics. Major U.S. corporations may pressure the government to repeal the blockade so they can join Spanish, Italian, Japanese, Canadian, and other foreign businesses in profiting from joint ventures with Cuba, especially in the lucrative tourism industry.

3. Jurists in the Ministry of Justice who worked closely with the Nicaraguans as part of the Ministry's technical collaborations have similarly expressed the frank and open nature of discussions between Cuban and Nicaraguan lawyers (Guintén, Pérez and Rodríguez Chacón, May 11, 1989). Nicaraguan jurists whom I interviewed in Managua in 1989 echoed these sentiments.

4. Since Mexico does not have a Ministry of Justice, the agreement is between the Cuban Ministry of Justice and a major Mexican university. Similarly, Cuba maintained close collaborative relations with Sandinista lawyers, even after Nicaragua's Ministry of Justice was dismantled in 1988 as part of that country's administrative reorganization. Nicaraguans were invited to Cuba, and Cuban legal specialists taught seminars in Nicaragua (Arteaga Abreu, April 19, 1989; Guintén, Pérez, Rodríguez Chacón, May 11, 1989).

5. No information is available for the years prior to 1967. The number of books in Table 5.1 does not match the number of law-related books in

Appendix G because Table 5.1 only includes books published by the major publishing house, *Editorial de Ciencias Sociales*. Books published by minor publishing houses and the Ministry of Higher Education are not included. Also, some socio-legal books included in Table 5.1 are listed under sociology or political science in Appendix G, and the category for law in Appendix G includes titles in additional areas.

6. Export data are from the *Anuario Estadístico de Cuba, 1985* (*Comité Estatal de Estadísticas*), Chapter 11, Table 11.7, pp. 384–387.

NOTES TO CHAPTER 6

1. President is used in two contexts in this chapter. First is the president of a panel of judges, indicated by a lower-case "p" in president. The second usage is President of a court, designated with the capital "P." The President of a criminal court oversees the administration of all criminal cases in the courthouse. This position is roughly equivalent to Chief Presiding Judge in U.S. courts.

2. In contrast, in the Soviet Union the appellate panels consist solely of professional judges, with no lay representation (Rand, 1991:96).

3. The percentage of professional judges in provincial courts has declined since 1988, when these data were collected. The 1990 Law of the Courts changed the composition of most provincial court panels from three professional and two lay judges (like the Supreme Court) to one professional and two lay judges (like the municipal courts). Recall from Chapter Three that lay judges serve one month per year, so twelve lay judges are needed to cover each lay position annually. Similarly, two professional judges may share a position if each serves as a judge for six months and works six months at her or his regular job. This is particularly likely in the case of law professors elected to judgeships.

4. My sources were somewhat ambiguous about whether a law-school graduate who works in some other profession could be a lay judge. The Law of the Tribunals states simply that the candidate cannot be a practicing jurist.

5. Candidates for positions as professional judges must have a law degree, be a Cuban citizen, enjoy a good public reputation, and evidence good moral conduct. They must have eight years of juridical experience to serve on the Supreme Court, five years for the provincial courts, and two years for the municipal courts (Article 41, 1990 Law of the Tribunals). Beginning in November 1991, professional judges must also pass written and oral qualifying exams prior to being named as a judge or promoted to a higher court (Ministry of Justice Resolution No. 39, April 10, 1991, and Ministry of Justice Resolution No. 96, August 8, 1991).

6. Uncertainty arose during the course of my research as to whether the Federation of Cuban Women (FMC) nominates candidates for judgeships. The Director of the Office of Preparation, Supervision, and Evaluation of Juridical Personnel, Francisco Javier Fernández Guerra, told me that the FMC was one of the nominating organizations (April 26, 1989). When I later met with two representatives of the FMC, Catherine Ribas and Ida González, they said that while the FMC might possibly nominate candidates at the municipal level, they had never heard of this occurring at the provincial or national level. They pointed out that the right to nominate judges was not a major issue for the FMC because most working women belong to this organization, and the majority of judicial

actors (i.e., judges, prosecutors, and criminal defense and civil attorneys) today are women. Consequently, the FMC "is actually very well represented in the courts" (May 10, 1989). They later checked with the FMC national office, reporting back to me, "The FMC definitively does not propose lay judges, but it can give an opinion about a person nominated" (May 16, 1989).

When I pursued this contradictory set of statements with María Luisa Arteaga Abreu of the Ministry of Justice, I learned that nominations are requested from the FMC and the Committees for the Defense of the Revolution (CDR). The FMC and CDRs occasionally submit names of candidates for municipal court lay judgeships, but most lay judges are elected from their workplaces (May 11, 1989). The final word on this controversy comes from the 1990 Law of the Courts, which states that candidates for lay judgeships are proposed in the workplace, places of study, and neighborhoods (Article 46).

7. There are a few exceptions to this rule. For example, one lay judge whom I interviewed was employed in the Ministry of Justice's Office of Preparation, Supervision, and Evaluation of Juridical Personnel (*Dirección de Cuadros y Capacitación*). This work experience, which included training judges, qualified her to become a provincial court judge without having served in municipal court.

8. This was unquestionably a "home video," rather than a professional production. For example, different colored lightbulbs were used to create varied background colors. The President of the Supreme Court was taped during regular working hours, as his desk phone rang incessantly while he was making his remarks.

9. Cubans work every second Saturday, for an average work week of 44 hours.

10. The only time I sensed any reluctance on the part of lay judges to adjudicate cases on an equal footing with their professional colleagues was when I asked some municipal court lay judges what they thought of a possible increase in the municipal court's jurisdiction to include more serious cases. While I was privy to discussions among top policy makers of the pros and cons of altering this court's jurisdiction (see Chapter Three), my mention of this possibility was the first these judges had heard of it. Accustomed as I am in the United States to people wanting to expand their power base, I was surprised when lay judges said that they would have to think about the idea, since they were not sure they had the practical experience or skill to adjudicate such cases. It is, perhaps, important to remember that with very few exceptions, lay judges in Cuba's provincial courts and Supreme Court must have prior experience in municipal court, and that lay judges serve only one month per year. The municipal court judges I interviewed were relatively inexperienced, and they were leery of accepting responsibilities that they were not certain they could adequately fulfill.

11. "... *Es claro que el Abogado ha de defender, en el proceso Civil, el interés de la parte que representa; y en el penal, al acusado de cuya defensa se encarga ... [en penal el abogado es] leal a su defendido, y leal, al mismo tiempo, a la sociedad*" (Lagunilla Martínez and Yanes Sosa, 1989:78–79).

12. "*El Abogado al ejercer su defensa, ha de exigir que se incorporen al proceso todos los elementos, proponer cuantas pruebas puedan favorecer el interés de su defendido pero sobre todo que ayude a revelar la verdad y esclarecer los hechos. El éxito de su función no es lograr la absolución, sino que se establezca la verdad ...*" (Lagunilla Martínez and Yanes Sosa, 1989:79).

NOTES TO CHAPTER 7

1. Note that unlike the grievance commissions which preceded them, the *consejos* had jurisdiction over wage disputes, evaluations, and promotions.

2. The data are as complete as possible, but some cases are pending and inaccuracies occur in recording and compiling data. It must be remembered that Cuba is a Third World country with limited access to computers. Data are compiled by hand at each courthouse, and then national-level statistics are calculated. At each stage, errors can occur. The data were made available by labor law specialist Lydia Guevara Ramírez from Supreme Court and State Committee for Work and Social Security (*Comité Estatal de Trabajo y Seguridad Social*) records.

3. Cases involving criminal charges go to criminal court, but also to labor court if they occurred in the workplace. Of the 4,642 labor cases involving crimes in 1990, 1,767, or 38.1 percent, were thefts and robberies, including embezzlement.

4. "*La facultad de las administraciones para imponer directamente medidas disciplinarias con efecto inmediato debe mantenerse, pero es conveniente darle una mayor participación al colectivo laboral . . .*" (fourth Whereas of Decree-Law No. 121, July 19, 1990).

APPENDIX

Appendix A. Mean Annual Salary,
             by Economic Spheres and Sectors [in pesos]

	1977	1978	1979
Total	1,645	1,680	1,721
Productive Sphere	1,628	1,669	1,712
Industry	1,788	1,854	1,862
Construction	1,745	1,843	1,923
Agriculture and livestock industry	1,330	1,357	1,418
Forestry	1,665	1,672	1,672
Transportation	2,083	2,094	2,139
Communications	1,723	1,726	1,763
Commerce	1,561	1,564	1,567
Other productive activities	2,152	2,103	2,151
Nonproductive Sphere	1,695	1,710	1,744
Communal and personal services	1,506	1,569	1,604
Science and technical	1,921	2,075	2,123
Education	1,577	1,618	1,682
Culture and art	1,981	1,858	1,996
Public health and social aid; sports and tourism	1,666	1,697	1,711
Finance and insurance	2,037	2,093	2,052
Administration	1,904	1,901	1,870
Other nonproductive activities	1,733	1,800	1,758

Sources: *Anuario Estadístico de Cuba*, 1978 (1977 figures),
          pg. 57, Table 1.
          Anuario Estadístico de Cuba, 1983 (1978–79 figures),
          pg. 108, Table IV.6.
          Anuario Estadístico de Cuba, 1985 (1980–85 figures),
          pg. 191, Table IV.7.

1980	1981	1982	1983	1984	1985
1,774	2,035	2,113	2,159	2,230	2,252
1,761	2,056	2,120	2,173	2,252	2,269
1,883	2,138	2,209	2,267	2,309	2,329
1,969	2,242	2,241	2,346	2,468	2,442
1,520	1,923	2,000	2,004	2,100	2,155
1,706	1,914	1,986	1,988	2,097	2,120
2,169	2,402	2,479	2,551	2,606	2,591
1,752	1,960	2,021	2,041	2,106	2,137
1,611	1,817	1,894	1,959	2,033	2,023
2,137	2,241	2,380	2,482	2,472	2,454
1,809	1,985	2,095	2,126	2,177	2,214
1,637	1,814	1,865	1,900	1,966	1,955
2,147	2,251	2,408	2,396	2,416	2,531
1,763	1,943	2,044	2,086	2,139	2,178
2,036	2,135	2,686	2,772	2,729	2,689
1,777	1,955	2,017	2,027	2,077	2,124
2,009	2,118	2,211	2,209	2,194	2,235
1,952	2,123	2,243	2,261	2,346	2,404
1,781	2,060	2,055	2,184	2,260	2,257

Appendix B. Medical Aid Facilities, Ministry of Public Health

	1958	1962	1963	1964	1965	1966	1967	1968	1969	1970	1971
Total	393	493	457	507	511	523	590	680	716	918	990
Medical Aid	393				481					872	
Hospitals	337	143	149	156	251	172	182	195	207	225	235
General	67	71	72	72	60	73	76	77	82	64	84
Surgical clinics	–				13					21	
Rural	1	35	38	41	43	44	44	48	47	48	51
Maternity	10	10	10	14	16	22	28	32	38	21	47
Other Medical Aid	56				230					647	
Polyclinics	52	141	152	162	171	197	239	282	290	308	314
Rural medical posts	–	–	–	43	40	38	60	94	91	96	121
Maternity homes	–	–	–	–	–	–	–	14	17	22	38
Blood banks	1	2	3	4	7	9	13	16	16	18	19
Social aid	•				30					46	
Homes for the elderly	*	*	27	27	29	30	31	35	37	40	44
Homes for the physically and mentally impaired	•	–	–	1	1	2	3	3	3	6	5

• Missing data do not affect calculations

– Refers to numbers equal to zero.

* Not available

Sources: *Anuario Estadístico de Cuba,* 1972 (1962–64, 1966–68 figures), pg. 252, Table 2.
Anuario Estadístico de Cuba, 1978 (1969, 1971–77 figures), pg. 256, Table 2.
Anuario Estadístico de Cuba, 1985 (1958, 1965, 1970, 1975, 1978–85 figures), pg. 526, Table XV.3.

1972	1973	1974	1975	1976	1977	1978	1979	1980	1981	1982	1983	1984	1985
1,036	1,086	1,095	1,104	1,143	1,160	1,196	1,232	1,243	1,331	1,399	1,530	1,672	1,788
		1,050				1,121	1,156	1,159	1,233	1,294	1,419	1,556	1,661
252	260	255	261	259	257	260	262	262	262	264	268	276	277
86	89	88	68	91	89	67	69	68	67	69	70	76	76
		22				22	22	23	23	23	22	27	27
56	56	56	58	57	56	52	53	53	52	52	54	56	57
51	53	53	23	56	57	23	22	21	20	20	21	20	20
		789				851	882	885	959	1,018	1,139	1,268	1,372
318	326	326	339	345	349	371	378	386	388	397	396	403	417
110	113	118	114	140	131	131	150	151	167	173	183	218	281
44	51	61	61	62	63	60	65	67	77	81	85	103	108
19	21	22	21	21	21	21	21	21	21	21	24	24	25
		54				75	76	84	98	105	111	116	127
45	47	47	48	49	50	66	67	74	82	87	94	98	109
6	6	6	6	6	7	9	9	10	16	18	17	18	18

Appendix C. Medical Personnel in the Ministry of Public Health

	1958(a)	1964	1965	1966	1967(b)	1968	1969	1970	1971	1972(f)	1973
Total	2,404	23,013	25,413	25,449	29,969	•	32,939	•	•	34,705	42,472
Doctors	1,125	6,655	6,238	7,036	6,608	*	6,028	6,152	6,204	6,549	7,043
Dentists	250	1,070	1,200	1,121	1,081	*	1,248	1,366	1,149	1,346	1,746
Pharmacists	46	57	519	438	380	*	709 (c)	*	*	790	731
Nurses and nurses' auxiliaries	826	8,347	9,637	10,253	12,459	*	14,372	4,803	13,155	13,871	17,210
Technicians and auxiliaries	157	6,404	7,819	6,601	9,441 (d)	*	10,852	*	3,238 (e)	12,149	15,742

- • Missing data do not affect calculations.
- * Not available.

Sources: *Anuario Estadístico de Cuba,* 1972 (1958–72 figures), pg. 256, Table 1.

Notes: (a) Excludes those in Mutual Health Societies.
(b) Includes positions contracted for as of December 31, 1967.
(c) Includes pharmacy and excludes production.
(d) Includes personnel from private practices that were nationalized.
(e) Refers to laboratory and x-ray technicians and aids.
(f) As of September 30.
(g) Taken from 1985 *anuario.*

Anuario Estadístico de Cuba, 1981 (1973–79 figures), pg. 273, Table 1.

Notes: The number of doctors and dentists corresponds to the total of the Registry of Professionals. Otherwise, only those working with the Ministry of Public Health are included.
Includes dental, pharmacy, laboratory, and X-ray technicians and assistants, and other intermediate health technicians.
Beginning with 1981, social workers are excluded.

Anuario Estadístico de Cuba, 1985 (1980–85 figures), pg. 525, Table XV.1

Notes: The number of doctors and dentists corresponds to the total of the Registry of Professionals

Cuba en Cifras, 1987 (1985–86 figures), pg. 115, Table 131

1974	1975	1976	1977	1978	1979	1980	1981	1982	1983	1984	1985	1986
47,965	54,089	60,206	66,815	72,351	75,033	71,176	73,797	79,758	89,191	103,563	115,989	125,955
8,190	9,328	10,671	13,908	14,388	15,038	15,247	16,210	16,836	18,828	20,490	22,910	25,567
2,029	2,319	2,425	3,130	3,356	3,549	3,646	4,188	3,986	4,380	4,711	5,335	5,752
689	741	737	769	777	773	733	730	700	714	633	610	650
19,131	21,193	23,725	24,900	26,249	26,457	27,193	29,399	31,855	35,058	38,793	42,740	48,339
17,926	20,508	22,648	24,108	27,581	29,216	24,357	23,270	26,381	30,211	38,936	43,653(g)	*

Appendix D. Housing

	1964	1965	1966	1967	1968	1969	1970	1971	1972	1973	1974
Total	7,088	5,040	6,271	10,257	6,450	4,817	4,004	5,014	16,807	20,710	18,552
Construction Firms:											
Ministry of Construction											
Number								2,475	15,813	20,108	18,293
Percent								49.4	94.1	97.1	98.6
Other Construction Firms											
Number								2,539	994	602	259
Percent								50.6	5.9	2.9	1.4
Total											
Percent of total											
Non-Construction Firms											
Percent of total											
Cooperatives											

Sources: *Anuario Estadístico de Cuba,* 1973 (1964–70 figures), pg. 150, Table 6
Anuario Estadístico de Cuba, 1978 (1971–75 figures), pg. 103, Table 4.
Anuario Estadístico de Cuba, 1981 (1976–80 figures), pg. 126, Table 4.
Anuario Estadístico de Cuba, 1985 (1981–84 figures), pg. 264, Table VII.6.
Cuba en Cifras, 1987 (1985–87 figures), pg. 51, Table 40.

1975	1976	1977	1978	1979	1980	1981	1982	1983	1984	1985	1986	1987
18,602	15,342	20,024	17,072	14,523	15,079	58,370	62,108	66,369	68,963	26,248	25,841	26,638
18,376	15,127	19,893	16,858	14,201	14,801	16,203	15,413	15,335	16,624	18,118	16,943	10,837
98.8	98.6	99.3	98.7	97.8	98.2							
226	215	131	214	322	278	623	1,895	2,389	1,676	1,775	2,383	5,914
1.2	1.4	0.7	1.3	2.2	1.8							
						16,826	17,308	17,724	18,300			
						28.8	27.9	26.7	26.5			
						1,421	3,903	6,366	4,529	4,302	3,806	5,085
						2.4	6.3	9.6	6.6			
						610	1,384	2,766	2,564	2,053	2,709	4,802

Appendix E. Middle Schools

	1958/59	1959/60	1960/61	1961/62	1962/63	1963/64	1964/65
Schools	•	184	315	284	315	330	357
Basic Secondary Rural	*	160	291	256	301	290	324
Pre–university Rural Vocational	21	24	24	28	14	33	33
Teaching Personnel	2,580	3,612	5,224	6,500	7,136	7,740	8,467
Basic Secondary Rural	1,400	2,349	4,055	5,438	5,914	6,460	7,079
Pre–university Rural	1,180	1,263	1,169	1,062	1,222	1,280	1,388
Enrollment	63,526	59,582	89,754	109,324	123,118	137,930	136,726
Basic Secondary Rural	26,278	35,100	71,057	91,482	107,598	121,090	118,109
Pre–university Rural	37,248	24,482	18,697	17,842	15,520	16,830	18,617
Graduates	•	2,455	11,806	10,877	10,563	15,700	18,310
Basic Secondary Rural	*	–	10,320	8,282	8,225	12,440	15,840
Pre–university Rural	1,272	2,455	1,486	2,595	2,338	3,290	2,470

• Missing data do not affect calculations
* Not available
– Refers to numbers equal to zero

Sources: *Anuario Estadístico de Cuba,* 1972 (1958/59–1966/67 figures), pg. 241, Table 8.
     Notes: The last two digits (far right) of all 1963/64 figures were difficult to read. In some cases, one or both were completely unreadable and zeros were used in their place
    Anuario Estadístico de Cuba, 1981 (1967/68–1978/79 figures), pg. 242, Table 11.
     Notes: (a) Corresponds to the number of rural basic secondary schools; the urban ones had no graduates due to a change in plan of study.
    Anuario Estadístico de Cuba, 1985 (1979/80–1984/85 figures), adapted from the following tables:
    Table XIII.5, pg. 483; Table XIII.6, pg. 485; Table XIII.8, pg. 487; Table XIII.10, pp. 488–489.
    Cuba en Cifras, 1987 (1985/86–1986/87 figures), pg. 104, Table 112.

1965/66	1966/67	1967/68	1968/69	1969/70	1970/71	1971/72	1972/73
378	416	424	435	413	410	478	498
344	378	390	400	380	376	441	459
		–	–	–	–	7	51
34	38	34	35	33	34	37	39
		–	–	–	–	–	–
		–	–	–	–	–	*
9,584	10,196	11,388	10,834	13,483	15,273	15,966	16,734
8,072	8,694	9,828	9,576	12,566	14,334	14,881	15,434
1,512	1,502	1,560	1,258	917	939	1,085	1,300
149,374	171,421	178,511	187,575	177,917	186,667	201,810	222,481
125,252	143,940	161,732	170,458	161,314	171,206	186,115	200,448
		–	–	–	–	3,438	24,891
24,122	27,481	16,779	17,117	16,603	15,461	15,695	22,033
		–	–	–	–	–	–
15,818	20,491	5,461	10,864	13,272	11,816	14,045	19,480
13,555	16,154	40(a)	6,574	8,073	7,589	12,243	14,957
		–	–	–	–	385	2,311
2,263	4,337	5,421	4,290	5,199	4,227	1,802	4,523
		–	–	–	–	–	–

Appendix E. Middle Schools (continued)

	1973/74	1974/75	1975/76	1976/77	1977/78	1978/79	1979/80
Schools	555	642	751	886	1,036	1,202	1,802
Basic Secondary	502	578	672	793	903	1,038	1,128
Rural	93	150	209	320	368	402	420
Pre-university	44	49	61	75	119	150	179
Rural	5	20	33	42	78	97	113
Vocational	9	15	18	18	14	14	11
Teaching Personnel	21,475	26,504	32,755	45,149	49,586	58,136	
Basic Secondary	19,813	24,541	30,052	41,311	42,222	49,357	51,990
Rural							17,277
Pre-university	1,662	1,963	2,703	3,838	7,364	8,779	9,940
Rural							4,718
Enrollment	265,589	337,524	420,315	535,100	645,588	759,288	
Basic Secondary	239,437	307,209	382,643	485,878	556,845	645,944	690,503
Rural	45,658	75,488	107,058	178,947	201,894	216,913	223,364
Pre-university	26,152	30,315	37,672	49,231	88,743	113,344	135,349
Rural	3,445	9,594	15,824	22,706	41,668	51,179	61,716
Graduates	22,472	35,020	45,190	146,023	126,788	157,849	
Basic Secondary	16,966	27,210	35,911	122,004	108,974	134,384	172,174
Rural	4,998	9,842	14,058	48,513	40,385	52,668	58,749
Pre-university	5,506	7,810	9,279	24,019	17,814	23,465	30,261
Rural	783	2,165	3,465	11,158	8,175	10,032	12,417

• Missing data do not affect calculations
* Not available
– Refers to numbers equal to zero

Sources: *Anuario Estadístico de Cuba,* 1972 (1958/59–1966/67 figures), pg. 241, Table 8.
   Notes: The last two digits (far right) of all 1963/64 figures were difficult to read.
     In some cases, one or both were completely unreadable and zeros were used
     in their place
   Anuario Estadístico de Cuba, 1981 (1967/68–1978/79 figures), pg. 242, Table 11.
   Notes: (a) Corresponds to the number of rural basic secondary schools;
     the urban ones had no graduates due to a change in plan of study.
   Anuario Estadístico de Cuba, 1985 (1979/80–1984/85 figures), adapted from the
   following tables:
   Table XIII.5, pg. 483; Table XIII.6, pg. 485; Table XIII.8, pg. 487; Table XIII.10,
   pp. 488–489.
   Cuba en Cifras, 1987 (1985/86–1986/87 figures), pg. 104, Table 112.

1980/81	1981/82	1982/83	1983/84	1984/85	1985/86	1986/87
1,902	1,956	1,914	2,059	2,086	1,234	1,293
1,132	1,115	1,054	1,008	1,018	1,027	1,025
415	414	384	362	351	340	342
220	238	246	253	248	260	268
141	157	183	202	209	204	213
10	11	19	30	30	37	39
					65,900	67,100
51,933	51975	51,512	50,583	50,473	51,200	50,900
16,774	15,795	15,679	15,080	14,545	14,200	14,900
11,752	13,113	13,589	14,100	14,022	14,700	16,200
5,761	6,059	7,626	8,673	9,314	9,300	9,700
					807,600	808,700
677,590	654,840	610,182	609,402	627,396	635,900	622,500
211,784	207,390	191,081	185,540	180,130	177,500	186,300
159,671	171,637	164,228	164,379	166,120	171,700	178,200
71,760	81,456	93,605	103,855	113,234	112,900	177,400
					193,300	217,600
170,484	178,473	173,360	170,816	162,655	153,100	174,400
50,610	54,412	53,317	51,942	46,968	41,200	46,000
33,123	39,202	45,063	42,836	41,911	40,200	43,200
13,609	16,139	22,168	23,206	26,690	26,800	28,700

Appendix F. Technical and Professional Schools, Faculty, and Students

	1958/59	1959/60	1960/61	1961/62	1962/63	1963/64	1964/65
Schools	40	37	50	49	57	120	120
Industrial (a)	20	13	21	25	31	40	36
Agriculture and animal husbandry (b)	–	6	6	–	–	6	9
Economy and administration	20	18	23	24	26	74	75
Teaching Personnel	1,267	1,108	1,300	1,759	2,564	3,373	2,930
Industrial (a)	834	526	625	1,189	1,476	2,185	1,676
Agriculture and animal husbandry (c)	–	83	105	–	–	103	139
Economy and administration	433	499	570	570	1,088	1,085	1,115
Enrollment	15,586	20,963	25,632	34,103	35,966	48,872	48,531
Industrial (a)	6,382	6,215	10,510	18,490	14,269	20,208	13,508
Agriculture and animal husbandry (d)	–	468	488	–	–	1,303	5,709
Economy and administration	9,204	14,280	14,634	15,613	21,697	27,363	29,314
Intermediate technician							
Qualified worker							
Graduates	1,594	2,520	781	589	5,475	9,120	5,708
Industrial (a)	590	1,066	351	61	694	5,460	3,342
Agriculture and animal husbandry (e)	–	81	57	–	–	90	–
Economy and administration	1,004	1,373	373	528	4,781	3,570	2,366
Intermediate technician							
Qualified worker							

– Refers to numbers that were equal to zero.

Sources: *Anuario Estadístico de Cuba,* 1972 (1958/59–1966/67 figures), pg. 240, Table 9

Notes: (a) Includes the schools of maritime offices and the Aeronautic Technology Institute and beginning in 1963/64 the schools of fishing.
(b) Includes centers for the study of the soil since 1964/65.
(c) Excludes the data of the Planning Council.
(d) Includes the enrollment of the Planning Council.
(e) Includes the graduates of the Planning Council. The last digit (far right) of all figures for 1963/64 was difficult to read; in cases where it was completely unreadable, a zero was substituted.

1965/66	1966/67	1967/68	1968/69	1969/70	1970/71	1971/72	1972/73
118	124	108	102	97	91	86	93
39	37						
16	24						
63	63						
2,970	3,328	3,122	3,329	4,200	4,645	4,355	4,805
1,969	2,278						
168	224						
833	826						
45,536	51,477	83,089	55,860	44,890	27,566	30,429	41,940
15,244	19,729						
17,120	18,172						
13,172	13,576						
		15,644	15,671	26,672	13,823	18,318	19,057
		67,445	40,189	18,218	13,743	12,111	22,883
4,286	5,537	9,726	9,247	8,881	10,533	11,973	12,567
1,787	2,186						
1,005	1,909						
1,494	1,442						
		3,509	3,745	3,604	4,414	4,789	4,798
		6,217	5,502	5,277	6,119	7,184	7,769

Anuario Estadístico de Cuba, 1981 (1967/68–1978/79 figures), pg. 243, Table 12.
  Notes: Beginning in 1974/75, figures for number of schools, teaching personnel,
    and enrollment include other organisms.
    Figures for the number of graduates include Ministry of Education and other
    organisms
Anuario Estadístico de Cuba, 1985 (1979/80–1984/85 figures), adapted from the
  following tables:
    Table XIII.5, pg. 484; Table XIII.6, pg. 485; Table XIII.8, pg 487; Table
    XIII.10, pg. 489.
Cuba en Cifras, 1987 (1985/86–1986/87 figures), pg. 195, Table 113.

Appendix F. Technical and Professional Schools, Faculty, and Students (continued)

	1973/74	1974/75	1975/76	1976/77	1977/78	1978/79	1979/80
Schools	113	134	239	266	329	337	357
Industrial (a)							
Agriculture and animal husbandry (b)							
Economy and administration							
Teaching Personnel	5,683	6,465	7,342	8,756	11,673	14,630	16,163
Industrial (a)							
Agriculture and animal husbandry (c)							
Economy and administration							
Enrollment	56,959	94,634	114,653	159,440	194,032	198,261	214,615
Industrial (a)							
Agriculture and animal husbandry (d)							
Economy and administration							
Intermediate technician	24,517	48,317	60,938	78,564	173,353	120,754	144,055
Qualified worker	32,442	46,317	53,715	80,876	20,679	77,507	70,560
Graduates	16,144	16,257	19,245	25,143	41,782	49,764	58,259
Industrial (a)							
Agriculture and animal husbandry (e)							
Economy and administration							
Intermediate technician	5,203	5,639	8,740	8,318	14,871	21,296	31,710
Qualified worker	10,941	10,618	10,505	16,825	26,911	28,468	26,549

– Refers to numbers that were equal to zero.
Sources: *Anuario Estadístico de Cuba,* 1972 (1958/59–1966/67 figures), pg. 240, Table 9
Notes: (a) Includes the schools of maritime offices and the Aeronautic Technology Institute and beginning in 1963/64 the schools of fishing.
(b) Includes centers for the study of the soil since 1964/65.
(c) Excludes the data of the Planning Council.
(d) Includes the enrollment of the Planning Council.
(e) Includes the graduates of the Planning Council. The last digit (far right) of all figures for 1963/64 was difficult to read; in cases where it was completely unreadable, a zero was substituted.

1980/81	1981/82	1982/83	1983/84	1984/85	1985/86	1986/87
401	426	431	605	632	639	634
17,602	19,901	21,679	23,356	25,304	27,500	27,000
228,487	263,981	285,765	312,867	305,556	307,100	317,600
162,279	195,276	214,493	238,181	248,231	261,900	283,100
66,208	68,705	71,272	74,686	57,325	45,200	34,500
57,584	74,643	91,014	107,528	81,023	88,900	71,900
28,619	38,912	52,212	62,032	63,431	62,900	58,200
28,965	35,731	38,802	45,496	17,592	26,000	13,700

Anuario Estadístico de Cuba, 1981 (1967/68–1978/79 figures), pg. 243, Table 12.
  Notes: Beginning in 1974/75, figures for number of schools, teaching personnel,
      and enrollment include other organisms.
      Figures for the number of graduates include Ministry of Education and other
      organisms
Anuario Estadístico de Cuba, 1985 (1979/80–1984/85 figures), adapted from the
  following tables:
      Table XIII.5, pg. 484; Table XIII.6, pg. 485; Table XIII.8, pg 487; Table
      XIII.10, pg. 489.
Cuba en Cifras, 1987 (1985/86–1986/87 figures), pg. 195, Table 113.

Appendix G. Book Titles Published, by Subject

Subjects	1971	1972	1973	1974	1975(a)	1976	1977
Total	629	764	737	734	827 734	726	942
General	63	45	44	47	47	38	43
Philosophy/psychology	13	13	16	3	5	11	34
Religion/theology	2	2	–	–	1	–	1
Sociology/statistics	11	11	10	7	9	6	20
Political science/ political econ.	29	31	22	38	90	86	79
Law/public admin./social assistance/social security	2	7	20	6	5	4	10
Military arts and sciences	4	1	2	1	–	1	4
Teaching and education	147	230	189	225	248 155	159	116
Business/communication/ transportation	19	14	10	2	4	4	3
Ethnography/ uses of costumes/folklore	–	4	1	–	–	–	–
Linguistics/ filology	6	16	27	17	12	23	32
Mathematics	19	18	18	15	11	6	32
Natural sciences	26	30	28	16	16	22	66
Medical science/ public hygiene	66	87	46	31	27	33	39
Engineering/ technology/ industry/art and crafts	49	56	39	42	51	41	64
Agriculture/forestry/ livestock/	20	14	27	23	7	20	24
Hunting and fishing							
Domestic economy	2	–	–	1	–	1	–
Urban design/	9	16	30	9		4	5
Architecture/art and film					5		
Recreation and sports	3	9	9	6	2	4	4
Literature	98	87	107	189	257 257	222	331
Geography and travel	5	9	8	1	2	–	5
History and biography	36	64	84	55	28	41	30
Urbanism/architecture/territorial/conditioning							
Plastic arts/graphics/photography							
Music/theater/films							

– Not Available

Sources: *Anuario Estadístico de Cuba,* 1978 (1971–73 figures), pg. 226, Table 6.
Anuario Estadístico de Cuba, 1981 (1974–81 figures), pg. 253, Table 6.
Anuario Estadístico de Cuba, 1985 (1975, 1979–84 figures), pg. 503, Table XIV.2.
(a) Figures from the 1981 and 1985 Anuarios are inconsistent; both are noted.
Cuba en Cifras, 1987 (1985–87 Figures), pg. 111, Table 124.

1978	1979(a)	1980(a)	1981(a)	1982	1983	1984	1985
937	1,095	1,031	1,319	1,455	1,672	1,684	1,713
	1,013	894	1,304				
11	32	51	128	64	102	191	91
18	7	11	2	21	12	27	29
1	–	1	–	1	1	2	1
14	4	2	1	3	11	6	25
91	84	40	94	18	12	44	76
6	11	3	7	4	9	18	13
–	6	–	–	–	–	9	2
201	356	519	565	937	531	320	228
	274	406	565				
6	7	–	18	13	21	13	34
4	3	1	10	2	1	1	8
19	4	–	24	–	65	112	137
21	8	–	16	–	28	71	58
13	7	4	8	8	57	72	92
28	47	16	64	16	113	113	169
54	61	11	66	14	288	158	160
12	17	7	23	2	42	44	22
1	4	3	3	2	2	9	3
5							
	7	9	13				
20	25	26	15	13	76	22	35
352	372	310	254	258	224	297	371
	372	286	239				
14	5	4	–	–	20	24	34
46	28	13	8	57	40	56	75
	–	–	–	6	5	7	6
	–	–	–	10	6	9	19
	7	9	13	6	6	59	25

Appendix H. Imports by Region—Thousands of Pesos

Category	1959	1968	1969	1970	1971	1972	1973	1974	1975
Total	814,407	1,102,506	1,221,621	1,310,968	1,387,502	1,189,844	1,462,594	2,225,959	3,113,089
Asia	113,060	96,664	112,188	131,696	166,007	131,783	187,295	340,251	489,890
Asia (excluding Middle East)	103,865	90,504	104,584	126,503	158,265	c	c	c	c
China	a	a	b	b	b	72,100	84,830	128,160	86,670
Korea	a	a	b	b	b	11,378	12,378	21,819	10,493
Viet Nam	a	a	b	b	b	428	409	763	521
Mongolia	98	0	164	156	157	149	139	–	416
Malaysia	1,135	258	758	2,085	–	522	1,178	–	132
Japan	11,291	3,354	9,630	33,384	60,215	45,276	86,663	175,039	360,691
Hong Kong	111	–	–	278	253	346	371	451	1,519
Singapore	–	–	–	1,147	2,411	7	226	8,734	22,625
Sri Lanka	20	–	–	–	88	39	11	69	103
India	7,634	–	–	–	26	–	–	197	–
Others	83,576								
Europe	566,545	985,092	1,084,127	1,136,042	1,166,974	994,194	1,201,929	1,701,282	2,345,320
EEC	53,798	131,020	121,266	172,822	156,841	66,129	182,359	381,572	570,351
Belgium	4,932	1,906	2,518	3,003	5,278	6,550	12,929	29,613	19,467
France	14,443	66,853	46,513	60,570	63,387	18,154	29,552	55,938	105,380
Holland	11,264	9,613	5,731	20,870	16,398	6,119	18,692	39,575	50,604
Italy	9,034	41,693	36,075	54,617	54,608	11,996	19,895	45,625	98,389
W. Germany	14,015	10,955	30,429	33,723	17,170	23,310	39,146	107	140,075
Luxembourg	110	–	–	39	–	–	–	–	574
Denmark	1,118	1,190	3,424	5,161	3062	4,391	3,499	14,963	27,741
United Kingdom	25,218	31,221	66,338	59,124	61,446	42,661	53,550	83,935	128,120
Ireland	196	–	0	7	7	14	5,096	4,720	1
A.L.C.E.	34,638	39,485	99,793	89,543	93,820	76,583	41,196	56,273	116,135
Austria	231	1,702	1,745	4,007	1,248	975	3,613	10,656	35,149
Norway	1,643	2,149	2,269	1,438	1,735	126	1,822	951	6,816
Sweden	3,744	2,466	18,874	6,712	16,327	12,419	13,757	26,155	44,985
Switzerland	2,379	757	7,143	13,101	10,002	16,011	20,430	15,286	23,991
Portugal	305	–	–	–	–	–	–	–	1,459
Iceland	187	–	–	–	–	–	–	–	–
Finland	662	1,434	1,034	844	1,147	1,642	1,574	3,225	3,735
Spain	25,690	20,505	48,076	37,294	33,039	15,534	40,111	61,818	152,268
Andorra	7	–	–	2	53	–	13	–	–
Liechtenstein	7	–	2,446	7,981	7,199	3,381	769	–	–
Other	26	–	–	–	–	97	13	69	40
Eastern Europe	447,583	787,646	808,430	826,575	874,392	830,571	935,161	1,196,516	1,500,906
Albania	a	a	1,108	1,260	1,132	1,334	738	3,712	1,805
Bulgaria	11,068	20,517	25,846	23,312	24,723	31,196	28,378	47,470	84,096
Czechoslovakia	33,029	39,041	28,096	30,249	30,931	30,107	33,287	41,066	45,146
Hungary	7,509	3,219	3,347	4,888	8,444	7,074	5,943	8,611	14,453

* Not Available
– Refers to numbers equal to zero

Sources: *Anuario Estadístico de Cuba*, 1972, Table 6, pg. 194–197.
(a) Not included in 1972 Anuario.
Anuario Estadístico de Cuba, 1973, Table 6, pg. 188–191.
(b) Not included in 1973 Anuario.
Anuario Estadístico de Cuba, 1978, Table X.7, pg. 167–168.
(c) Not included in 1978 Anuario.
Anuario Estadístico de Cuba, 1981, Table XI.7, pg. 193–194.
(d) Not included in 1981 Anuario.
Anuario Estadístico de Cuba, 1985, Table XI.8, pg. 388–391.
(e) Not included in 1985 Anuario.
Cuba en Cifras, 1987, Table 95, pg. 92 and 94.

1976	1977	1978	1979	1980	1981	1982	1983	1984	1985	1986
3,179,679	3,461,590	3,573,844	3,687,530	4,626,964	5,114,003	5,530,604	6,222,137	7,227,480	8,035,000	7,569,000
309,242	370,134	266,082	240,469	312,398	319,909	385,467	265,443	514,696	492,000	414,100
d	d	d	d	d	e	e	e	e	e	e
70,238	64,727	94,976	97,647	105,225	139,011	218,810	152,628	244,757	228,882	
4,809	8,926	11,481	9,126	7,411	9,051	6,837	9,688	9,315	12,661	
991	1,123	4,750	5,519	5,955	9,422	21,104	17,193	32,133	21,869	
38	430	781	621	776	386	1,125	736	991	684	
–	–	–	–	–	–	–	–	–	–	
230,349	291,938	150,491	125,740	182,168	160,275	135,997	85,193	217,373	219,201	
481	1,938	2,330	1,816	1,919	1,575	744	–	267	3,299	
1,922	955	–	–	5,889	–	850	–	–	–	
4	21	–	–	–	–	–	–	–	–	
–	22	–	–	–	–	–	5	4,931	2,975	
2,527,038	2,850,795	3,148,327	3,355,834	4,103,799	4,638,065	5,031,321	5,740,386	6,371,163	7,131,200	6,827,400
443,710	353,544	275,752	244,090	367,008	402,389	209,856	335,060	395,970	366,900	472,900
18,117	65,843	32,380	16,298	22,404	28,100	10,883	11,929	8,903	11,400	
58,696	70,271	40,247	40,215	118,838	105,157	33,734	100,329	98,275	93,942	
41,012	28,551	29,684	28,454	34,508	58,925	32,388	37,028	34,670	25,022	
65,189	34,271	28,214	22,540	28,043	41,067	24,283	18,949	62,329	43,169	
80,349	64,769	74,751	73,494	82,904	99,297	54,032	64,560	91,374	81,611	
144	218	184	20	630	180	173	285	189	234	
26,362	41,928	13,575	2,219	5,510	6,786	4,693	5,430	5,452	6,449	
153,711	47,664	56,719	60,850	77,171	62,877	49,670	92,631	92,244	105,078	
130	29	–	–	*	*	*	3,919	2,534	–	
108,918	77,096	57,444	64,300	102,798	116,117	66,651	64,308	82,678	80,400	87,700
24,617	18,083	11,113	10,750	10,784	14,641	11,012	9,712	20,332	30,876	
503	174	217	559	746	1,357	1,074	1,342	433	426	
34,600	33,879	15,344	19,253	37,219	36,985	31,852	16,720	31,507	23,789	
34,073	21,992	21,755	28,392	39,836	50,246	17,275	31,936	21,356	22,655	
1,304	648	1,784	2,490	5,989	7,046	2,466	4,049	3,866	2,184	
–	27	4,056	–	4,901	334	–	–	–	–	
13,821	2,293	3,175	2,856	3,323	5,508	2,972	549	5,184	504	
186,187	154,267	74,571	105,038	139,072	163,005	95,184	106,982	107,719	176,889	
–	0	16	–	–	*	*	–	–	*	
–	439	1,103	2,085	656	–	*	–	–	38	
–										
1,781,922	2,232,382	2,731,686	2,933,268	3,488,938	39,511,481	4,655,676	5,223,513	5,771,732	6,472,000	6,239,900
5,558	6,263	4,104	848	1,655	5,487	3,649	5,874	4,444	4,096	
84,211	90,150	126,479	116,388	145,966	174,730	170,261	198,021	191,490	191,012	
38,240	50,003	52,248	64,516	100,818	137,471	182,222	186,399	182,396	196,687	
37,881	39,854	47,531	47,152	51,437	62,026	97,316	124,447	127,446	167,455	

Appendix H. Imports by Region—Thousands of Pesos (continued)

Category	1959	1968	1969	1970	1971	1972	1973	1974	1975
Eastern Europe (ctd.)									
Poland	13,210	4,211	3,826	3,356	2,357	1,803	7,631	8,860	15,373
E. Germany	26,592	38,744	42,979	49,987	63,400	35,958	40,101	51,909	76,228
Rumania	4,816	8,818	34,172	22,945	12,599	8,721	8,109	9,977	13,546
Greece	135	–	–	–	–	–	–	–	–
Turkey	3	–	–	–	–	–	–	–	–
USSR	350,757	671,796	669,056	690,578	730,806	714,378	810,974	1,024,911	1,250,259
Yugoslavia	3,613	5,002	3,082	974	476	243	2,307	5,034	5,620
Others	602	1,300	b	b	b	c	c	c	c
Middle East	9,195	6,124	7,604	5,193	7,742	c	c	c	c
Saudi Arabia	114	0	0	–	98	–	–	–	–
Iran	3	–	–	–	–	–	–	–	–
Iraq	6	–	–	–	–	–	–	–	–
Israel	39	–	3	44	7	–	0	–	–
Lebanon	1	–	–	–	582	–	798	3,755	4,606
Syria	342	1,268	2,134	3,225	1,852	1,517	288	532	338
Yemen Republic	0	–	–	–	–	–	–	–	94
Others	71	0	415	–	100	21	4	732	1,682
Africa	7,732	8,805	11,436	10,728	5,627	5,255	3,465	7,988	9,993
Algiers	663	1,619	2,381	4,263	1,739	1,662	219	1,048	1,862
Morocco	5,763	7,002	8,877	6,025	3,648	1,781	1,558	6,634	4,439
Egypt	8,619	4,856	5,052	1,924	5,103	1,762	1,488	11	1,373
Sudan	4	0	–	0	–	–	–	–	–
Congo	87	184	178	440	239	39	62	–	173
Others	1,215	–	–	–	1	11	138	295	2,146
Americas	126,975	11,945	13,870	32,502	44,306	51,468	64,102	171,276	266,754
Canada	17,811	8,837	13,860	27,968	27,375	18,497	34,144	93,677	98,084
United States	88,876	–	–	–	–	–	–	–	7
Latin Intergration Cat.	16,487	3,108	10	4,534	16,931	32,971	29,760	75,085	157,950
Chile	1,425	–	–	4,418	12,834	10,952	14,707	2,334	–
Mexico	3,938	2,610	10	116	51	12,450	6,413	11,808	2,626,703
Peru	75	498	–	–	3,223	9,569	1,594	1,723	17,796
Argentina	a	a	a	b	b	–	7,038	56,018	105,520
Venezuela		a	a	b	b	–	–	3,202	5,922
Others	11,049	–	0	–	823	–	8	–	2,009
Central Amer.									
Common Mkt.	1,552	–	–	–	–	–	–	–	0
Caribbean Community	41	–	–	–	–	–	197	283	3,529
Rest of Latin Amer.	140	–	–	–	–	–	1	993	5,392
Rest of America	2,068	–	–	–	–	–	–	1,238	1,792
Oceania	95	–	–	–	4,588	7,144	5,803	5,162	1,132
Australia	51	–	–	–	4,588	3,910	5,803	5,162	1,132
Others	44	–	–	–	–	3,234	–	–	–

* Not Available
– Refers to numbers equal to zero

Sources: *Anuario Estadístico de Cuba*, 1972, Table 6, pg. 194–197.
  (a) Not included in 1972 Anuario.
Anuario Estadístico de Cuba, 1973, Table 6, pg. 188–191.
  (b) Not included in 1973 Anuario.
Anuario Estadístico de Cuba, 1978, Table X.7, pg. 167–168.
  (c) Not included in 1978 Anuario.
Anuario Estadístico de Cuba, 1981, Table XI.7, pg. 193–194.
  (d) Not included in 1981 Anuario.
Anuario Estadístico de Cuba, 1985, Table XI.8, pg. 388–391.
  (e) Not included in 1985 Anuario.
Cuba en Cifras, 1987, Table 95, pg. 92 and 94.

1976	1977	1978	1979	1980	1981	1982	1983	1984	1985	1986
9,959	20,116	32,300	46,063	68,872	52,214	68,383	92,171	66,969	75,812	
98,897	152,917	139,214	135,678	165,334	171,218	205,698	250,647	267,629	280,172	
16,945	14,809	2,129	9,183	51,156	114,379	183,756	120,610	148,948	130,923	
–	21	2,390	–	–	–	–	–	–	–	
150	–	–	206	67	–	–	–	–	–	
1,490,231	1,858,270	2,327,681	2,513,440	903,700	3,233,956	3,744,391	4,245,344	4,782,410	5,373,025	
6,154	33,046	5,365	6,847	5,260	4,813	3,954	10,523	13,064	34,958	
d	d	d	e	e	e	e	e	e	e	
d	d	d	e	e	e	e	e	e	e	
–	42	–	–	–	–	–	–	–	–	
–	–	–	–	–	–	–	–	–	–	
–	–	1,246	–	–	–	–	–	–	–	
–	–	–	–	–	–	–	–	–	–	
–	–	–	–	–	–	–	–	–	–	
410	–	–	–	–	–	–	–	–	–	
–	–	–	–	–	–	–	–	–	–	
–	12	27	–	3,055	189	–	–	–	1,055	
18,921	17,943	4,186	6,109	4,477	7,530	1,704	9,046	9,247	23,800	17,700
1	1	0	3	479	550	301	1,088	523	14,816	
1,309	911	652	21	–	–	–	–	–	–	
1,091	433	930	22	–	–	–	–	–	260	
–	–	–	–	–	–	–	–	–	–	
30	–	–	139	–	–	–	–	402	341	
16,490	16,598	2,604	5,924	3,998	6,980	1,403	7,958	8,322	8,374	
322,954	220,664	154,425	84,106	205,228	147,219	110,832	205,601	318,560	379,500	302,200
103,234	55,027	39,255	35,384	111,008	78,994	47,290	37,277	56,457	58,800	53,400
–	–	–	–	–	–	–	–	–	–	–
212,573	160,305	111,646	36,140	62,960	44,972	37,992	132,236	232,113	281,700	209,400
–	–	–	–	–	–	–	–	–	–	
29,433	29,388	20,533	7,362	22,765	11,026	15,930	22,992	72,746	77,125	
10,059	11,022	11,014	12,112	19,044	14,175	1,889	2,962	4,732	2,968	
164,793	115,183	77,522	13,749	15,210	17,845	12,548	83,062	146,887	193,339	
1,503	973	487	1,565	22,431	236	293	7,246	7,517	5,790	
6,785	3,739	2,090	1,352	3,510	1,690	7,332	15,974	231	2,443	
1,957	78	1,620	0	3	9,691	1,036	13,284	10,852	8,600	11,300
170	840	395	121	302	79	2	197	1,370	1,400	1,900
3,706	1,903	1,509	12,461	e	e	e	e	e	e	
1,314	2,511	–	–	30,955	13,483	24,512	22,607	17,767	29,000	26,200
1,524	2,054	824	1,012	1,062	1,280	1,280	1,661	13,814	8,500	7,600
1,524	2,054	824	1,012	1,062	1,280	1,280	1,661	7,777	8,457	
–	–	–	–	–	–	–	–	6,037	–	

Appendix I. Day Care

	1970	1971	1972	1973	1974	1975	1976	1977
Number of units	606	620	633	642	654	658	674	713
Capacity at end of year	47,458	42,968(a)	42,516	42,172	43,581	47,147	50,463	57,788
Average yearly enrollment		45,547	45,967	51,807	54,570	59,856	64,086	65,598
Final enrollment	47,370	42,705	48,778	52,235	56,717	60,424	65,236	62,928
Average yearly attendance	33,719	30,679	31,870	34,630	36,633	40,361	42,312	44,957
Educational and technical personnel	4,719	5,185	5,655	6,330	6,964	8,463	9,113	10,698
Number of mothers benefited	32,307 (b)	30,277 (b)	40,837	45,136	50,043	54,179	60,119	58,007

Sources: *Anuario Estadístico de Cuba,* 1978 (1971–78 figures), pg. 209, Table 1.
Anuario Estadístico de Cuba, 1985 (1970, 1979–85 figures), pg. 482, Table XIII.1.
(a) The figure given for 1971 corresponds to the yearly average; the 1982 figure corresponds to the last figure of the year.
(b) Excludes outdoor day care.
Cuba en Cifras, 1987 (1986–87 figures), pg. 102, Table 106.

1978	1979	1980	1981	1982	1983	1984	1985	1986	1987
766	802	832	839	839	835	837	844	854	927
70,639	80,509	87,913	90,358	91,380	91,667	92,215	92,911	95,800	109,500
72,730									
86,263	92,103	91,736	91,772	93,933	97,596	102,346	103,352	109,900	120,100
47,267	55,398	59,312	62,176	66,108 (a)	68,230	72,129	72,480	76,500	79,000
12,461	13,706	14,174	14,982	18,339	18,793	19,137	19,749	21,000	21,200
77,333	83,439	82,951	85,235	85,995	89,900	94,025	95,694	101,500	110,800

Appendix J. Distribution of the Work Force, by Occupational Category and Gender (in thousands)

	1973	1974	1975	1976	1977	1978
(Both Sexes)						
Total	2,245.7	2,313.3	2,393.8	2,469.2	2,397.5	2,540.8
Workers	1,271.8	1,311.4	1,343.3	1,372.2	1,326.1	1,379.6
Technicians	266.1	290.1	314.5	338.7	370.9	424.0
Administrators	95.7	113.5	125.7	135.6	142.5	161.4
Service jobs	439.4	395.9	378.2	368.2	335.6	349.8
Managers	148.8	178.8	207.6	224.7	222.4	226.0
(Women Only)						
Total						762.1
Workers						183.7
Technicians						218.2
Administrators						124.1
Service jobs						196.2
Managers						39.9

Sources: *Anuario Estadístico de Cuba,* 1978 (1973–77 figures), pg. 58, Table 4.
Anuario Estadístico de Cuba, 1983 (1978–82 figures), pg.110, Table IV.11.
Anuario Estadístico de Cuba, 1985 (1983–84 figures), pg. 193, Table IV.12.
Cuba en Cifras, 1987 (1985–86 figures), pg. 37, Table 25

1979	1980	1981	1982	1983	1984	1985	1986
2,611.7	2,599.9	2,632.8	2,875.2	3,047.3	3,122.0	3,173.3	3,317.6
1,387.8	1,354.3	1,362.3	1,485.5	1,561.3	1,591.6	1,604.4	1,673.3
464.7	484.5	506.1	555.1	591.2	604.0	635.1	671.0
175.9	180.3	192.2	213.7	230.3	244.8	248.5	257.8
352.3	348.0	353.6	390.2	422.8	431.0	431.4	450.2
231.0	232.8	218.6	230.7	241.8	250.6	253.9	262.3
814.0	843.1	890.8	1,010.6	1,098.6	1,156.2	1,189.5	1,261.2
191.2	194.0	209.9	246.8	276.8	293.1	293.6	320.8
242.1	256.4	265.2	298.9	324.1	332.9	354.7	378.3
139.1	146.0	157.8	176.5	190.1	201.2	208.5	213.8
200.1	201.0	211.6	236.2	252.7	267.4	268.2	279.5
41.5	45.7	46.3	52.2	54.9	61.6	64.5	68.8

REFERENCES

Abel, Richard L. 1981. "Conservative Conflict and the Reproduction of Capitalism: The Role of Informal Justice." *International Journal of the Sociology of Law* 9:245–267.

———. 1982a. "Introduction." Pp. 1–13 in Richard L. Abel (ed.), *The Politics of Informal Justice, Volume 1: The American Experience*. New York: Academic.

———. 1982b. "The Contradictions of Informal Justice." Pp. 267–430 in Richard L. Abel (ed.), *The Politics of Informal Justice, Volume 1: The American Experience*. New York: Academic.

———. 1989. "Comparative Sociology of Legal Professions." Pp. 80–153 in Abel, Richard L. and Philip S. C. Lewis (eds.), *Lawyers in Society: Comparative Theories, Volume 111*. Berkeley: University of California Press.

Althusser, Louis. 1971. *Lenin and Philosophy*. New York: Monthly Review Press.

Amaro Salup, José Raúl. 1989. Interview in *Granma*, May 3:4.

Amherst Seminar. 1988. "From the Special Issue Editors." *Law and Society Review* 22:629–636.

Aniyar de Castro, Lola. 1987. *Criminología de la liberación*. Maracaibo: Instituto de Criminología de la Universidad de Zulia.

Arranz Castillero, Vicente Julio. 1989. "Los sujetos y las partes en la fase preparatoria del juicio oral. Los sistemas de instrucción." *Revista Cubana de Derecho* 18(38):41–56.

Azicri, Max. 1985. "Crime, Penal Law, and the Cuban Revolutionary Process." *Crime and Social Justice* 23:51–79.

Balbus, Isaac D. 1977. *The Dialectics of Legal Repression: Black Rebels Before the American Criminal Courts*. New York: Russell Sage Foundation.

Beirne, Piers and Alan Hunt. 1988. "Law and the Constitution of Soviet Society: The Case of Comrade Lenin." *Law and Society Review* 22:575–614.

Berman, Jesse. 1969. "The Cuban Popular Tribunals." *Columbia Law Review* 69:1317–1354.

Biancalana, Flora and Cecilia O'Leary. 1988. "Profile of U.S. Press Coverage of Cuba." *Social Justice* 15(2):63–71.

Bodes Torres, Jorge. 1988. *La detención y el aseguramiento del acusado en Cuba*. La Habana: Editorial de Ciencias Sociales.

Bottomley, A. and J. Roche. 1988. "Conflict and Consensus: A Critique of the Language of Informal Justice." In R. Matthews (ed.), *Informal Justice?* London: Sage.

Bracamonte, José A. 1987. "Foreword: Minority Critiques of the Critical

Legal Studies Movement." *Harvard Civil Rights, Civil Liberties Law Review* 22(2):297–299.

Brady, James P. 1977. "Political Contradictions and Justice Policy in People's China." *Contemporary Crises* 1:127–162.

———. 1981. "Sorting Out the Exile's Confusion: Or Dialogue on Popular Justice." *Contemporary Crises* 5:31–38.

———. 1982. *Justice and Politics in People's China: Legal Order or Continuing Revolution?.* New York: Academic.

Brigham, John. 1988. "The Bias of Constitutional Property: Toward Compensation for the Elimination of Statutory Entitlements." *Law and Inequality: A Journal of Theory and Inequality* 5:405–429.

Burawoy, Michael. 1985. *The Politics of Production.* London: New Left Books (Verso).

Cain, Maureen. 1985. "Beyond Informal Justice." *Contemporary Crises* 9:335–373.

Calavita, Kitty. 1992. *Inside the State: The Bracero Program, Illegal Immigrants, and the INS.* New York: Routledge.

Cantor, Robert. 1974. "New Laws for a New Society." *Crime and Social Justice* 2:12–23.

Castro Ruz, Fidel. 1992a. "Speech by President Fidel Castro Ruz, First Secretary of the Central Committee of the Communist Party of Cuba at the 13th Regular Session of the National Assembly of People's Power, Held at the International Conference Center October 29, 1992." Reprinted in *Granma International,* November 15:7–10.

———. 1992b. "This Law Will Improve Our System and People's Power As A Whole. Fidel's Remarks at the Recently Concluded National Assembly Session." Reprinted in *Granma International* November 8:4.

———. 1991. "We Have the Right to Dream of the United Latin America of Which Bolívar and Martí Dreamed. Fidel's Message to the First Ibero-American Summit." Reprinted in *Granma Weekly Review,* August 4:2–7.

———. 1990. "The Unity of the People, That Is the Most Sacred Thing and the Number One Weapon of the Revolution!" Speech at the special session of the National Assembly of People's Power, February 20. Reprinted in *Granma Weekly Review* March 4:2–3.

Chambliss, William J. 1988. *Exploring Criminology.* New York: Macmillan.

———. 1979. "On Law Making." *British Journal of Law and Society* 6:149–171.

——— and Robert Seidman. 1982. *Law, Order, and Power.* Reading, PA: Addison-Wesley.

——— and Marjorie S. Zatz. 1993. *Making Law: The State, the Law, and Structural Contradictions.* Bloomington: Indiana University.

Chase-Dunn, Christopher K. (ed.). 1982. *Socialist States in the World-System.* Beverly Hills: Sage.

Cohen, Leonard J. 1985. "Judicial Elites in Yugoslavia: The Professionalization of Political Justice." *Review of Socialist Law* 11:313–344.

Cohen, Stanley. 1985. *Visions of Social Control: Crime, Punishment and Classification.* New York: Polity Press.

Comité Estatal de Estadísticas. 1972. *Anuario Estadístico de Cuba.* La Habana.

———. 1976. *Anuario Estadístico de Cuba.* La Habana.

———. 1978. *Anuario Estadístico de Cuba*. La Habana.

———. 1981. *Anuario Estadístico de Cuba*. La Habana.

———. 1983. *Anuario Estadístico de Cuba*. La Habana.

———. 1985. *Anuario Estadístico de Cuba*. La Habana.

———. 1987. *Cuba en Cifras*. La Habana.

———. 1990. *Boletín Estadístico de Cuba*. La Habana.

Communist Party of Cuba. 1983. *Resolución del VI Pleno del Comité Central del Partido Comunista de Cuba*. La Habana: Editora Política.

———. 1984. *Resolución del VIII Pleno del Comité Central del Partido Comunista de Cuba*. La Habana: Editora Política.

Counihan, Carole. 1986. "Antonio Gramsci and Social Science." *Dialectical Anthropology* 11:3–10.

Cuba Fernández, José Santiago. 1973. "Discurso pronunciado por el Fiscal General de la República, Dr. J. Santiago Cuba Fernández: El nuevo sistema judicial en Cuba." *Revista Cubana de Derecho* 2(6):88–91.

———. 1974. "El Día de Trabajador Jurídico." *Revista Cubana de Derecho* 3(8):81–90.

Cuba, Republic of. 1976. *Constitución de la República de Cuba: Tésis y resolución*. La Habana: Departamento de Orientación Revolucionaria del Comité Central del Partido Comunista de Cuba.

———. 1990. *Experiencia en la provincia de Villa Clara sobre la constitución, competencia y funcionamiento de órganos de justicia laboral de base*, August.

Danzig, Richard. 1982. "Towards the Creation of a Complementary, Decentralized System of Criminal Justice." In Roman Tomasic and Malcolm M. Feeley (eds.), *Neighborhood Justice: Assessments of an Emerging Idea*. New York: Longman.

Dávalos Fernández, Rodolfo. 1990. *La nueva ley general de la vivienda*. La Habana: Editorial de Ciencias Sociales

de la Cruz Ochoa, Ramón. 1985. "Comentario oficial." Pp. 48–52 in Colectivo de autores (eds.), *Política, ideología y derecho*. La Habana: Unión Nacional de Juristas de Cuba, Ministerio de Justicia, and Editorial de Ciencias Sociales.

de la Fuente López, Jorge. 1989. "Necesidad y posibilidad de un nuevo Código de Familia. Ideas en torno a esta polémica." *Revista Cubana de Derecho* 18(38):71–106.

del Olmo, Rosa. 1981. *América Latina y su criminología*. México: Siglo Veintiuno Editores.

Delgado, Richard. 1987. "The Ethereal Scholar: Does Critical Legal Studies Have What Minorities Want?" *Harvard Civil Rights-Civil Liberties Law Review* 22(2):301–322.

Dórticos Torrado, Osvaldo. 1973. "Discurso pronunciado por el Dr. Osvaldo Dórticos Torrado, Presidente de la República: El nuevo sistema judicial en Cuba." *Revista Cubana de Derecho* 2(6):75–83.

Edelman, Murray. 1964. *The Symbolic Uses of Politics*. Urbana: University of Illinois Press.

Erisman, H. Michael. 1985. *Cuba's International Relations: The Anatomy of a Nationalistic Foreign Policy*. Boulder: Westview.

Editorial de Ciencias Sociales. 1985. *Catálogo general de títulos publicados 1967–1984*. La Habana: Editorial de Ciencias Sociales.

———. 1985. *Catálogo 85*. La Habana: Editorial de Ciencias Sociales.

————. 1988. *Catálogo 87–88*. La Habana: Editorial de Ciencias Sociales.

————. 1988. *Precatálogo de publicaciones 1989*. La Habana: Editorial de Ciencias Sociales.

Escalona Reguera, Juan. 1985. "Discurso pronunciado por el Dr. Juan Escalona Reguera, miembro del Comité Central del Partido y Ministro de Justicia, en el acto nacional por el Día del Trabajador Jurídico efectuado el día 5 de junio de 1985 en el municipio de Viñales, provincia de Pinar del Río." *Revista Jurídica* 3(9):259–270.

————. 1987. "Discurso del miembro del Comité Central y Ministro de Justicia, Dr. Juan Escalona Reguera, en la clausura del III Congreso de la Unión Nacional de Juristas de Cuba." *Revista Jurídica* 16:186–195.

————. 1988. "Una política consecuente en la prevención del delito y la justicia penal. Palabras del diputado a la Asamblea Nacional y Ministro de Justicia, compañero Juan Escalona Reguera, al presentar el Proyecto de Ley de Modificaciones al Código Penal, Tercera Legislatura ANPP, 1987." La Habana: Departamento de Diseño y Fotografía, Ministry of the Interior.

Escasena Guillarón, José Luis. 1984. *La evolución de la legalidad en Cuba*. La Habana: Editorial de Ciencias Sociales.

————. 1988. "Apuntes sobre algunas modificaciones al libro I del Código Penal." *Revista Cubana de Derecho* 17(34):123–145.

Evanson, Debra. 1990. "The Changing Role of Law in Revolutionary Cuba." Pp. 53–66 in Sandor Halebsky and John M. Kirk (eds.), *Transformation and Struggle: Cuba Faces the 1990s*. New York: Praeger.

————. 1994. *Law and Revolution in Cuba*. Boulder, Colo.: Westview.

Fernández Bulté, Julio. 1985. "La legalidad socialista." Pp. 39–48 in Colectivo de autores (eds.), *Política, ideología y derecho*. La Habana: Unión Nacional de Juristas de Cuba, Ministerio de Justicia, and Editorial de Ciencias Sociales.

————. 1989. *Acerca del programa de progreso científico-técnico del sector jurídico en el quinquenio 1990–1995* (Draft). La Habana.

Fernández-Rubio Legra, Angel. 1985. *El proceso de institucionalización de la Revolución Cubana*. La Habana: Editorial de Ciencias Sociales.

Fiscalía General de la República de Cuba (ed.). 1988. *Ley de la Fiscalía*. July.

Fitzpatrick, Peter. 1983. "Law, Plurality and Underdevelopment." Pp. 159–182 in David Sugarman (ed.), *Legality, Ideology and the State*. New York: Academic.

————. 1988. "The Rise and Rise of Informalism." In R. Matthews (ed.), *Informal Justice?* London: Sage.

————. 1992. "The Impossibility of Popular Justice." *Social and Legal Studies* 1(2):199–215.

Frank, Andre Gunder. 1967. *Capitalism and Underdevelopment in Latin America*. New York: Monthly Review Press.

————. 1969. *The Development of Underdevelopment*. New York: Monthly Review Press.

Friedman, Lawrence M. 1989. "Lawyers in Cross-Cultural Perspective." Pp. 1–26 in Abel, Richard L. and Philip S. C. Lewis (eds.), *Lawyers in Society: Comparative Theories, Volume III*. Berkeley: University of California Press.

———— and Jack Ladinsky. 1967. "Social Change and the Law of Industrial Accidents." *Columbia Law Review* 67:50–82.

Fuller, Linda. 1987. "Power at the Workplace: The Resolution of Worker-Management Conflict in Cuba." *World Development* 15(1):139–152.

Galanter, Marc. 1979. "Legality and Its Discontents: A Preliminary Assessment of Current Theories of Legalization and Delegalization." In E. Blankenburg, E. Klausa, and H. Rottleuthuer (eds.), *Alternative Rechtsformen und Alternative zum Recht*. Bonn: Westdeutscher Verlag.

García Hernández, Gilberto E. 1989. *Constitución: Deberes y derechos*. La Habana: Editorial de Ciencias Sociales.

Garcini Guerra, Héctor. 1976. "La Constitución del estado socialista cubano." *Revista Cubana de Derecho* 5(12):103–117.

Galeano, Eduardo. 1989. "Cuba, 30 Years Later: A Work of This World." *Granma Weekly Review* January 22:3.

Giddens, Anthony. 1982. *Profiles and Critiques in Social Theory*. London: Macmillan.

Ginsburgs, George. 1985. "The Soviet Judicial Elite: Is It?" *Review of Socialist Law* 11(4):293–311.

Goldberg, Stephan B., Eric D. Green, and Frank E. A. Sander. 1985. *Dispute Resolution*. Boston: Little, Brown, and Co.

Gómez Treto, Raúl. 1988. "¿Hacia un Nuevo Código de Familia?" *Revista Cubana de Derecho* 17(34):31–74.

Gramsci, Antonio. 1971. *Prison Notebooks*. New York: International Publishers.

Granma International. 1993. "Varadero Now." June 16:13.

Greenberg, David F. 1989. "Law and Development in Light of Dependency Theory." *Research in Law and Sociology* 3:129–159.

Guevara Ramírez, Lydia. 1992. Personal communication, November 6.

Guillén Landrián, Franscisco. 1987. *La codificación del derecho laboral en Cuba*. La Habana: Editorial Ciencias Sociales.

Gundersen, Aase. 1990. "Popular Justice and Equal Rights: Gender and Social Change in Mozambique." Presented at the Law and Society Association meetings, June.

———. 1992. "Popular Justice in Mozambique: Between State Law and Folk Law." *Social and Legal Studies* 1(2):257–282.

Harrington, Christine B. 1985. *Shadow Justice*. Westport, CT: Greenwood Press.

——— and Sally Engle Merry. 1988. "Ideological Production: The Making of Community Mediation." *Law and Society Review* 22:709–737.

Hart Dávalos, Marina. 1985. "Comentario oficial." Pp. 202–208 in Colectivo de autores (eds.), *Política, ideología y derecho*. La Habana: Unión Nacional de Juristas de Cuba, Ministerio de Justicia, and Editorial de Ciencias Sociales.

Hayden, Robert M. 1986. "Popular Use of Yugoslav Labor Courts and the Contradictions of Social Courts." *Law and Society Review* 20:229–251.

Hazard, John N. 1969. *Communists and their Law—A Search for the Common Core of the Legal Systems of the Marxian Socialist States*. Chicago: The University of Chicago.

Henry, Stuart. 1985. "Community Justice, Capitalist Society, and Human Agency: The Dialectics of Collective Law in the Cooperative." *Law and Society Review* 19:303–327.

Hipkin, Brian. 1985. "Looking for Justice: The Search for Socialist Legality and Popular Justice." *International Journal of the Sociology of Law* 13:117–132.

Hirst, Paul. 1985. "Socialism, Pluralism, and Law." *International Journal of the Sociology of Law* 13:173–190.

Huggins, Martha. 1985. "Approaches to Crime and Societal Development." *Comparative Social Research* 8:17–35.

Hunt, Alan. 1985. "The Ideology of Law: Advances and Problems in Recent Applications of the Concept of Ideology to the Analysis of Law." *Law and Society Review* 19:11–39.

Ietswaart, Helen F. P. 1982. "The Discourse of Summary Justice and the Discourse of Popular Justice: An Analysis of Legal Rhetoric in Argentina." In Richard L. Abel (ed.), *The Politics of Informal Justice, Volume ii: Comparative Studies*. New York: Academic.

Isaacman, Barbara and Allen Isaacman. 1982. "A Socialist Legal System in the Making: Mozambique Before and After Independence." Pp. 281–323 in Richard L. Abel (ed), *The Politics of Informal Justice, Volume ii: Comparative Studies*. New York: Academic.

Kairys, David (ed.). 1982. *The Politics of Law: A Progressive Critique*. New York: Pantheon.

Kautzman Torres, Víctor L. 1988. *Prevención del delito y tratamiento al delincuente en Cuba revolucionaria*. La Habana: Editorial de Ciencias Sociales.

Kellner, Douglas. 1978. "Ideology, Marxism, and Advanced Capitalism." *Socialist Review* 42:37–65.

Kertzer, David I. 1979. "Gramsci's Concept of Hegemony: The Italian Church-Communist Struggle." *Dialectical Anthropology* 4:321–328.

Kidder, Robert L. 1988. "From the Editor." *Law and Society Review* 22:625–627.

Laclau, Ernesto. 1971. "Feudalism and Capitalism in Latin America." *New Left Review* 67:19–38.

Lage, Carlos. 1992. "Cuba Has Had to Rethink Her Economic Strategy." *Granma International* November 15:11.

Lagunilla Martínez, Manuel and Daniel Alberto Yanes Sosa. 1989. "La ética del abogado en el socialismo." Pp. 71–98 in Organización Nacional de Bufetes Colectivos (eds.), *Enfoques jurídicos de abogados cubanos*. La Habana: ONBC.

Lempert, Richard. 1989. "The Dynamics of Informal Procedure: The Case of a Public Housing Eviction Board." *Law and Society Review* 23(3):347–397.

Leng, Shao-Chuan and Hungdah Chiu. 1985. *Criminal Justice in Post-Mao China*. Albany: State University of New York.

Lorey, David E. 1988. "Professional Expertise and Mexican Modernization: Sources, Methods, and Preliminary Findings." Pp. 890–912 in James W. Wilkie, David E. Lorey, and Enrique Ochoa (eds.), *Statistical Abstract of Latin America*. Los Angeles: UCLA Latin American Center Publications.

Lynch, Dennis O. 1981. "Legal Roles in Colombia: Some Social, Economic, and Political Perspectives." Pp. 26–75 in C. J. Dias, R. Luckham, D. O. Lynch, and J. C. N. Paul (eds.), *Lawyers in the Third World: Comparative and Developmental Perspectives*. Uppsala, Sweden: The Scandinavian Institute of African Studies and the International Center for Law in Development.

Machado Ventura, José Ramón. 1984. "Discurso del miembro del Buró Político del PCC, Dr. José Ramón Machado Ventura, en la inauguración de la Facultad de Derecho de la Universidad de Las Villas." *Revista Jurídica* 5:209–221.

Makhnenko, A. Kh. 1976. *The State Law of Socialist Countries.* Moscow.

Marimón Roca, Enrique. 1981. "¿A quiénes debe servir la justicia revolucionaria? (Algunos apuntes sobre la experiencia Cubana)." Pp. 157–169 in Corte Suprema de Justicia de Nicaragua (ed.), *La justicia en la revolución: memoria del seminario jurídico Sílvio Mayorga.* México: Editorial Popular de los Trabajadores.

Markovits, Inga. 1982. "Law or Order—Constitutionalism and Legality in Eastern Europe." *Stanford Law Review* 34:513–613.

———. 1989. "Law and Glasnost: Some Thoughts About the Future of Judicial Review Under Socialism." *Law and Society Review* 23(3):399–447.

Marx, Karl. 1971. *The Grundrisse* (translated by David McLellan). New York: Harper and Row.

McCaughan, Ed and Tony Platt. 1988. "Tropical Gulag: Media Images of Cuba." *Social Justice* 15(2):72–104.

McDonald, James H. 1993. "Whose History? Whose Voice? Myth and Resistance in the Rise of the New Left in Mexico." *Cultural Anthropology* 8(1):96–116.

——— and Marjorie S. Zatz. 1992. "Popular Justice in Revolutionary Nicaragua." *Social and Legal Studies* 1(2): 285–307.

Merino Brito, Eloy G. 1972. "La organización del sistema judicial cubano." *Revista Cubana de Derecho* 1(2): 63–80.

Menkel-Meadow, Carrie. 1989a. "Feminization of the Legal Profession: The Comparative Sociology of Women lawyers." Pp. 196–255 in Abel, Richard L. and Philip S. C. Lewis (eds.), *Lawyers in Society: Comparative Theories, Volume III.* Berkeley: University of California Press.

———. 1989b. "Exploring a Research Agenda of the Feminization of the Legal Profession: Theories of Gender and Social Change." *Law and Social Inquiry* 14:289–319.

Merry, Sally Engle. 1982. "Defining 'Success' in the Neighborhood Justice Movement." In Roman Tomasic and Malcolm M. Feeley (eds.), *Neighborhood Justice: Assessment of an Emerging Idea.* New York: Longman.

———. 1988. "Legal Pluralism." *Law and Society Review* 22:869–896.

———. 1990. *Getting Justice and Getting Even: Legal Consciousness Among Working-Class Americans.* Chicago: University of Chicago Press.

———. 1992. "Popular Justice and the Ideology of Social Transformation." *Social and Legal Studies.* London: Sage.

Michalowski, Raymond J. 1992. "Crime and Justice in Socialist Cuba." Pp. 115–138 in John Lowman and Brian MacLean (eds.), *Realist Criminology.* Toronto: University of Toronto Press.

———. 1989. "Socialist Legality and the Practice of Law in Cuba." Presented at "Cuba: 30 Years of Revolution," November 23–24, Halifax, Nova Scotia.

Miller, Tom. 1992. *Trading With the Enemy: A Yankee Travels Through Castro's Cuba.* New York: Atheneum.

Ministry of Justice, Republic of Cuba. 1987. *Material de estudio sobre pre-vención y atención social para la superación de los jueces legos*. La Habana: Dirección de Cuadros y Capacitación, July.
――――. 1985. *Leyes del pueblo: Cuba 1959–1985*. La Habana: Departamento de Divulgación.
Molina, Gabriel. 1992. "The Direct Election of Deputies Amounts to a Kind of Plebiscite, Says Juan Escalona." *Granma International* November 8:3.
National Assembly of People's Power, Republic of Cuba. 1981. *Bodies of People's Power*. Havana: Department of Revolutionary Orientation of the Central Committee of the Communist Party of Cuba.
――――. 1988. *Informe sobre las modificaciones al proyecto de acuerdo para regular el proceso de elaboración y presentación de los proyectos de leyes*. La Habana, December.
Neave, Guy. 1989. "From the Other End of the Telescope: Deprofessionalization, Reprofessionalization, and the Development of Higher Education, 1950–1986." Pp. 154–195 in Abel, Richard L. and Philip S. C. Lewis (eds.), *Lawyers in Society: Comparative Theories, Volume III*. Berkeley: University of California Press.
Ollman, Bertell. 1986. "The Meaning of Dialectics." *Monthly Review* 38:42–55.
O'Malley, Pat. 1987. "Regulating Contradictions: The Australian Press Council and the 'Dispersal of Social Control.'" *Law and Society Review* 21:83–108.
Ordóñez Martínez, Francisco. 1982. *La legalidad socialista, firme baluarte de los intereses del pueblo*. La Habana: Editorial de Ciencias Sociales.
Pepinsky, Harold E. 1982. "A Season of Disenchantment: Trends in Chinese Justice Reconsidered." *International Journal of the Sociology of Law* 10:277–285.
Pérez Sarmiento, Eric. 1989. "Estudio de la fase preparatoria en el proceso penal cubano." *Revista Jurídica* 7(23):71–107.
Poulantzas, Nicos. 1973. *Political Power and Social Classes*. London: New Left Books.
Prieto González, Alfredo. 1990. "Cuba en la prensa norteamericana: La 'conexion cubana'" *Cuadernos de Nuestra America* 7(15):223–257.
Prieto Morales, Aldo. 1982. *Derecho procesal penal, primera parte*. First Edition. La Habana: Ediciones ENSPES.
――――. 1985. *Derecho procesal penal, primera parte*. Second Edition. La Habana: Ediciones ENSPES.
Provine, Doris Marie. 1986. *Judging Credentials: Nonlawyer Judges and the Politics of Professionalism*. Chicago: University of Chicago Press.
Quirós Pírez, Renén. 1985. "La política penal en la etapa contemporánea de nuestro desarrollo social." Pp. 105–113 in Colectivo de autores (eds.), *Política, ideología y derecho*. La Habana: Unión Nacional de Juristas de Cuba, Ministerio de Justica, and Editorial de Ciencias Sociales.
――――. 1987. "La despenalización y la sanción." *Cuaderno de Legalidad Socialista*. Year 5, 17(3):5–12.
――――. 1988. "Las modificaciones del Código Penal." *Revista Cubana de Derecho* 17(33):3–26.
Rand, Robert. 1991. *Comrade Lawyer: Inside Soviet Justice in an Era of Reform*. Boulder: Westview Press.
Randall, Margaret. 1979. "Introducing the Family Code." Pp. 296–298 in

Zillah R. Eisenstein, ed., *Capitalist Patriarchy and the Case for Socialist Feminism*. New York: Monthly Review Press.

Revista Cubana de Derecho. 1976. Special issue on the Constitutional referendum, 5(11).

Roca Calderío, Blas. 1974. "Discurso por Blas Roca, miembro del Secretariado del Comité Central del Partido Comunista de Cuba en clausura del Congreso, 13 enero, 1974." *Discursos en el Congreso de Constitución de los Bufetes Colectivos*. La Habana: Editorial Orbe.

———. 1975. "La jornada del trabajador jurídico." *Revista Cubana de Derecho* 4(9):65–73.

Rodríguez Calderón, Mirta. 1990. "Women Heads of Household in Cuba: Going Beyond Diagnosis." Paper presented at the United Nations Expert Group Meeting on Vulnerable Women, Vienna, November 26–30.

Rodríguez Gavira, Antonio. 1988. "Algunas ideas sobre la modificacion de nuestra ley de procedimiento penal." *Revista Cubana de Derecho* 17(33):99–104.

Rodríguez, Carlos Rafael. 1987a. "La reforma universitaria." Pp. 495–516 in *Letras con filo*, tomo 3. Ciudad de La Habana: Ediciones UNION. Reprinted from *Cuba Socialista*, February, 1962.

———. 1987b. "La universidad en el socialismo," (talk given in Magna Hall upon receipt of the title "Professor of Merit" by the University of Havana, May 27, 1983). Pp. 561–582 in *Letras con filo,* tomo 3. Ciudad de La Habana: Ediciones UNION.

Rodríguez, Maimundo. 1990. "Family Doctor Services Extended." *Granma Weekly Review* April 1:2.

Rosaldo, Renato. 1989. *Culture and Truth: The Remaking of Social Analysis*. Boston: Beacon Press.

Sachs, Albie. 1992. "The Future of Roman Dutch Law in a Non-Racial Democratic South Africa: Some Preliminary Observations." *Social and Legal Studies* 1(2):217–227.

———. 1985. "The Two Dimensions of Socialist Legality: Recent Experience in Mozambique." *International Journal of the Sociology of Law* 13:133–146.

——— and G. H. Welch. 1990. *Liberating the Law: Creating Popular Justice in Mozambique*. London: Zed Books.

Salas, Luis. 1979. *Social Control and Deviance in Cuba*. New York: Praeger.

———. 1983. "The Emergence and Decline of the Cuban Popular Tribunals." *Law and Society Review* 17:587–612.

Santos, Boaventura de Sousa. 1977. "The Law of the Oppressed: The Construction and Reproduction of Legality in Pasargada." *Law and Society Review* 12:5–126.

———. 1980. "Law and Community: The Changing Nature of State Power in Late Capitalism." *International Journal of the Sociology of Law* 8:379–397.

———. 1982a. "Popular Justice, Dual Power, and Socialist Strategy." In Piers Beirne and Richard Quinney (eds.) *Marxism and Law*. New York: John Wiley and Sons.

———. 1982b. "Law and Community: The Changing Nature of State Power in Late Capitalism." In Richard L. Abel (ed.), *The Politics of Informal Justice, Volume 1: The American Experience*. New York: Academic.

———. 1982c. "Law and Revolution in Portugal: The Experiences of Popular Justice After the 25th of April 1974." Pp. 251– 280 in Richard L. Abel (ed.), *The Politics of Informal Justice, Volume 11: Comparative Studies*. New York: Academic.

Schneider, Anne and Helen Ingram. 1990. "Behavioral Assumptions of Policy Tools." *Journal of Politics* 52(2):510–529.

Schonholtz, D. 1985. "Neighborhood Justice Systems: Work, Structure, and Guiding Principles." In Stephen B. Goldberg, Eric D. Green, and Frank E. A. Sander (eds.), *Dispute Resolution*. Boston: Little, Brown, and Co.

Seidman, Robert. 1984. "Research Priorities: The State, Law, and Development." *Contemporary Crises* 8:329–344.

Selva, Lance H. and Robert M. Bohm. 1985. "A Critical Examination of the Informalism Experiment in the Administration of Justice." *Crime and Social Justice* 23:43–57.

Smith, Carol A. 1987. "Culture and Community: The Language of Class in Guatemala." Pp. 197–217 in Mike Davis, Manning Marable, Fred Pfiel, and Michael Sprinker (eds.), *The Year Left 2: An American Socialist Yearbook*. London: Verso.

———. 1986. "Reconstructing the Elements of Petty Commodity Production." *Social Analysis* 20:29–46.

———. 1984. "Local History and Global Context: Social and Economic Transitions in Western Guatemala." *Comparative Studies in Society and History* 26(2):193–228.

———. 1983. "Regional Analysis in World-System Perspective: A Critique of Three Structural Theories of Uneven Development." In Sutti Ortiz (ed.), *Economic Anthropology: Topics and Theories*. New York: University Press of America.

Smith, Wayne S. 1987. *The Closest of Enemies: A Personal and Diplomatic Account of U.S.-Cuban Relations Since 1957*. New York: W. W. Norton.

Spitzer, Steven. 1982. "The Dialectics of Formal and Informal Control." Pp. 167–205 in Richard L. Abel (ed.), *The Politics of Informal Justice, Volume 1: The American Experience*. New York: Academic.

Sumner, Colin. 1982. "Crime, Justice and Underdevelopment: Beyond Modernization Theory." Pp. 1–39 in Colin Sumner (ed.), *Crime, Justice and Underdevelopment*. London: Heinemann.

Thompson, E. P. 1978. "Eighteenth-century English Society: Class Struggle Without Class?" *Social History* 3(2):133–198.

Tiruchelvam, Neelan. 1984. *The Ideology of Popular Justice in Sri Lanka: A Socio-Legal Inquiry*. New Delhi: Vikas.

University of Havana, Law School. 1989a. *Modelo del profesional plan de estudios "C"* (March Draft). La Habana.

———. 1989b. *Modelo del profesional plan de estudios "C"* (May Draft). La Habana.

Unión Nacional de Juristas de Cuba. 1987. *Tésis sobre la vida jurídica del país*. La Habana: Departamento de Impresos Dirección Administrativa, June.

Valdés Temprana, Minerva. 1985. "El derecho y la protección a la familia en la nueva sociedad." Pp. 193–202 in Colectivo de autores (eds.), *Política, ideología y derecho*. La Habana: Unión Nacional de Juristas de Cuba, Ministerio de Justicia, and Editorial de Ciencias Sociales.

van der Plas, Adele G. 1987. *Revolution and Criminal Justice: The Cuban Experiment, 1959–1983*. Providence, R.I.: FORIS Publications.

Varona y Duque de Estrada, Francisco. 1972. "Sobre la enseñanza del derecho en el período de transición." *Revista Cubana de Derecho*. 1(2):81–86.

Vega Vega, Juan. 1987. "La prevención delictiva: tarea de todos." *Cuaderno de Legalidad Socialista*. Year 5 16(2):5–9.

Viera Hernández, Margarita. 1986. *Criminología*. La Habana: Ministerio de Educacion Superior.

———. 1987. "Estrategias teóricas de reflexión sobre la prevención de la criminalidad en la criminología socialista cubana." *Cuaderno de Legalidad Socialista*. Year 5, 16(2):35–40.

Watson, Alan. 1974. *Legal Transplants: An Approach to Comparative Law*. Charlottesville: University Press of Virginia.

Weber, Max. 1968. *Economy and Society, Volume 11*. Berkeley: University of California Press.

Wright, Patricia J. 1987. "Alchemical Notes: Reconstructing Ideals From Deconstructed Rights." *Harvard Civil Rights-Civil Liberties Law Review* 22(2):401–433.

———. 1991. *The Alchemy of Race and Rights: Diary of a Law Professor*. Cambridge: Harvard University Press.

Zatz, Marjorie S. and Su-li Zhu. 1991. "Legal Formalism, Legal Pluralism, and Social Control: A Reconsideration in Light of Research from the Third World." Paper presented at the annual meetings of the American Society of Criminology.

PERSONAL INTERVIEWS CITED

Arranz Castillero, Vicente Julio. (University of Havana law professor, specialist in criminal law; member of commission to draft a new law of criminal procedure): November 9, 1989; May 2, 1989.

Arteaga Abreu, María Luisa. (Director of International Relations, Ministry of Justice; former President of the National Organization of Law Collectives): July 5, 1990; April 19, 1989; May 11, 1989; December 1, 1989.

Carreras y Cuevas, Delio J. (professor and historian of the University of Havana): July 5, 1990.

Castanedo Abay, Armando. (University of Havana law professor, specialist in administrative law): May 3, 1989; July 4, 1990.

Castro Cabrera, Dolores. (labor law specialist, Ministry of Justice): May 22, 1991.

Ceballos Arrieta, Mario A. (criminal defense attorney specializing in Supreme Court; member of commission to draft a new law of criminal procedure): November 22, 1989.

Couto Robert, Carlos. (assistant to vice-president of the State Committee for Economic Cooperation): May 11, 1989.

de la Cruz Ochoa, Ramón. (Attorney General of the Republic of Cuba; former First Vice-Minister of Justice): December 5, 1989.

de la Fuente López, Jorge. (civil law attorney; member of commission to draft a new Family Code): December 4, 1989.

del Junco Allayón, Martín. (labor law specialist, Ministry of Justice): May 22, 1991.

Díaz Pinillo, Marcelino. (University of Havana law professor, specialist in criminal law; member of commission to draft a new law of criminal procedure; provincial court judge; former President of a regional criminal court and of a municipal court): May 9, 1989; November 17, 1989; June 28, 1990.

Fernández Guerra, Francisco Javier. (Director of Office of Preparation, Supervision, and Evaluation of Juridical Personnel, Ministry of Justice): April 26, 1989; December 1, 1989.

Fernández Bulté, Julio. (Dean of the University of Havana Law School; legal advisor to National Assembly's Commission on Constitutional and Legal Affairs): March 31, 1989; May 22, 1989; November 28, 1989.

Fernández Jiménez, Omar. (Vice-Dean of the University of Havana Law School; member of National Union of Cuban Jurists international relations committee): April 7, 1989; April 13, 1989; April 18, 1989; May 9, 1989; November 14, 1989.

García Alzugaray, Miguel Angel. (Director of International Relations, Office of the Attorney General of the Republic of Cuba): April 27, 1989; May 23, 1991.

Garrido Lugo, Jorge. (lawyer): December 3, 1989.

Gómez Arias, Milagros. (University of Havana law professor, specialist in international law): May 2, 1989.

González, Ida. (official in the National Office of the Federation of Cuban Women): May 10, 1989; May 16, 1989.

Guevara Ramírez, Lydia. (legal advisor to the Cuban Labor Confederation; member of National Union of Cuban Jurists international relations committee): April 18, 1989; May 29, 1991.

Guintén, Amado. (Vice-Minister of Justice): May 11,1989.

Hernández Ramírez, Félix. (University of Havana law school professor): April 13, 1989; March 30, 1989.

Hernández Sosa, Héctor Fidel. (professional judge in Las Tunas Provincial Court): November 24, 1989.

Kautzman Torres, Víctor L. (Assistant Director of Legal Affairs for the Foreign Ministry; legal advisor to the Ministry of Justice; member of the National Union of Cuban Jurists juridical affairs and international relations committees; adjunct professor of constitutional law at the University of Havana Law School): May 8, 1989; May 12, 1989; May 18, 1989.

Laou, Miriam. (University of Havana law professor, specialist in labor law): April 21, 1989; November 10, 1989.

Martín, Raudilio. (Vice-President of the National Union of Cuban Jurists and chair of its international relations committee): April 18, 1989.

Martínez Rubio, Francisco. (President of the National Assembly's Commission on Constitutional and Legal Affairs): May 17, 1989.

Pérez Sarmiento, Eric. (assistant to Vice-Minister of Justice Amado Guintén): May 11, 1989.

Pérez Sixto, Nancy. (University of Havana law professor, specialist in family law; working with comission to draft a new Family Code): November 9, 1989; May 9, 1989; June 21, 1990.

Quirós Pírez, Renén. (legal advisor to Minister of Justice; University of Havana law professor, specialist in criminal law): May 15, 1989.

Rega, Elia Ester. (University of Havana law professor, specialist in criminal law; professional judge in City of Havana Provincial Court): April 12, 1989.

Ribas Hermelo, Catherine. (official in the foreign relations section of the National Office of the Federation of Cuban Women): May 10, 1989.

Rivero, Dánilo. (President of the City of Havana Provincial Criminal Court): March 22, 1989.

Rodríguez Chacón, Pedro. (Director of Notary Department, Ministry of Justice): May 11, 1989.

Rodríguez Gavira, Antonio. (criminal law specialist, Ministry of Justice; member of commission to draft a new law of criminal procedure): December 4, 1989; May 22, 1991.

INDEX